BASEBALL IN FLORIDA

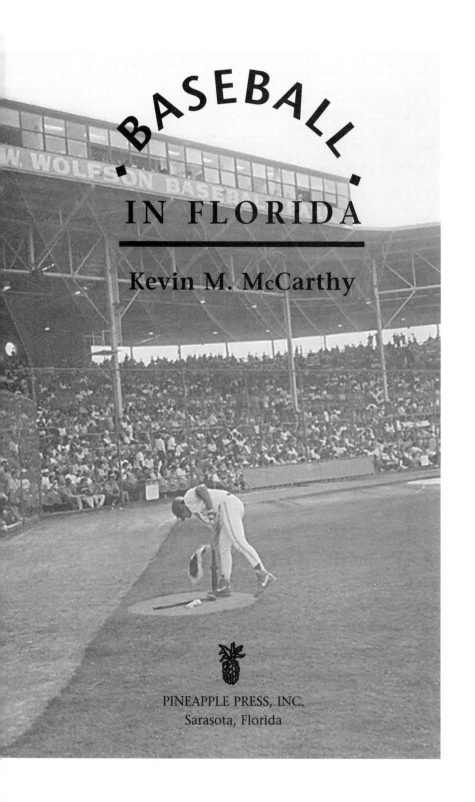

BASEBALL

IN FLORIDA

Kevin M. McCarthy

PINEAPPLE PRESS, INC.

Sarasota, Florida

Inquiries should be addressed to:
Pineapple Press, Inc.
P.O. Box 3899
Sarasota, Florida 34230-3899

LIBRARY OF CONGRESS CATALOGING-IN-PUBLICATION DATA

McCarthy, Kevin.
        Baseball in Florida / by Kevin M. McCarthy. — 1st ed.
                p.   cm.
        Includes bibliographical references (p. 241) and index.
        ISBN 1-56164-097-2. — ISBN 1-56164-089-1 (pbk.)
        1. Baseball—Florida. 2. Baseball—Florida—History. I. Title.
GV863.F6M33   1996
796.357'09759—dc20   95-41260
                                                        CIP

First Edition
10 9 8 7 6 5 4 3 2 1

Design by Carol Tornatore
Printed and bound by Quebecor Printing/Fairfield, Fairfield, Pennsylvania

CONTENTS

INTRODUCTION

"Whoever wants to know the heart and mind
of America had better learn baseball, the rules
and realities of the game."

— Jacques Barzun

When the owners of major league baseball voted unanimously in March 1995 to add an expansion team to Tampa Bay, baseball in Florida reached a pinnacle that many would not have predicted 100 years ago. That decision seemed appropriate based on demographics, climate, and geographical proximity to Latin America, but more importantly because of the century-long bond between baseball and Floridians. That bond goes back to a time in the late 19th century when settlers here could finally rest after fighting the Seminole Indian Wars of the 1830s, achieving statehood in 1845, enduring the Civil War and Reconstruction in the 1860s, and gradually making use of the state's forests and waterways in the 1870s.

That those new residents often chose baseball for their recreation said much about both their desire to become more Americanized after 300 years of Spanish control and their intent to take advantage of the state's climate, which allowed year-long exercise outdoors. It also reminds us that many if not most Floridians come from someplace else, and often that someplace else had a professional baseball team they had grown up with. That fact can explain the fascination with having new teams in Miami and Tampa Bay and why television ratings in Florida for national games are among the highest in the country.

Nineteenth-century newspapers showed what an important role baseball played in the social life of Floridians. Newspapers described holidays like Independence Day, when townspeople closed up their shops for the day, packed picnic lunches, went to the local diamond, and watched the hometown nine take on a visiting squad. The sport joined such traditional festivities as a parade and maybe some fireworks as a way to enjoy a day off with the family.

Baseball was relatively new to the South, having made its way here after the Civil War, but Floridians adopted it with enthusiasm because they could easily afford to play the sport — all they needed was an open field and a small amount of equipment — and it allowed them to compete against neighboring towns and even barnstorming squads from other states.

This then is the story of that sport: how it evolved slowly but steadily in the Sunshine State, how it took off when northern teams chose the warm Marches of St. Petersburg and Vero Beach for spring training, how colleges and universities developed into baseball powerhouses able to attract high school talent from around the country, and how the lure of the major league attracted more and more Florida youth — with varying degrees of success. That history includes outstanding college ball, the Negro Leagues, women playing baseball, and the minor leagues. It deals with the segregation of spring training sites and the integration of major league baseball. It mentions baseball camps, old-timers' leagues, even movies and novels about the sport.

Recent years have seen a great proliferation of baseball books, averaging about one new book every four days, a rate far greater than for football, basketball, soccer, or any other sport. Why? What is it about baseball that causes Americans to lay down their gloves and take up their word processors? What kind of connection is there between American culture and the values represented by baseball? How could Tallahassee's Red Barber keep millions of radio listeners spellbound for 12 years, even if they didn't like baseball, with his weekly four-minute conversations about the subject with host Bob Edwards on National Public Radio?

Many Americans can trace their love of the game to that time when their parents took them as youngsters to a game. Some say baseball has not adapted to the television age, that watching a game in the privacy of your home is boring and monotonous compared to the experience of attending a game in person. The games may not have nonstop action, but they still have fans cheering, booing, doing the wave, eating hot dogs, drinking a brew, stretching, arguing politely with complete strangers on the comparative strengths and weaknesses of today's ballplayers compared with those of past heroes, singing "Take Me Out to the Ball Game," keeping a watchful eye on the scoreboard for other games, and generally forgetting the cares of the day.

I began this book when much of America was watching the heroics of Cal Ripken Jr., Frank Thomas, and Tony Gwynn in the major leagues; I researched it during the bitter baseball disputes of the 1994–95 strike; worked on it when replacement players were taking the place of the striking players; and finished it when players and owners decided that they would play the 1995 season after all, although by that time more and more fans were deciding they could do without baseball. Whether the sport would resume its attraction to Americans remained to be seen.

During the past year, I've watched T-ball and college games in Gainesville; a high school game at Doubleday Field in Cooperstown, New York; single-A games of the Florida State League in Fort Myers and Daytona Beach; a double-A game of the Southern League in Jacksonville; a replacement game in Dunedin; met Don Miles (formerly of the Los Angeles Dodgers for eight games), Peter Bragan Sr. (president of the minor league Jacksonville Suns), and Andy Lopez (coach of the Florida Gators); and taught sections of a course entitled "Writing about Baseball" at the University of Florida.

This book is dedicated to my 55 college students, who shared a semester with me learning and writing about the sport; to my grandfather and father, who took me to the ballpark; to my mother, who took me to the library; to my twin brother, who always had time to play catch with me; to my four children, whom I helped teach how to catch high fly balls and run the bases; and to my wife, a Classics professor who studies Homer while I write about homers, but who went with me to college and to minor league and spring training games, and spurred me on to write this book.

For research help and suggestions, I would like to thank Richard Crepeau, David Fuller, Terri Ganim, Jake Jacoway, James Jones, Joe Justice, Peter Malanchuk, Stuart McIver, David Nolan, Kathy Norris, Harold Nugent, Tina Ray, Mike Rosenthal, Wes Singletary, members of the Society for American Baseball Research, and the very helpful staff at the National Baseball Hall of Fame Museum and Library in Cooperstown, New York. Sources of quotations in the text can be found at the end of the book.

BASEBALL IN FLORIDA

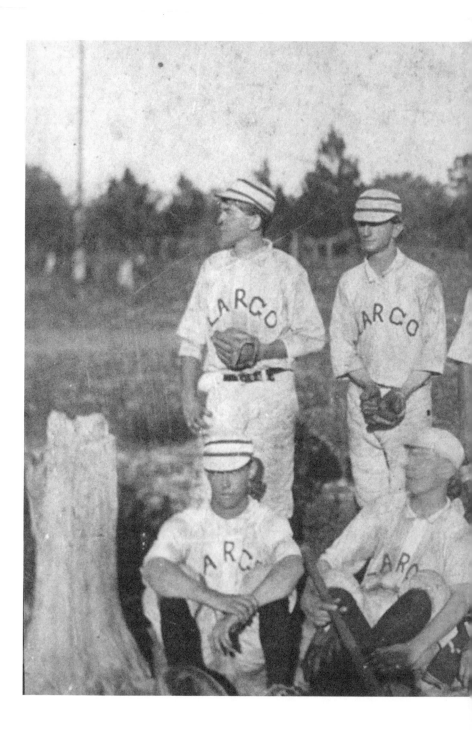

Chapter One

EARLY BASEBALL IN FLORIDA

"The national game of baseball is a manly out-door sport, always to be encouraged and patronized and always relishable, especially when so well played as that on Wednesday."

— *The Weekly Floridian*, 1874

◀ Abner Doubleday, Civil War general and purported inventor of baseball.

Dictionary of American Portraits, Dover Publications, 1967

◀ Alexander J. Cartwright, the man responsible for establishing rules for baseball.

Dictionary of American Portraits, Dover Publications, 1967

ABNER DOUBLEDAY IN MIAMI

If **Abner Doubleday** had invented baseball, which scholars no longer believe, he might have done so in Miami, since he was stationed there at Fort Dallas on the Miami River during the Third Seminole War (1855–58). Then Miami might have laid claim to the National Baseball Hall of Fame, had its own Doubleday Field, and not had so many doomsayers when the city made a bid for a major league team.

Today scholars believe that **Alexander J. Cartwright** was responsible for devising a set of rules for baseball, which, like cricket, was based on the English boyhood stick-and-ball game known as rounders and its derivative, town ball. On June 19, 1846, Cartwright had his New York Knickerbockers play the first game at Elysian Fields in Hoboken, New Jersey, under the new rules, and it then grew in popularity throughout the country. Cartwright himself took it west to California's gold fields in 1849. Twenty years later, the game became professional when the Cincinnati Red Stockings paid its players. After that, cities formed their own professional teams. Baseball soon spread southward and made its way to the new state of Florida, which was eager to become as Americanized as possible.

BASEBALL IN 19TH-CENTURY FLORIDA

The social, cultural, and athletic scene in 19th-century Florida played a major role in the development of baseball, as it did in many developing parts of the United States, as people struggled to make a living and raise their families. The Florida peninsula, although the earliest American site settled by European adventurers, was slow to develop, partly because Spain, which controlled it, was reluctant and unable to establish large towns and partly because early settlers had to battle Native Americans, mosquitoes, and unexpected storms.

As was true throughout the rest of America, however, Floridians looked to sports to entertain themselves after long days of work. Among the sports they liked was baseball, because of its low start-up costs and its outdoor setting. As might be expected, though, the rules of the game were not always clear to players in those early games. In 1874, for example, in the first game between a Tallahassee team and one from a neighboring town, one visiting player might have won the game for his team if he had been more aware of the rules. As reported in a local newspaper, he hit a clean home run, but failed to

▲ The great Ted Williams in the spring of 1941 plays cricket with British Royal Air Force cadets who were in primary flight school at Lakeland's Lodwick School of Aeronautics. *Special Collections Room, Lakeland Public Library*

Gainesville residents could pull their surrey right up to the field ▶ to watch a game around 1900. *Florida State Archives*

touch first base as he rounded the diamond; the reporter then explained, for readers unfamiliar with the newly imported sport, that "each separate base must be *actually touched* in its regular order by some portion of the base-runner's body."

The teams often wore uniforms in those early days, but not the safety equipment in use today. Players on the Garden City team of Tallahassee in 1874 were typical in their white shirts with blue collars, white pants, checked caps, and a rosette of scarlet and blue on their uniform. Besides snappy uniforms, some of those early teams also had popular names, like Jacksonville's Boot and Shoe Base Ball Club (clerks from shoe stores), Dixies, Longfellows (every player was over six feet tall), Muffers, Mechanics, Mystics, Osceola Mutuals, Quicksteps, Reliables, and Rubbers. The men on one team, nicknamed "The Fat Nine," each weighed at least 200 pounds; they could rival Lake City's Fat Man's Club, whose total for its first nine players was 2,083 pounds, or 231 pounds a player. A Palatka team in 1894 changed its name from Never Sweat to Big Injuns, although a 30–0 loss to Jacksonville in a five-inning game might have prompted a reporter to suggest the team change its name to Not Sweat Enough. The Jacksonville players in that game became so tired of running around the bases, scoring 19 runs in one inning alone, that they simply stopped in exhaustion and allowed the Palatka players to make a triple play.

HIRING PROFESSIONAL PLAYERS

As towns became more serious about baseball, especially in their determination to beat rival towns, they had to have the best players, and that usually meant hiring athletes from other towns, players they referred to as "from a distance." Such a practice often resulted in complaints from losing teams. When a Tallahassee team, the Garden City Club, played the Jacksonville Lees in 1874, the newspaper of the former complained that it was not fair for the Lees to bring in a professional from Palatka: "If the sole object is to *beat* our club, without regard to who gains the honor and credit . . . let the Lees send North and import a professional nine at once." A letter in that issue of the newspaper said that the Jacksonville Lees, named after Robert E. Lee, would do more credit to their namesake by fielding their own players.

Professional Teams Tour Florida

Local teams and fans learned a lot by watching professional players compete against each other on barnstorming trips through the state in the late 19th century. In 1888, 12,000 fans turned out in Jacksonville to watch New York play Washington in what was probably the first major league game played in the area. Similar interest was aroused in local Jacksonville fans when the New York Giants spent several weeks of spring training there in 1895 and again the following year. Later, such teams as the Philadelphia Athletics, Cincinnati Reds, Boston Nationals, and Brooklyn Superbas held spring training in Jacksonville and did much to encourage local ballplayers. All this resulted in a Jacksonville team's becoming a charter member of the South Atlantic League (SALLY League) in 1904 and, despite a disappointing 58–59 record the first year, attracting some 1,000 fans per game. Four years later, the Jacksonville Scouts would win their first SALLY League pennant with a 77–34 record.

LOCAL RIVALRIES DEVELOP

As happened throughout this country, once local teams tired of playing each other and felt good enough to challenge outsiders, intertown games became popular. Florida towns like Fernandina took pride in fielding a team made up of the best players from individual teams and having it compete against other towns.

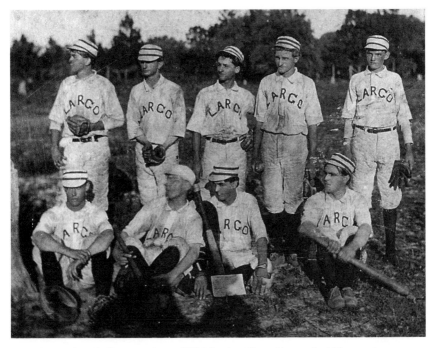

▲ A Largo baseball team about 1900 had spiffy uniforms but flimsy gloves.
Heritage Park-Pinellas County Historical Museum

One of the fiercest Florida rivalries was between Fernandina and Jacksonville, especially when Fernandina consistently failed to show up for games in 1893 after accepting a challenge from the larger town, and kept flaunting a championship bat the Fernandina players had won several years before in a regional tournament. As the town teams improved, especially those in north Florida, they adopted a new slogan: "Let's compete against Georgia teams."

Competing was one thing; losing to a Georgia team was another. In 1893, after the Jacksonville Mystics lost to the Savannah Oglethorpes, the whole Florida team disbanded and, for the fee of a suit of clothes for each ballplayer, they agreed to wear the name of a local bookstore on their uniforms. A Jacksonville newspaper did not like what it saw: ". . . in all times, in all ages and all lands, true sportsmen have scorned to lend themselves to the vulgar devices of the advertiser." At a time decades before shoe contracts and endorsement provisions in contracts, the newspaper went on at some length to pour scorn on those players:

▲ A baseball game in St. Petersburg about 1904 was literally played on a sand-lot. *Heritage Park-Pinellas County Historical Museum*

If the young men who have lent themselves to this cheap advertising scheme needed to do it because they were poor, and received for it compensation in cash to help them and their parents along, the act would be an honorable one, and no one who respects honest poverty would open his lips in derogation of it. But, that young persons, growing up in a community where shortly they expect to take the honorable places of their fathers and elders, should so compromise their gentlemanly dignity is certainly matter for profound regret. It hurts the pride of every other amateur who hears of it; it matters not who or what the thing advertised may be, whether a great patriarchal trades house or a petty tenement shop; the loved name of amateur, which touches the better part of man, his pride of physical and mental excellence, his love of art for art's sake; of science, for its benefits to man; of skill, for the beauty which displays itself in deft movements, is outraged and abused when it is made merchandise for gain and greed, or betrayed to the common uses of the advertiser.

▲ Spectators watch the baseball rivalry between West Tampa and Temple Terrace teams at McFarlane Park in West Tampa in 1922. *Tampa-Hillsborough County Public Library*

It would not be the last time that money would play a role in Florida baseball. Several years later, seven members of a Jacksonville team quit, took their uniforms with them, and formed their own team when they believed they were not receiving enough of the gate receipts.

SPORTS REPORTING

At a time when people received most of their news, reading material, and contact with the outside world through newspapers, reporters and editors often waxed eloquent in describing otherwise-mundane events like sports. Early baseball reporters had a style that verged on the hyperbolic, but must have pleased readers eager for news of how their Mudville Nine trounced a hated rival. A reporter for Jacksonville's *Florida Times-Union* covering an 1887 baseball game between a Jacksonville team, the Citizens, and one from Palatka seemed to take great pleasure in describing the game:

> Palatka hit the ball until it was lopsided, pretty near where and when they pleased, ran the bases until their tongues

hung out of their mouths, worked up a thirst that a barrel of Billey Beers' oatmeal water took to quench, and as the rooster said, "had a gilt-framed picnic." When the Palatka boys didn't earn runs from the Citizens, they were given runs, this being the home club's conception of the proper and sportsmanlike way to turn over the keys of the city to honored and respected guests.

WOMEN, BETTING, AND CHARITABLE CAUSES

Women usually attended those 19th-century Florida games and, in fact, were sometimes the majority in the stands. In one 1897 game, women were blamed for the loss when the Jacksonville nine paid more attention to the ladies than to the game. The women often had to sit in carriages that ringed the field, since many ball fields had no regular seats, and those ballparks with bleachers often had very poor facilities for spectators. Once when a torrential downpour interrupted a game and the flimsy roof of the grandstand leaked badly, the women spectators resolved not to attend another game unless officials built better accommodations.

▲ The DeLand Baseball Team around 1905 didn't have much in the way of uniforms, but they did have a canine mascot. *Florida State Archives*

In those early days, the whole town would close down to let everyone attend the game, especially if an out-of-town team had arrived. The early games also had betting, some of it to excess. In one 1895 game between teams from Gainesville and Palatka, at least $200 — a sizable sum in those days — was lost by the visitors. In an earlier game in Jacksonville, a member of the Mystics team was so disgusted at his teammates' playing that he left the game and bet two-to-one that his opponents would win.

Money raised by a baseball game sometimes went to charitable causes. An 1882 game between teams from Jacksonville and Fernandina, for example, raised over $300 for victims of a yellow fever epidemic in Pensacola. An 1889 game between the "railroad boys" and the "steamboat boys" raised money for Jacksonville's St. Luke's Hospital.

Even so, not everyone felt sanguine about the sport. One person complained in 1893 that boys playing baseball in the streets of Jacksonville frightened horses passing by. Another person wrote that, if he had a dog that went to a ballgame on a Sunday, "I'd fill him full of shot, and if he went on Wednesday, I'd give him one hundred lashes. There is nothing more corrupt this side of hell than baseball."

Others, however, took their dogs with them to games and used them to intimidate the opposition. One player trained his dog to sit erect, growl, and make threatening gestures toward the batter, which apparently worked in at least one instance by totally distracting the batter. Another person taught his mule to encourage a local player by braying whenever the man came to bat. Somehow today's "tomahawk chop" and "wave" seem mild by comparison.

UMPIRES

The rampant betting going on at games bothered many spectators, but the poor treatment of umpires was even more disturbing. Selecting the umpire was often a delicate matter, since someone from one of the two opposing towns might be accused of favoring his home team. Angry players bold enough to take a game into their own hands were known to substitute a new umpire midway through the game if they were displeased with the original umpire's calls. All of this helped the men in blue develop a toughness necessary for longevity in the game.

In a Palatka game between the Fats and the Leans, whose players looked accordingly, one of the umpires had pistols, bowie knives, and a large dog to enforce his decisions. At one point he had to draw his gun to make sure the players obeyed his directives. Gun-toting occurred in this century, too. Once in the 1920s, when the DeLand team was playing in Crescent City, the local town policeman was the umpire. When the DeLand catcher clearly tagged out the runner from third base at least five feet from home plate, the umpire called him safe. When the DeLand nine started to protest, the umpire/policeman pulled his pistol, declared that he had called him safe, and would not allow any more discussion of the matter.

When Fort Lauderdale's first team traveled by wood-burning train to the little town of Fellsmere 11 miles west of Sebastian in 1913, the manager of a local farm welcomed them. He then announced, first, that he was going to umpire and, secondly, that the local boys expected to win — which is what the Fellsmere team did, helped perhaps a little by the umpire and by the shotgun-wielding farmer who sat menacingly behind first base. The locals felt great pride in beating the boys from the big city on the east coast of Florida. The latter probably felt good just to get out of Fellsmere alive.

Other umpires had a sense of humor and an involvement in the game that are missing today. Once when a player took one of the opposing team's bats to sit on in the damp outfield, the umpires fined him one watermelon. The local newspaper reported that the umpires in that game acknowledged clever play with "wild applause."

In time, umpires became known for their fairness and justice — and lack of firepower. In fact, the local newspaper considered one Fort Lauderdale umpire, **W. J. "Cap" Reed**, the best in the South, which may have led to his being elected mayor five times. Other towns reversed the umpire-to-mayor scenario and made their mayors umpires. When teams from Jacksonville and Fernandina played in 1899, for example, the mayor of Fernandina called balls and strikes, and, despite a long-running feud between the two towns, was considered honest and impartial by both sides throughout the game.

As umpires cracked down on illegalities in play, players had to resort to new, legal strategies for a winning edge. Once in the small town of Welaka on the St. Johns River, during a game between the locals and the Norwalk team, one of the visiting players used a new tactic. When "first baseman Bard heard that Allen was known as a very polite clerk in a store, he waited till Allen got on his base, and then asked him to cut him off a piece of bacon about the size of a pitcher, and sure enough Allen started in the direction of the store to do as requested, and Bard put the ball on him."

John J. McGraw

Among the 19th-century umpire-hating players who got his start in Florida was the great **John J. McGraw** (1873–1934), a Hall-of-Famer who set 24 records as a manager, 13 of which have never been broken. In 1891, the 17-year-old McGraw arrived in Gainesville to play shortstop for a team called the All-Stars, which former National League pitcher **Alfred W. Lawson** had organized. McGraw's contract stipulated that he would be fed and housed, given money for shaving and washing, and provided with one cigar a week. When his team, nick-named the "Champions" of Florida," went to Jackson-

▲ The great John J. McGraw played baseball in Gainesville in 1891.

Dictionary of American Portraits,
Dover Publications, 1967

ville to play the Cleveland Spiders, who had their spring training there, McGraw did so well that he received offers to play baseball for different teams. Much later as manager of the New York Giants, McGraw returned to Gainesville in 1918 to hold spring training on the campus of the University of Florida. In 1937, he was inducted into the Baseball Hall of Fame, an honor that recognized his many contributions to the game.

THE BOARD

Floridians became enamored with baseball, especially as news-gathering services gave them more immediate access to what was going on in distant cities. Historian James McGovern wrote that Pensacola "was wild about big league baseball. Fans gathered at the offices of the *Journal* at World Series time in the early 1920s to obtain immediate news of the game from Associated Press Service. Games were afterwards described on the *Journal's* front page. The newspaper also ran features on how to play baseball, replete with pictures of star players."

At World Series time in cities around America, including Jacksonville and Miami, fans would gather outside local newspaper offices to see the board, a large replica of a baseball diamond, on which operators would indicate the progress of the game. Before radio and television enabled stay-at-homes to enjoy the game in some privacy, thousands of devoted baseball fans could enjoy World Series action through the board.

The board gave a play-by-play record of the game just seconds after each play. Sometimes an announcer with a megaphone would tell the assembled fans what was going on, while his colleague moved the pieces on the board. If a city had more than one newspaper, each

▼ Miami's version of the board.
Florida State Archives

▲ Watching play-by-play in the World Series on the board in Jacksonville.
Florida State Archives

▼ Baseball scoreboard in front of the *St. Petersburg Times* in 1924.
St. Petersburg Museum of History

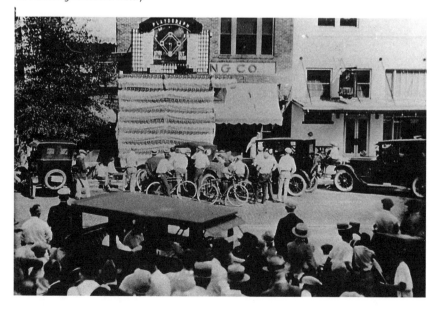

might try to lure more spectators by using bigger boards and more elaborate paraphernalia to indicate the bases, the diamond, and the outfield. Reporters at the game would relay by telegraph wire each pitch, each play just as it happened. The operators would then move the "ball" and "ballplayers" around the board to indicate what had happened.

Newspaper boards might follow a local team's away games, but most cities used the boards at World Series time, usually in late September. This was especially true after newspapers began covering baseball more extensively in the first decade of the 20th century. The boards were usually outside and free, but occasionally, especially where a newspaper did not have any other competition, the board would be inside a casino or local club, and fans had to pay a quarter to "see" the game inside. After radio station KDKA in Pittsburgh broadcast the first major league game on August 5, 1921, the boards began to disappear, especially as more and more people bought radios.

BASEBALL IN SOUTH FLORIDA

Baseball in south Florida developed slowly because of the low population and the lack of good roads or a railroad to take teams to other towns. The first game in the Biscayne Bay area did not take place until 1892, when the Lemon City team played the Coconut Grove team. In 1896, Miami still had fewer than 300 residents, although the jump to 1,681 four years later presaged the town's rapid growth. The early 1890s saw only a few games a year between towns in south Florida, but that changed as rivalries intensified.

Guy Metcalf, publisher of *The Juno Tropical Sun* in Juno, the county seat of Dade County, did much to interest local readers in the sport in the late 1890s by printing details of the National Baseball League and profiles of such players as **George E. Andrews, Cap Anson, Ed Delahanty, Wee Willie Keeler, "Iron Man" Joe McGinnity**, and **John J. McGraw**.

George E. Andrews was born in 1859 in Painesville, Ohio, and went on to play for the Phillies (1884–89), Indianapolis of the National League (1889), Brooklyn of the Players League (1890), and Cincinnati of the American Association (1891), before retiring in the mid-1890s to his pineapple plantation near Fort Pierce. Instead of being able to enjoy his retirement, however, he was ruined by the 1895 freeze and had to return to the National League as an umpire to earn a livelihood. Around 1897, developer Henry Flagler hired him to organize and run guest entertainment and care for guests' yachts at large hotels on the lower southeast coast, which Andrews did for 12 years. He lived at 310 Pine Street in West Palm Beach, which was named Andrews Terrace after he died in 1934 (Fort Lauderdale officials had honored him with Andrews Avenue in 1895). Flagler's railroad, which reached West Palm Beach and Miami and eventually Key West, finally enabled baseball teams and fans to travel between towns and make the games a festive outing with families.

Fort Lauderdale Establishes a Baseball Team

When Fort Lauderdale began growing steadily after its 1913 incorporation, it organized a baseball team, something civic leader Frank Stranahan encouraged by donating land and building a baseball field that later became the athletic field for the old Fort Lauderdale High School. Baseball games, usually played on weekends and holidays, brought out the whole town and gave the people a sense of identity, even a common foe for the day.

Playing such towns as Fort Pierce, Palm Beach, and Stuart was fun and good-natured competition for the Fort Lauderdale players, but playing Miami was a different story and produced spirited games. That rivalry spilled over into the newly formed East Coast Baseball League, which the Fort Lauderdale team joined in 1913. The teams in that league were so determined to win the pennant that year that they used professionals in the final weeks of the season. The *Fort Lauderdale Sentinel* reported just how those final weeks went: "More real interest has been aroused over this pennant chase in Lauderdale than any event in the history of the town. . . . Fort Lauderdale is known all over the South as a live one and her fame as a baseball town is established."

One of the best players for the Fort Lauderdale team was pitcher **Lester Sweetland** (1901–74), who went on to play for the Phillies (1927–30) and Cubs (1931) for a disappointing 33–58 record.

Nicknames, Lady Bellringers, and Mayors

Some of the local teams, like the Miami Seminoles and West Palm

Beach Invincibles, had nicknames, but Fort Lauderdale's did not; what it did have were the Lady Bellringers, a group of 15 to 20 cheerleaders, led by Frank Stranahan's niece, Grace Dunlap, who rattled dinner bells, cowbells, sleigh bells — anything that could make a loud noise. The Bellringers could really get into the mood of a game. Once when the locals were playing the hated Miami team and Miami's **Red Snedigar**, who had reached third, started to run for home plate on a grounder, Miss Dunlap ran along with him, ringing her bell, all of which distracted Snedigar so much that the Fort Lauderdale boys were able to tag him out, and the locals won another game. Snedigar must have thought that baseball had prepared him for the travails of politics, because, as happened with several other umpires, he later became mayor, of Miami Beach.

BASEBALL IN THE 1920s

The outbreak of World War I ended those early baseball teams, but locals organized new teams after the war, at which time the Fort Lauderdale team finally decided on a nickname, the Tarpons. So determined were they to win that the rival towns would hire "ringers," former big leaguers, even those who had been banned from the game for some infraction. Businesses would close for the afternoon as everyone trooped out to the ball field to cheer on the local team with cries like "Beat Miami" and "Trounce the Tarpons."

As time went on, players played for more than local pride, sometimes splitting the gate receipts between both teams; for example, when the Miami Magicians went to Palm Beach for a game in October 1920, each player received $12.80 after the game.

Managers in south Florida had to contend with problems that present-day managers do not have. Blue laws that outlawed baseball on Sundays were a particular problem for the teams. The local clergy had strong feelings about what one called "Sunday baseball and other forms of Sabbath desecration." In April 1921, for example, after the Tarpons had beaten the Invincibles in West Palm Beach, police arrested both teams for "violating the Sabbath" and would not release them until the manager of the Invincibles posted a $50 bond for each player.

▲ (Top) The Miami baseball team around 1921. *Florida State Archives*

(Bottom) The Coral Gables team in 1924. *Florida State Archives*

Seminole Indian Teams

Among baseball teams in south Florida were several Seminole teams made up of local Indians. **Tony Tommy**, a young man who broke tribal precedent by entering a local school in Fort Lauderdale, helped organize other Indians into a team that occasionally played "white" teams like the Hopkins–Lake Placid School of Coconut Grove. A local newspaper commented on the type of baseball played: "When it comes to playing baseball[,] the Seminoles of Florida are highly civilized, for their teams put up a [good] game and one that would win games in many of the minor league organizations of the United States."

▲ The Coral Gables team in 1925 traveled by bus to away games.
Florida State Archives

SPRING TRAINING IN FLORIDA?

As the major league teams discovered the benefits of having spring training in Florida, away from the cold, pollution, and hectic pace of the North, Floridians came to like the "boys of spring" and began to hope that one of the teams would relocate to Florida for the regular season. The Boston Braves came to Miami in 1916 and were later followed by the Cincinnati Reds, New York Giants, St. Louis Browns, Brooklyn Dodgers, and Baltimore Orioles. It would take another seven decades, however, before a major league team would finally locate in south Florida.

▲ Early Pensacola teams had women sporting outfits of the teams they supported. *Pensacola Historical Society*

Chapter Two

YOUTH BASEBALL

The Mayport team had their own canine mascot in 1901.

YOUTH BASEBALL IN THE 19TH AND EARLY 20TH CENTURIES

When Floridians began playing baseball in the 19th century, the game attracted its share of youngsters eager to show their skills and maybe even beat their elders. In one early newspaper report, the Grasshoppers, a team consisting of boys aged 8 to 12 beat a group of men by a score of 21–12, prompting a reporter to write, "There is evident material among the little ones for first-class ballists." When that same group of youngsters later lost 41–38 to another youth team, the Jacksonville Duvals, the losers, perhaps having learned something from the adults, complained that the umpire had been biased against them. In any case, the tradition grew of Florida youngsters playing baseball from an early age and all year round.

Many young Floridians participated in city baseball leagues, where local companies fielded teams to compete against each other. That sometimes led to situations where youngsters like **Manuel "Curly" Onis** of Tampa were scouted by the pros and signed to the big leagues. Onis's career "took him from the sandlots of Ybor City to the glory that was Ebbets Field." Writers often noted how baseball in Florida towns in the early part of this century was thriving.

▲ An early Quincy team. *Florida State Archives*

Babe Ruth and Youth Baseball in Florida

The great Yankee slugger was well-known for his solicitude for youngsters, perhaps as a result of his growing up in St. Mary's Industrial School for Boys, a reformatory in Baltimore. In 1934, at the height of the Depression and toward the end of his career, Ruth became involved in a project that brought 50 boys on a free trip to St. Petersburg. At a time when he was featured nationally on cereal boxes and a weekly radio program, he announced that the 50 winners of a contest sponsored by Standard Oil as a promotion for its new Esso brand would be his guests at the Yankees' spring training camp in Florida. One of those boys, **Norman L. Macht**, described what that experience-of-a-lifetime was like, traveling by train (for some of the boys their first train ride) on the Orange Blossom Special and arriving at the Huntington Hotel, which still exists on Fourth Avenue North. For the next three days, Ruth talked to them about baseball and had them compete in games, swim in the Gulf, and enjoy the sunshine and beautiful weather. Later, he shipped each of them a crate of grapefruit and oranges. Although none of the boys became major leaguers, they had fond memories of that visit south to see Ruth.

Little League

Besides school baseball teams, many boys and girls compete on Little League teams throughout the state. Since 1939, when Little League baseball began in Williamsport, Pennsylvania, thousands of players have competed at different levels of play in well-organized leagues throughout the world. In order to accommodate the young players, Little League baseball scaled down its playing field to two-thirds regulation size, reduced the distance between the pitcher's mound and home plate to 46 feet, and selected players from well-defined geographic areas. Hundreds of former Little Leaguers eventually made their way into the major leagues, making up more than two-thirds of the then-major leaguers. Among the boys who have played in Florida Little League and gone on to the majors are **Vince Coleman**, **Steve Garvey**, **Dwight Gooden**, **Mike Greenwell**, **Boog Powell**, and **Don Sutton**.

Williamsport hosts the annual Little League World Series. Over its 48-year history through 1995, several hundred teams from around the United States have participated in the World Series, including 16

▲ Babe Ruth with arms around two young boys in the early 1930s.
St. Petersburg Museum of History

▲ A Clearwater baseball team about 1914. The letters "P.C." stand for Pinellas County. *Heritage Park-Pinellas County Historical Museum*

teams from Florida. Tampa has supplied most of the Florida entries, including two from the West Tampa Little League (1967, 1969), four from the Belmont Heights Little League (1973, 1975, 1980, 1981), and one from the Northside Little League (1989). Other Florida teams that qualified for the World Series were from St. Petersburg (1948), Pensacola (1949, 1950, 1951), Lakeland (1954), Sarasota (1982, 1986), Altamonte Springs (1984), and Dunedin (1991).

Although no Florida team has won the Little League Baseball Championship, Florida teams were runner-ups six times: 1948, 1949, 1975, 1980, 1981, and 1984. The Belmont Heights Little League team from Tampa did win the 1982 Junior League Baseball World Series with future major leaguers **Derek Bell** and **Gary Sheffield**.

From time to time, the organization recognizes individuals and companies that have successfully encouraged local youth to join the Little League. The first recipient of the Little League Baseball President's Award was **Ted Ferreira**, a very successful high school baseball coach in Florida for more than 30 years. He helped bring

Little League baseball to Sarasota County, directed the Little League Baseball Camp in Williamsport for many years, and coached Little League for 25 years in Fort Myers, which named a playing field there after the popular coach. The Little League Good Sport Award, which recognizes a Little Leaguer who has demonstrated superior qualities of sportsmanship, leadership, a commitment to teamwork, and a desire to excel, was awarded to regional honoree **James McGuinness** of Boynton Beach in 1994.

In recent years, the Little League organization has adapted to the physically and mentally handicapped by establishing the Challenger Division, a special league for players many thought would never be able to play the sport. Players in that division use a softer ball and smaller bat because many of them swing with only one hand. Boys and girls on the league's regular teams assist the Challenger players by pushing their wheelchairs, guiding them around bases, and fielding balls, which they then give to the Challenger player to make the throw. The national organization introduced the division in 1989 to coincide with its 50th anniversary, and Jacksonville added it in 1990.

In 1991, some 600 leagues offered the Challenger Division and about 20,000 youngsters participated. One hundred-twenty Jacksonville-area youngsters from ages 6 to 18 got to play a sport they might never have had the chance to play, something bound to increase their self-confidence and determination. The Jacksonville parent of an 8-year-old with cerebral palsy expressed the feelings of many when he said, "We're really glad they put this together. He's excited now and he wants to play basketball. We never thought he'd be able to participate in sports."

PONY Baseball

PONY (Protect Our Nation's Youth) Baseball was established by Little League officials in Washington, Pennsylvania, to provide another program for boys and girls to play baseball. Today, different divisions allow youngsters of a similar age to play. The Shetland League is for the youngest players, who then advance to the Pinto League (7- and 8-year-olds), Mustang League (9- and 10-year-olds), Bronco League (11- and 12-year-olds), Pony League (13- and 14-year-olds), Colt League (15- and 16-year-olds), and Palomino League (17- and 18-year-olds). The dimensions of the diamond are slowly

increased until regulation size is reached, and rules about base steal-
ing and innings pitched are enforced to enable the youngsters to
develop at an appropriate pace.

Florida teams that won the PONY World Series, including the
Bronco, Pony, and Colt leagues, were:

LEAGUE	YEAR	LOCATION	CHAMPION TEAM
Bronco	1967	Kingsville, TX	Monchy de Arcos, Miami
Bronco	1974	Washington, PA	Lake Worth
Bronco	1976	Oak Park, IL	Miami
Bronco	1978	St. Joseph, MO	Miami
Bronco	1982	St. Joseph, MO	Miami (Southwest)
Bronco	1986	Pinole, CA	Miami (Carlos Pascual)
Pony	1958	Washington, PA	Miami
Pony	1976	Washington, PA	Tampa (N. Palomino)
Colt	1958	Springfield, IL	Miami
Colt	1959	Ontario, CA	Pensacola
Colt	1976	Lafayette, IN	Tampa
Colt	1990	Lafayette, IN	Tampa (Forest Hills)

▼ The ball fields of today differ sharply from that used by these
Boy Scouts in 1921. *Tampa-Hillsborough County Public Library*

The only time one of the championship games was played in Florida was the 1972 Colt League World Series in Tampa. PONY Baseball also offers a sportsmanship award to one Pony League baseball player and one Pony League softball player; Tampa's **John Curry**, who won the 1994 baseball award, received a $1,000 higher-education scholarship.

Babe Ruth Baseball

Babe Ruth Baseball was founded in 1951 in Hamilton Township near Trenton, New Jersey, to provide amateur baseball opportunities for 13- to 15-year-old players. In 1994, 760,000 played in the organization, which had 5,500 leagues and 38,900 teams. In 1968, the International Babe Ruth League established a Hall of Fame to honor those organizations and persons who played an important role in the development of that baseball program. Among those inducted into this Hall of Fame was the Athletic Institute of Florida (1971), as well as the following individuals from Florida: **J. Jervey Gantt** (1983) and **William A. Axtell** and **Howard Rohrbacher** (both in 1989).

Babe Ruth Baseball has established several divisions over the years to allow more youth to participate. The World Series of the 13–15 age group has had two Florida boys who won Most Outstanding Player honors: **Andy Vickery** of Pensacola (1957) and **George Cruz** of Sarasota (1989). And the World Series of that age group has had two Florida boys win the batting championship: **Floyd Blackman** of Pensacola (1957, .667 average) and **Craig Calhaun** of Sarasota in (1989, .526 average). In the 1993 World Series three boys from Sarasota made the All-Tournament Team: second baseman **Kevin Pillifant** and outfielders **James Jenkins** and **Matt Cannon**; third baseman **Gino Tutera** of Sarasota won the 1993 Most Outstanding Glove Award in the World Series.

In 1966, the organization established the 16- to 18-year-old division for older players. The World Series of that age group has had three Florida boys who won Most Outstanding Player honors: **David Miller** of Pensacola (1983); **Roger Miller** of Sarasota (1984), who shares the record for fewest hits allowed in a World Series game (0); and **Chris Casels** of Pensacola (1986). Chris also won the World Series Batting Championship that year with a .667 average and shares the record for most hits in a World Series game (5). **Joe Sims** of Pensacola shares the record for most home runs in a World Series game (2) in 1983.

In 1974, the organization formed the Babe Ruth Prep League for 13-year-olds to provide more participation for younger players. The World Series of this division has had three Florida boys who won Most Outstanding Player honors: **Kirk Dulom** of Miami (1980); **David Hunt** of Sarasota (1988), and **Jose Nodal** of Miami (1989). Among the Florida boys with records in the World Series (1980) were **Manual Rivas** of Miami: most hits in a game (4); **George Casanove** of Miami: most hits in a series (13); **Kirk Dulom** of Miami: most home runs in a game (2); Kirk also shares the record for most home runs in a series (3). That 1980 Miami team shares the World Series record of Most Games Won in the Series (6) and had the highest batting average in a World Series: .368.

▲ Future major leaguer Don Sutton (second from the right, standing) was on this 1961 All Stars of the Babe Ruth League team. *Pensacola Historical Society*

▲ The dugout, stadium, and equipment were not very elaborate for this Pensacola team around 1920. *Pensacola Historical Society*

In 1982, Babe Ruth Baseball established the Bambino Division for players aged 5–12; Alachua, Florida, hosted the 1992 World Series of this division. Among the Babe Ruth League graduates from Florida, with an asterisk indicating they were born here, on recent major league rosters were **Howard Johnson*** from Clearwater; **Mike Greenwell** from Fort Myers; **Jay Bell*** and **Travis Fryman** from Pensacola; **Derek Lilliquist*** from Sarasota; **Dean Palmer***, **Reggie Jefferson***, and **Bobby Thigpen*** from Tallahassee; and **Mark Guthrie** from Venice.

The Big League World Series

Fort Lauderdale has been for over two decades the scene of the Big League World Series, the championship event for international youth baseball that matches 11 teams of 16- to 18-year-olds from around the world in a double-elimination series. This World Series, part of Little League Baseball, began 30 years ago when **Floyd Hull**, an associate municipal judge in Fort Lauderdale, contracted with the city to build a facility, nicknamed Little Yankee Stadium, to host the Annual Big League World Series, beginning in 1970. At that time, the series had 10 volunteers; today it has over 100. And the bleachers in what is today Floyd Hull Stadium went from wooden to cement, and one sky box went to three. So successful was this World Series that the Freedom Foundation of Valley Forge awarded its prestigious annual national award in 1979 to the organization because of the benefits the series provides to youth, the country, and international understanding. In 1980, Floyd Hull won the same award for his 25 years of service with the Federal Little League. Another person who has done much to run the World Series is **Kathy Norris**, who has been working with the Series for over 25 years.

Florida teams have participated in all the tournaments, not only because Broward County is the host team, but also because the quality of Florida baseball is so high. In 1985 and 1992, the Broward County All Stars won the world title. Other Florida teams that have represented the USA SOUTH are Jacksonville (1977, 1990); Miami-Carol City (1981); Orlando (1972, 1983, 1984, 1985, 1991); and Tampa (1978, 1979, 1980, 1982). Beginning in 1995, the broadcasting of the championship game by ESPN 2 did much to publicize the event nationally.

Khoury Association

The Khoury Association is a non-profit, non-denominational organization of affiliated youth baseball and softball leagues, some of which play in Florida. The organization, which began in St. Louis, Missouri, in 1937, is one of the few year-round baseball programs in this country and has over 3,000 volunteers, including coaches, umpires, and officials. The Khoury League began in south Florida in 1955, starting in Dade County at St. Brendan's School fields and later moving to Tropical Park. Some 25,000 boys and girls, aged 5 to 17, from Broward and Dade counties play baseball and softball throughout the year. The Khoury League International World Series began in 1989 at the Griffin Sports Center in Davie, Florida, with the Midget Division. The second series was played at Miami's Tamiami Park with the addition of the Juvenile Division; Hialeah Khoury League won first and second place that year. The third World Series, which Hialeah won in both the Midget and Juvenile divisions, was held at Broward County's Brian Piccolo Park at 9501 Sheridan Street in Cooper City. The state headquarters of the George Khoury Association of Baseball Leagues is 10271 Southwest 108th Street, Miami, Florida 33176.

REVIVING BASEBALL IN INNER CITIES (RBI)

Miami and Tallahassee have also been involved in Reviving Baseball in Inner Cities (RBI), a program that gives inner-city youngsters the chance to learn and enjoy the sport. Begun in 1989 in south central Los Angeles by **John Young**, who would later work for the Florida Marlins as a major league scout in the West, the program encompasses some 40 cities and nearly 10,000 players. Young began the program when he discovered that many inner-city youngsters quit playing baseball between the ages of 13 and 16 because of poorly organized leagues, the lack of funding and community support for baseball, the presence of street gangs, and the attraction of drugs and alcohol. With much effort, Young established the community-based program that combined education and baseball.

As an example of how effective the program can be, in 1994 more than 45 Miami-area teens participated in a city-wide league, which the Florida Marlins sponsored. Those youth, many of whom had spent time in jail for crimes, played at Wynwood's Roberto Clemente Park, a rehabilitated drug haven that seemed destined to remain underutilized until the RBI program infused new life into it. The RBI program provides players with free uniforms, transportation, and whatever equipment they need to play the sport. Park director **Jorge Jaen**, who has spent much time and effort in organizing local RBI teams, said, "A lot of kids have heard about this [baseball program], and every day they ask about baseball. It's incredible what baseball has done here." Florida Marlins right fielder **Gary Sheffield** felt so strongly about the program that he vowed in 1994 to donate to RBI $100 for every double and triple and $200 for every home run he hit over the next four seasons.

HIGH SCHOOL BASEBALL

High school baseball in Florida has done well, especially at a number of schools which have consistently fielded excellent teams. Among the strongest high school teams in 1995 are the following (in alphabetical order):

1. The BOLLES SCHOOL, a small AAAA school in Jacksonville, has produced some excellent ballplayers; for example, **Steve Carver**, who was named Baseball America's Summer Player of the Year in 1994; **Chipper Jones** of the Atlanta Braves; and **Rick Wilkins**, who has

▲ St. Petersburg High School team of 1904. *St. Petersburg Museum of History*

played for the Cubs since 1991. Head Coach **Don Suriano** has a 300–84 record after 14 seasons there and has won the district championship 11 times and the state championship once. **Chipper Jones** may have been the first number-one pick from this state in the amateur draft.

2. SARASOTA HIGH SCHOOL was ranked Number 1 in 1994 with a 33–4 record and won consecutive state championships (1993–94). Coach **Clyde Metcalf**'s teams have compiled an impressive 352–64 record in his 13 seasons there. Among promising players in the recent past is **Doug Million**, the 1994 USA Today High School Player of the Year and Baseball America's High School Player of the Year; he was 12–2 that year with a 1.21 ERA and 149 strikeouts in 87 innings in his senior year of high school and was picked seventh in the 1994 draft by the Colorado Rockies.

3. SEMINOLE HIGH SCHOOL in Largo, 27–5 in 1994 and the victor over top-ranked Sarasota High School twice, is consistently good.

4. SOUTHWEST HIGH SCHOOL in Miami was 25–4 in 1994 and won the 1994 American Legion World Series. The 1995 team had two pitchers who had defected from Cuba's junior national team and joined Coach **J. C. Diaz**, whose own family had come over from Cuba in 1961. J. C. Diaz replaced his brother, **Jorge**, who had compiled a 126-63-1 record at Southwest from 1988 through 1994 before joining the Cleveland Indians as a scout. Thirty-seven Eagles players went on to play college baseball, six went into minor league ball, and four went into the majors: **Dave Augustine**, who played outfield for Pittsburgh (1973–74); **Ray Bare**, who pitched for St. Louis (1972–74) and Detroit (1975–77); **Andre Dawson**, both Rookie of the Year (1977) and Most Valuable Player (1987) before returning to Miami to finish his career with the Florida Marlins; and **Dane Johnson**, who was promoted to the White Sox in 1994.

5. ST. THOMAS AQUINAS HIGH SCHOOL in Fort Lauderdale was 20–7 in 1994. Coach **Ed Waters**, who has spent 20 years at St. Thomas Aquinas, recorded his 400th coaching victory as his Raiders won their fifth straight conference title, the sub-district crown, and a second place in the regionals. The 404–163 record of the Raiders (.714) is truly outstanding. Among the 14 former Raiders drafted or signed by the majors was **Mike Stanley** (1981), whom *Newsday* named Yankee Player of the Year in 1993.

▼ St. Thomas Aquinas High School, like many schools today, has modern facilities and an experienced coaching staff. *Coach Ed Waters*

6. WESTMINSTER CHRISTIAN HIGH SCHOOL in Miami consistently ranks high in the polls. One of its best players in recent years was **Alex Rodriguez**, the first high school All-American named by *Baseball America* to reach the majors, where he played for the Mariners (1994–95).

For a list of the state high school champions, see Appendix A.

Three of the top 25 high school recruits in 1994, according to *Baseball America*, were from Florida high schools: **Charles Alley** of Palm Beach Lakes High School in Palm Beach, **Jeff Manser** of Tampa's Hillsborough High School, and **David Ross** of Tallahassee's Florida High School. The final National High School Top 25 for 1995, as reported in *Baseball America* (July 10–23, 1995, p. 52), contained three Florida high schools: #4 – Key West High School (35–2), #10 – St. Thomas Aquinas High School of Fort Lauderdale (27–4), and #13 – Sarasota High School (27–5).

Sarasota and Tampa Youth Baseball

Various Florida sites can claim to be baseball powerhouses at the high school level, but two in particular, Sarasota and Tampa Bay, can proudly point to their long-established baseball programs. One reporter praised Sarasota in glowing terms: "Maybe it's in the water. Maybe this city's passion for baseball, especially youth baseball, courses through underground pipes, out of faucets and into the community's glasses and recipes."

Besides mentioning the above-cited Sarasota High School team, that writer mentioned Riverview High School, coached by former major leaguer **Hugh Yancy**, who had played seven games for the Chicago White Sox in the 1970s. The fact that Riverview's shortstop, **Brian Spiezio**, is the nephew of former big leaguer **Ed Spiezio** (Cardinals, 1964–68, Padres, 1969–72, and White Sox, 1972) reinforces the long baseball tradition in the city.

The other strong area for high school baseball is Tampa. Typical of how that city honors its best ballplayers is the Tony Saladino Award, given each year to Hillsborough County's top senior high school baseball player. The award, begun by Tony Saladino in memory of his late father, has been given to the following players in its 25-year history (with the eight who made the majors indicated with an *): **Rick Faulkner** and **Davian Menendez** (1971), **Anthony Lazzara** and **Dan**

Bazarte (1972), **Mike Heath*** (1973), **Nick Ray** (1974), **John Shouse** (1975), **Sammy Spence** (1976), **Danny Pickern** (1977), **Lenny Faedo*** (1978), **Rick Figueredo** (1979), **David Magadan*** (1980), **Vance Lovelace*** (1981), **Rich Monteleone*** (1982), **John Ramos*** (1983), **Chuck Donahue** (1984), **Tino Martinez*** (1985), **Gary Sheffield*** (1986), **Chris Meyers** (1987), **Min Park** (1988), **Kiki Jones** (1989), **Salvy Urso** (1990), **Bruce Thompson** (1991), **Troy Kent** (1992), **Troy Carrasco** (1993), **Scott Glaser** (1994), and **Mike Valdes** (1995).

The annual Saladino Baseball Tournament at Tampa King High School highlights some of the best players in the area. Founded in 1981 by Tony Saladino to honor his late father, the tournament has featured such future major leaguers as **Dwight Gooden** and **Gary Sheffield** (Hillsborough High), **Wade Boggs** (Tampa Plant), **Fred McGriff** (Tampa Jefferson), and **Derek Bell** (King).

Finally, the fact that Floridians begin playing ball at a young age

▲ Joe DiMaggio shows 3-year-old Larry Valencourt in 1948 that one is never too young to start learning baseball.
Florida State Archives

and are able to play year-round has often enabled them to excel on the national level. For example, in 1994 **Jason Wright** of Seffner won the title in the 13-year-old division, the highest-age group, at the national finals of baseball's revived Pitch, Hit, and Run competition in Arlington, Texas. Other winners in that competition included a second-place finish for **Ryan De Vars** of Tampa in the 10-year age group and a third-place finish for **Ben Sykes** of Lakeland in the 11-year age group.

Florida's Cuban Connection

The proximity of Florida to Cuba has helped baseball in the state. Floridians received early exposure to major league teams passing through on their way to games in Cuba. Also, Florida is attractive to Cubans wishing to emigrate, such as major leaguer **Jose Canseco**, who came to Miami with his family when he was a child. Other Cuban defectors include **Rene Arocha**, a top pitcher on Cuba's national team who asked for asylum in Miami in 1991 and eventually played for the St. Louis Cardinals (1993–95); **Ariel Prieto**, who was able to fly out of Cuba because his father-in-law is a U.S. citizen living in Florida; and **Euclides Rojas**, who escaped from Cuba in a homemade boat in 1994 headed for Florida and eventually wound up being drafted by the Florida Marlins.

High School Coaches in Florida

When Miami's Westminster Christian High School Coach **Rich Hofman**, who has coached at the school since 1969, won his state-record 600th career game in 1994, he broke the record of 599 set by **Buddy Lowe**, who had coached at Mount Dora (1990) and Leesburg (1960–87). Among the other winningest high school coaches not already mentioned are **Bill Brinker** of St. Petersburg's Seminole (1967–), **John Brown** of Jacksonville's University Christian (1975–), **Ralph Davis** of Miami's Senior (1955–82), **Bob Hawkins** of Gainesville's P.K. Yonge (1967–), **Jack Kokinda** of West Palm Beach's Cardinal Newman (1970–), **Howard May** of Jacksonville's Terry Parker (1970–), and **Greg Nichols** of Dunedin (1972–). Another successful high school coach who deserves mention is **Danny Allie** of Dr. Phillips High in Orlando.

American Legion Baseball

The American Legion describes its purpose in promoting baseball as fourfold: to inculcate in American youth a better understanding of the American way of life, promoting 100% Americanism; to instill in our nation's youth a sincere desire to develop within themselves a feeling of citizenship, sportsmanship, loyalty and team spirit; to aid in the improvement and development of the physical fitness of the country's youth; and to build for the nation's future through the youth.

The success of the program is clear from the fact that more graduates have been inducted into Baseball's Hall of Fame from the American Legion than from any other amateur baseball program. The Legion also takes pride in the hundreds of young men who have played in its programs and then attended college on a baseball scholarship and become successful in other professional fields. Florida ranks eighth in the number of American Legion teams it fields, behind Pennsylvania, Nebraska, Minnesota, California, Oklahoma, Missouri, and New Jersey. The number of registered Florida teams in the last few years is: 1987, 73; 1988, 74; 1989, 77; 1990, 99; 1991, 117; 1992, 146; 1993, 148; 1994, 154.

In 1994, **Fernando Rodriguez** of Miami Post 346 was named the American Legion National Player of the Year after he pitched a five-hitter to beat Chino (California) Post 299 in the title game of the Legion World Series. The right-handed Rodriguez was 15–1 for the season. Miami was the fourth Florida team to win the National Championship, the others being Hialeah (1978), West Tampa (1981), and Jensen Beach (1986).

▲ This youngster, Jimmy "Smoker Jr." Mott, has all that it takes to play baseball. *Florida State Archives*

Chapter Three

COLLEGE BASEBALL

"As the games begin, the best of college baseball
seems to largely reside in one place — Florida."
— Rick Lawes, *USA Today Baseball Weekly*, 1992

COLLEGE BASEBALL IN FLORIDA

College baseball has done well here because the state's climate has allowed players to compete all year long, its high schools have been a good source of talent, and its colleges have established strong baseball programs. Several cities have developed very strong traditions: Jacksonville (Florida Community College at Jacksonville, Jacksonville University, and the University of North Florida — one writer boasted that "Jacksonville could be the college baseball capital of the world") and Miami (Barry University, Florida International University, Miami-Dade Community College, and the University of Miami). In addition, several colleges in the state have a rivalry comparable to that of football or basketball; for example, the Florida State–Miami baseball rivalry, which Baseball America calls one of the five best in the nation. And while professional teams are established mostly in Northern and Western cities, more and more colleges in all parts of the country have players from warm-weather states on their rosters.

The fact that so many major league teams have held spring training in Florida has allowed the state's youth to see top-notch play and

▲ The Summerlin Institute Baseball team of 1908 with future senator Spessard Holland (standing second from the left) and future Miami Beach mayor Louis "Sned" Snedigar (sitting at far right in second row). *Florida State Archives*

has occasionally enabled local teams to play the pros in exhibition games. The New York Yankees, for example, under owner **George Steinbrenner**, a strong supporter of college baseball programs throughout the state, have played some of those teams in the spring, which allowed scouts to measure college players against the pros and sometimes to sign good prospects.

In 1916, when the University of Florida team faced **Connie Mack's** Philadelphia Athletics, the pitcher for the Gators was **Spessard L. Holland**. After Holland had struck out five of the big-league batters,

▲ Manager Connie Mack of the Philadelphia Athletics was known for his gentlemanly manners and his hats.

Dictionary of American Portraits, Dover Publications, 1967

Mack was impressed enough to offer the young man a chance at the majors: "I don't know whether you could make the grade with the majors or not, but I'd like to offer you the chance." Holland did not take Mack up on the offer, but instead went on to become a governor and U.S. senator. Some of those in a similar situation who did go on to the majors were **Johnny Burnett** of the Cleveland Indians, **Al Lopez** of the Brooklyn Dodgers, and **Lance Richbourg** of the Boston Braves.

Florida Winners of Baseball Awards

Each year the American Baseball Coaches Association (ABCA) honors with the Dick Howser Memorial Award the nation's outstanding college baseball player. Begun by the St. Petersburg Area Chamber of Commerce Baseball Committee soon after Howser's death in 1987, the trophy is given to the athlete who best demonstrates the baseball skills, moral character, and courage of its namesake. **Dick Howser,** who was born in Miami in 1936 and grew up in West Palm Beach, became a two-time All-American shortstop at Florida State University (1957–58). He played in the minors for three years and the majors for eight years (Kansas City, 1961–63; Cleveland, 1963–66; and the New York Yankees, 1967–68), coached at Florida State University (1979), and became a manager of the Yankees and Royals, winning the World Championship with the Royals in 1985. He died after a battle with cancer in 1987.

Officials select a Player of the Year in NCAA Divisions I, II, and III, the National Association of Intercollegiate Athletics (NAIA), and the National Junior College Athletic Association (NJCAA). These players become the finalists for the trophy and undergo final scrutiny by a committee formed by the ABCA. Nominees for the first trophy in the 1987 season were limited to players from Florida colleges because of a shortage of time in the selection process, but since then, players from around the country have been eligible.

Mike Fiore, a University of Miami outfielder, won the first trophy in 1987, followed by **Robin Ventura** of Oklahoma State (1988), **Scott Bryant** of Texas (1989), **Alex Fernandez** of Miami-Dade Community College-South (1990), **Frankie Rodriguez** of Howard College in Texas (1991), and **Brooks Kieschnick** of the University of Texas, the first two-time winner (1992–93).

Another important award is the Golden Spikes Award, which the United States Baseball Federation presents each year to the nation's best amateur player. Three baseball players at Florida schools have won this award: **Mike Fuentes** (1981), **Mike Loynd** (1986), both of Florida State University, and **Alex Fernandez** of Miami-Dade Community College-South (1990). A high school player from Florida who later won the Golden Spikes Award was **Oddibe McDowell**, who graduated from McArthur High School in Hollywood, Florida, before attending Miami-Dade North Junior College and Arizona State University; *Baseball America* also named him its 1984 College Baseball Player of the Year.

TWO-YEAR COLLEGES

The two-year public colleges in Florida, which for the most part belong to one of four conferences in the Florida Community College

Activities Association, have consistently fielded strong baseball teams, a fact proved by the number of their graduates who have gone on to play at four-year schools and in the professional ranks. Those conferences and the number of state baseball champions from them are: Panhandle (3), Mid-Florida (5), Suncoast (15), and Southern (10). (For a listing of the State Two-Year-College Baseball Champions, see Appendix B.) The two-year colleges that have won the most championships are Manatee (10), Miami Dade North (5), and Brevard (3). Among the two-year colleges in Florida that play baseball, several deserve special mention (in alphabetical order):

1. INDIAN RIVER COMMUNITY COLLEGE at Fort Pierce has sent 75 players into the pros; the Pioneers have been state champions twice (1979, 1993) and Southeast District champions once (1993); Their head coach, **Mike Easom**, has a career record at IRCC for the past 19 seasons of 644–321 for a .667 winning percentage.

2. MANATEE COMMUNITY COLLEGE at Bradenton has been state champion 10 times (1960, 1961, 1962, 1963, 1968, 1969, 1972, 1982, 1991, 1994); the college has won more state championships (10) and Southeastern Regional championships (7), and had more trips to the national tournament (7) than any other Florida two-year college. It has had 29 junior college All-Americans, 115 players who advanced to the professional level, and 21 players who made it to the majors. The school has had two head coaches. The first was **Bob Wynn** (1959–81, a 576–273 record), a member of the NJCAA Hall of Fame who retired as head coach in the fall of 1981 to serve as athletic director until he retired in 1993; the ballpark, Robert C. Wynn Field, is named after him. The second coach is **Tim Hill** (1982–), with a 445–189 record at Manatee and 84–66 at South Florida Junior College. The president of the school, Dr. **Stephen Korcheck**, is a former two-sport All-American (baseball and football) at George Washington University and a major league ballplayer (Washington Senators, 1954–55, 1958–59).

3. SANTA FE COMMUNITY COLLEGE's head coach, **Harry Tholen**, won his 500th career game in 1994 and has an overall record of 506–287 for a splendid .638 winning percentage. He has led his teams to 23 winning seasons, and his 1992 Saints won the Mid-Florida Conference.

◆

TWO NO-HITTERS IN ONE GAME

In what may have been the first college game to have two no-hitters by opposing pitchers, the 1995 game between Sanford's Seminole Community College and Orlando's Valencia Community College featured two great pitchers: **Tony Von Dolteren** of Seminole and **David Rivera** of Valencia. Seminole won when a walk, a throwing error, and a wild pitch scored a run.

National Junior College Athletic Association

Most of the two-year or community colleges (CC) in Florida belong to the National Junior College Athletic Association (NJCAA), which sponsors various athletic contests and crowns the champions of each. Among the NJCAA champions in baseball are the following local schools: Miami-Dade Community College-North (1964), Miami-Dade Community College-South (1981), and Hillsborough Community College (1988).

Among the NJCAA records set by state schools and players are: Longest Single Game: Hillsborough 6 vs. Manatee 4, 32 innings (1987); Shutouts: 10 by **Joe Arnold** at Miami-Dade CC-North (1967); and Most Triples: 12 by **Steve Cook** of Miami-Dade CC-North (1974). Among the NJCAA Division-I Baseball Tournament Records are: Triples: 4 by **Howard May** of Gulf Coast CC (1965); Home Runs in one Game: 3 by **Steve Cook** of Miami-Dade CC-North (1974); stolen bases: 11 by **Humbert Acosta** of Miami-Dade CC-Downtown (1976); and innings pitched: 30 2/3 by **Joe Arnold** of Miami-Dade CC (1966).

The NJCAA Baseball Hall of Fame includes these members:

1983 - **Demie Mainieri**, Miami Dade CC-North, Miami
1984 - **Leroy Wheat**, Broward CC, Fort Lauderdale
1988 - **Robert C. Wynn**, Manatee CC, Bradenton
1991 - **Charles P. Greene**, Miami-Dade CC-South, Miami
         Frank J. Torre, Major League Baseball, Palm Grove Garden
1994 - **Bill Frazier**, Gulf Coast CC, Panama City
1995 - **Howard Roey**, Florida CC, Jacksonville

The NJCAA Men's Baseball Records for active coaches include these:

NAME	SCHOOL	YEARS	WINS	LOSSES	RANKING
Charles Greene	Miami-Dade CC-South	27	879	458	4
Edward Davis	St. Petersburg JC	26	656	574	18
Mike Easom	Indian River CC	18	614	304	22
Tim Hill	Manatee CC	17	529	270	28
Harry Tholen	Santa Fe CC	24	506	287	31
Roger Martinsen	Central Florida CC	24	474	410	41

The NJCAA Men's Baseball Records for inactive coaches include these:

NAME	SCHOOL	YEARS	WINS	LOSSES	RANKING
Demie Mainieri	Miami-Dade CC-North	30	1012	409	2
Bill Frazier	Gulf Coast CC	17	600	242	11
John C. Tindall	St. Johns River CC	30	591	495	12
Robert C. Wynn	Manatee CC	23	576	251	13
Buddy Kisner	Pensacola JC	20	524	383	16
Leroy Wheat	Broward CC	13	455	121	22

The JUCO Baseball World Series

The Florida participants in the JUCO Baseball World Series, Division I, 1958 through 1995, were Brevard CC (1986, 1989), Florida CC in Jacksonville (1987), Gulf Coast CC (1965, 1973), Hillsborough CC (1988), Indian River CC (1993, 1995), Manatee CC (1961-63, 1965, 1968, 1972, 1991, 1994), Miami-Dade CC-Downtown (1976), Miami-Dade CC-North (1964, 1966, 1967, 1971, 1974), Miami-Dade CC-South (1978, 1981), and Santa Fe CC (1985).

The leaders of final baseball statistics include Strikeout Leader: **Ricardo Jordan** of Miami-Dade CC-South with 154 strikeouts, 1.10/inning (1989); Total Strikeout Leaders: **Ricardo Jordan** of Miami-Dade CC-South with 154 strikeouts (1989) and **Alex Fernandez** of Miami-Dade CC-South also with 154 strikeouts (1990); and Stolen Base Leader: **Michael Ward** of Valencia CC with 67, a .90 percentage (1993). **Emile Brown** of Indian River CC won the 1994 Rawlings Big Stick Batting Award with a .421 average. The top community-college teams in the Florida division in 1994 were Manatee (42–17), Florida CC in Jacksonville (43–12), Indian River (29–16), Tallahassee (42–11), and Gulf Coast (47–12).

FOUR-YEAR COLLEGES AND UNIVERSITIES

Collegiate Baseball, the journal that describes college baseball, consistently highlights Florida schools at the two- and four-year levels. Like other state schools throughout the nation, Florida colleges at first recruited mostly from in-state ballplayers, but eventually the excellence of the programs attracted out-of-staters. Among the local four-year colleges and universities that deserve mention in this baseball history (in alphabetical order) are:

1. FLORIDA ATLANTIC UNIVERSITY, which was founded in 1961 and has a student enrollment of 16,500, plays baseball in the NCAA Division I and the Trans America Athletic Conference (TAAC). The Owls' head baseball coach is **Kevin Cooney**, who has an overall record of 332–192–4 and a six-year record (1988–) at FAU of 182–142–4. The other head coach was **Steve Traylor** (1981–1986, 268–107–2 record). The school has had four All-Americans: **Keith Foley** (1983), **Scott Hay** (1986), **Jack Penrod** (1988), and **Mike Ryan** (1984). Seventeen alumni have played professional baseball.

2. FLORIDA INTERNATIONAL UNIVERSITY in Miami, which jumped to Division I in 1983, has had to compete for years with the perennial regional powerhouse, the University of Miami. Coach **Danny Price**'s Golden Panthers of FIU have averaged nearly 38 wins a season since making the move to Division I and split with Miami in 1995. One of the team's 1995 stars was second baseman **Mike Lowell**, who hit .307 with a wood bat in the Cape Cod summer league and was named the league's all-star second baseman. The final Top-25 *Baseball America* poll for 1995 ranked the team, which finished with a 50–11 record, 22nd in the nation.

3. FLORIDA SOUTHERN COLLEGE, one of the strongest colleges in Division II baseball competition, made post-season playoffs a record 25 straight years, only missing the initial year (1968) and finally ending that streak in 1993. The Moccasins or Mocs have won eight championships, including three under coach **Hal Smeltzly**, who was inducted into the American Association of Baseball Coaches Hall of Fame in 1980 and the Florida Sports Hall of Fame in 1987 and who has served as Florida Southern's Director of Athletics since 1972. The Moccasins, the nation's best in their division in 1971, 1972, 1975, 1978, 1981, 1985, 1988, and 1995, have been led by **Hal Smeltzly** (1958–66 and 1968–76, record: 391–166–4), **Joe Arnold** (1977–83,

▲ The Stetson University team about 1910. *Florida State Archives*

▼ The Florida Southern College baseball team about 1919.
Heritage Park-Pinellas County Historical Museum

316–69), and **Chuck Anderson** (1967 and 1984–present, 563–155–1). Their combined record of 1,265–392–5 was an amazing .763 winning percentage.

Coach **Joe Arnold**, who went on to coach at the University of Florida (1984–94), won two Division II national titles (1978, 1981), was Division II Coach of the Year twice (1978, 1981), and had an NCAA record six consecutive World Series appearances during his tenure at Florida Southern. Arnold had been an All-American baseball player at Miami-Dade Community College-North (1966, 1967) before going on to play well at Arizona State University, where in 1968 as a pitcher he had an 11–1 record and an 0.68 ERA; he then went on to play in the Houston Astros organization (1968–70) before returning to Arizona State to earn a master's degree (1971).

Coach **Chuck Anderson**, from Avon Park, Florida, has spent much of his career at FSC. He played baseball there (1959–62), won Most Valuable Player awards there twice (1961, 1962), and stayed on as an assistant coach (1963–83), interim head coach (1967), and then head coach (1984–present). During his tenure as assistant and head coach, he was involved in the school's 25 NCAA tournaments and an unprecedented seven national championships, two as head coach (1985, 1988). In 1994, he won his 500th game.

The Florida Southern baseball team has as its home base Tigertown, which is also the spring training headquarters of the Detroit Tigers; the four practice diamonds as well as the 7,000-seat Joker Marchant Stadium also serve the Lakeland Tigers, Detroit's Class

The Florida State ▶
Seminoles baseball team in
1968 was ranked number one
in the nation during a
21-game winning streak.
Florida State Archives

A affiliate in the Florida State League. An amazing 94 Mocs have signed with the pros, and the school has had 61 All-Americans. Coach Anderson served in 1995 as the first vice president of the American Baseball Coaches Association (ABCA), an organization founded in 1945 by college coaches to promote and improve the college game. Membership today includes seven divisions: NCAA I, II, III, NAIA, NJCAA, High School, and Youth. Over 5,000 members belong to the ABCA. It includes coaches from every state and many foreign nations.

▲ The Florida Southern College baseball emblem.
Florida Southern College

Florida Southern is a member of the Sunshine State Conference, which was founded in 1975 and has an annual baseball championship. Other state schools in the conference are Barry University in Miami Shores, Eckerd College in St. Petersburg, Florida Tech in Melbourne, Rollins College in Winter Park, Saint Leo College in Saint Leo, the University of North Florida in Jacksonville, and the University of Tampa in Tampa.

4. FLORIDA STATE UNIVERSITY has consistently had one of the best baseball teams in the nation, although its 1948 start was relatively late. Its coaches were **Charles Armstrong** (1948–51, record: 49–29), **Ralph Matherly** (1952–54, 43–22–1), **Danny Litwhiler**

(1955–63, 189–82), **Fred Hatfield** (1964–68, 161–57–1), **Jack Stallings** (1969–74, 248–107–3), **Woody Woodward** (1975–78, 170–57), **Dick Howser** (1979, 43–17–1), **Mike Martin** (1980-, 814–280). In 1948, its first year, the baseball team joined other Florida schools (Stetson and Tampa) in the nine-member Dixie Conference. Its first All-American was **Dick Howser**, who went on to become manager of the Yankees and later manager of the world-champion Kansas City Royals in 1985. By the spring of 1995, FSU had the most appearances in the College World Series (13) of any school without winning a national championship, and its 17 consecutive regional appearances form the second-longest streak, behind only Miami's ongoing record (22).

By 1995, FSU was ranked 22nd, and first in Florida, among universities in having the most players make it to the majors, despite having such a late start in baseball. Its string of 326 consecutive games in which it scored at least one run was the second-longest in NCAA Division I history. It has finished second in the College World Series (1970, 1986), tied for third (1989), came in fourth (1962), and most recently tied for fifth (1995) with a final record of 53–16. The final Top-25 poll for 1995 as published in *Baseball America* ranked the team third in the nation. In the 1970 Series, FSU pitcher **Gene Ammann** was named MVP.

FSU pitcher **Paul Wilson** from Orlando received the second-highest bonus in draft history when, as the first player picked in the 1994 draft, he signed for $1.55 million with the New York Mets. The 6′5″, 215-pound fast-baller went on to play in the Gulf Coast League and at St. Lucie of the Class A Florida State League.

The school has fielded excellent baseball teams over the years. Coach **Mike Martin** became only the third coach in Division I history to win 800 games in just 15 seasons. His teams won at least 50 games in each of his first 12 seasons, a streak that may be unmatched in college baseball. A 1966 graduate of FSU and a player on the 1965–66 Seminole teams, Martin became head coach in 1980, when **Dick Howser** left FSU for the New York Yankees.

Among the excellent players at FSU are several who deserve special mention. **Mike Fuentes**, who set an NCAA record in 1981 of 64 career home runs in college baseball, won the Golden Spikes Award, the baseball equivalent of the Heisman Trophy. A year later, FSU's **Jeff**

Ledbetter broke the record with a career mark of 97 homers; his 42 homers in 1982 broke the NCAA record of 29 in one season and led to his being the Sporting News Player of the Year, an honor that FSU player **Terry Kennedy** had won in 1977. FSU pitcher **Mike Loynd** won the Golden Spikes Award in 1986 for his 20–3 record.

5. ROLLINS COLLEGE in Winter Park was founded in 1885 and ten years later participated in its first intercollegiate event: a baseball game with Stetson, which Rollins won, 11–10. The early baseball rivalry between Rollins and Stetson was so intense that in 1903 both teams brought in outside players with superior skills. Stetson imported some University of Illinois players, while Rollins used the great major-league pitcher and future Hall-of-Famer **Rube Waddell** and his Philadelphia Athletics catcher **Ossee "Schreck" Schreckengost**, both of whom registered as students at Rollins and signed up for at least one course. Waddell had the habit of hanging from a bar in the top of the dugout between innings to stretch his arm, although many at the time thought he was just strange. When the Stetson team arrived in Winter Park to play Rollins, the Hatters saw the formidable Waddell, refused to take the field, and caught the next train back to DeLand. Waddell, who pitched for and coached the Rollins team, is said to have called in the outfielders on at least one occasion and then thrown strikes past the bewildered batters. Waddell and Schreck joined their Philadelphia teammates in Jacksonville that spring, the first time the Athletics trained in the state.

The Tars baseball team, which is in the NCAA Division II and the Sunshine State Conference, has a long tradition of excellence. In 1954, for example, the Rollins team was the first from a Florida college or university to play in the College World Series in Omaha, finishing as a runner-up, despite having only 300 male students enrolled and possibly being the smallest college ever to make the World Series. Enthusiasm in Winter Park was so high for the team that year that officials had loudspeakers set up around town so people could hear the broadcasts.

The school may also be the only one to play in three different national championships: the NCAA (1954), the NAIA (1957, 1959), and the NCAA Division II (1989). One of its alumni, **John Castino** of the Minnesota Twins (1979–84), was the 1979 American League Rookie of the Year.

▲ The Stetson University team with a visiting member of the University of Chicago team around 1910. *Florida State Archives*

The Rollins coaches have been **Jack McDowall** (1930–42, [there was no team during the war years]), **Joe Justice** (1947–71, record: 482–287–13, 12 conference titles and nine post-season games), **Boyd Coffie** (1972–91, 586–419–6 and eight post-season games), **John Fulgham** (1992–94, 63–52 and one post-season game), and interim head coach **Bob Rikeman** (1995–). The Tars, who play home games at Alfond Stadium at Harper-Shepherd Field, host the oldest collegiate tournament in the nation each year (begun in 1948) in what they call "Baseball Week." Rollins has 57 alumni in the pros, some of them as players and others as managers and scouts.

6. STETSON UNIVERSITY, founded in DeLand in 1883, has had strong athletic teams over the years. When the school affiliated with the University of Chicago for 12 years (1898–1910), the two institutions had comparable courses, so the students from Chicago could attend Stetson, especially in the mild winters of central Florida. This

enabled ballplayers from the two schools to train and play together.

The Stetson baseball team excelled in the early years of the school and took particular delight in beating the larger schools, for example, the University of Florida. The players were eager to take on any other team, including professional teams, and usually did well. Its 1916 team, for example, had five players go on to professional baseball and lost to the Brooklyn Dodgers by just one run, 7–6. The college boys were actually winning that game 6–2 in the sixth inning when the Stetson pitcher got into a heated argument with the umpire and was ejected.

Today, the Hatters play baseball in the Trans America Athletic Conference, which was founded in 1978, as do three other Florida universities: Central Florida in Orlando, Florida Atlantic in Boca Raton, and Florida International in Miami. In 1936, DeLand became a charter member of the Class A Florida State League (FSL) and remained in the FSL until 1954.

Head Coach **Pete Dunn**, who played at Stetson (1969–70), became the head baseball coach in 1980 after being an assistant at Georgia Southern College (1973–74), head coach at Apopka (Florida) High School (1975–77), and an assistant at Stetson under **Jim Ward** (1978–79). When he won his 500th game in 1993, he became the fourth-winningest active NCAA I baseball coach with 15 years or less experience.

Four Hatters were All-Americans: **Mike Fulford** (1970), **Tom Hickox** (1988, 1989), **Tony Latour** (1970), and **Mike Wolfe** (1975); 41 alumni have gone on to the pros. The school has had a remarkable record over the years: 22 seasons with 20 or more wins, 16 seasons with 30 or more wins, and two seasons with 40 or more wins. They have won 63% of the 1,178 NCAA I games played in a span of 22 years.

7. The UNIVERSITY OF CENTRAL FLORIDA, founded in Orlando in 1963, has had four baseball coaches: **Doug Holmquist** (1973–75, record: 66–41–1), **Jack Sexton** (1976–77, 43–41), **Bill Moon** (1978–82, 124–120–3), and **Jay Bergman** (1983–, 422–267–3). Bergman, a Rollins College graduate, also coached at Seminole Community College and the University of Florida before beginning at UCF in 1983. Twenty-one Knights have gone into the pros; four were All-Americans: **Tim Barker** (1985), **Tim Foskett** (1983), **Chad**

Mottola (1992), and **Sam Swanger** (1975). In 1995, the Knights won 29 games in a row, just five games short of the all-time Division I record set by Texas in 1977. The final Top-25 poll for 1995 as published in *Baseball America* ranked the team, which finished with a 49–13 record, 19th in the nation.

8. The UNIVERSITY OF FLORIDA baseball program sometimes seemed to play second fiddle to the more popular football program, but it consistently produced major league talent. The school has had 19 head coaches: **H. D. McLeod** (1912, record: 9–4–2), **R. P. Hoffman** (1913, 11–9–1), **Pat Flaherty** (1914–16, 15–29–1), **Hugh Wicher** (1917, 8–3), **Artie Phelan** (1919–20, 14–16–1), **William Kline** (1921, 4–10), **Lance Richbourg** (1922–23, 1926, 39–21), **Rex Farrior** (1924, 5–14), **James White** (1925, 3–6), **Brady Cowell** (1927–33, 61–65–2), **Ben Clemons** (1934–36, 20–29–1), **Lew Hardage** (1937–39, 35–24–1), **Sam McAllister** (1940–42, 1946–47, 40–56–4), **Bob Pittman** (1945, 2–9), **Dave Fuller** (1948–75, 557–354–6), **Jay Bergman** (1976–81, 216–113), **Jack Rhine** (1982–83, 72–39–1), **Joe Arnold** (1984–94, 434–244–2), and **Andy Lopez** (1995–).

The two winningest coaches at UF have been **Dave Fuller**, whose teams won 557 games during his 28 years as head coach, and **Joe Arnold**, whose teams won 434 games during his 11 years as head coach. Arnold was the only one to lead the school to the College World Series (1988, 1991). Former Gator stars like **Mike Stanley** of the New York Yankees testified to his success. Florida's overall winning percentage (.613) in its 58 years in the Southeastern Conference (SEC) ranked it number one in All-Time SEC Standings.

Andy Lopez, who won the 1992 College World Series at Pepperdine, became head coach in 1994 and brought high hopes. Lopez had coached baseball for six years at Cal State-Dominguez Hills and six years at Pepperdine; he was the consensus National Coach-of-the-Year in 1992 and four-time West Coast Conference coach of the year. Part of the reason he came to the University of Florida was the high caliber of the baseball program at the school. He said, "If you're the best team in Florida, you have a legitimate chance to compete for a national championship." The baseball program was able to use some of the money that the school's successful football and basketball teams generated in 1994 to build a $3.5 million clubhouse and plaza for the baseball program.

▲ The playing field at the University of Florida is modern and comfortable.

Jeffrey L. Gage, University of Florida

9. The UNIVERSITY OF MIAMI, which began in 1926 and is the largest independent teaching and research university in the Southeast, has a long tradition of excellence in its sports programs, a tradition that has attracted excellent athletes and coaches; for example, Hall-of-Famer **Jimmie Foxx**, who coached the UM baseball team in 1956 and 1957. The school has had a long, successful history of baseball, especially after **Ron Fraser** became head coach in 1963 and went on to become one of the best-known and most successful baseball coaches in the United States. He was inducted into the Florida Sports Hall of Fame in 1986. Fraser, who pitched for FSU in the 1950s, is also a member of the Florida State University Athletic Hall of Fame.

After coaching at Miami for 30 years, Fraser retired at the end of the 1992 season with 1,271 victories, the second highest in NCAA Division I history; his total record was 1,271–438–9 for an amazing .747 percentage of wins. His Hurricanes won the College World Series twice (1982, 1985) and led college baseball in home attendance for six years in the 1980s. He won the World Amateur Coach of the Year honors (1973) and became the first American to win the International Baseball Association's Coach of the Year Award (1987).

Fraser helped to spread baseball to other countries, teaching it in such places as Germany, Holland, the Soviet Union, and Spain. He served as Holland's director of baseball, leading that country to the

European championship in his first year, and he took part in the Soviet Union's first international baseball tournament. Fraser coached the 1992 U.S. Olympic baseball team in Barcelona, Spain, where his team finished fourth in the first Olympics in which baseball was a full-fledged medal sport.

The other Hurricane head coaches have been **Jack Harding** (1940, 1959, record: 16–15–1), **Eddie Dunn** (1946–54, 81–72–2), **Perry Moss** (1955, 15–7), **Jimmie Foxx** (1956–57, 20–20), **Whitey Campbell** (1958, 1960–62, 69–36–3), **Brad Kelley** (1993, 36–22), and **Jim Morris** (1994–95, 97–31). One hundred fifty-five Hurricanes have made it into the pros, and 17 have made it to the major leagues. The University of Miami's baseball recruiting coordinator, **Turtle Thomas**, has been called "the hardest-working recruiter in college baseball." In 1994, he logged 20,000 air miles flying all over the country, attending 19 baseball tournaments and scouting the best high school seniors he could find. Such hard work for Thomas, then in his eighth year at Miami, resulted in highly skilled players for the university and eventually for the majors. For example, Miami tied with Arizona State for having the most players (nine) drafted by the majors in 1994.

Miami won the national title twice (1982, 1985), came in second (1974, 1986, 1992-tied), tied for third (1995), and came in fourth (1978, 1980). The final Top-25 *Baseball America* poll for 1995 ranked the team, which had a 48–17 record, fourth in the nation. Two of its players were named MVP in the College World Series: pitcher **Danny Smith** (1982) and designated hitter **Greg Ellena** (1985). Miami leads the nation in all-time consecutive regional appearances in the College World Series (23).

10. The UNIVERSITY OF SOUTH FLORIDA in Tampa has had four head baseball coaches: **Beefy Wright** (1966–75, record: 131–127–2), **Jack Butterfield** (1975–76, 61–24–1), Hall-of-Fame pitcher and former Phillie **Robin Roberts** (1977–85, 262–240–2), and **Eddie Cardieri** (1986–, 301–190). The team ranked first in its conference, which was either the Sun Belt Conference (1978–91) or the Metro Conference (1992–present) four times: 1982, 1986, 1990, and 1993. USF's All-Americans include **Mike Campbell** (1973), **Lou Garcia** (1975), **Scott Hemond** (1984, 1986), and **Darren Stumberger** (1993). The university, which ranks 24th in the nation with its 34,000-plus students and

is rapidly on its way to becoming the largest university in Florida, should get stronger in baseball and may very well challenge the other powerhouses of the state in the sport.

11. The UNIVERSITY OF TAMPA, despite having a low enrollment of only 1,500 students, has a stellar baseball tradition, much of it due to the excellent coaching of **Lelo Prado**, who had a 237–107–1 (.689) record through 1994. In his six years at UT, he won two NCAA Division II national championships (1992, 1993), a remarkable feat for a coach who is in his early 30s. He coached 16 All-Americans, two Academic All-Americans, 39 All-South region picks, and 28 all-SSC selections. In 1994, he was named the American Baseball Coaches Association National Coach of the Year for the second year in a row.

One of the school's best players, **Sam Militello**, was named the Small College Player of the Year (1990) as well as first team All-American (1989, 1990) and third team All-American (1988). In 1995, one of the school's graduates, **Terry Rupp**, was named head baseball coach to replace Prado, who went on to Louisville.

College Tournaments

Among the college regular-season baseball tournaments in Florida are the following: the Olive Garden Classic in Orlando, the Jacksonville Greyhound Racing BB Classic in Jacksonville, Rollins Baseball Week in Winter Park, the ECAC Florida Baseball Invitational in Fort Myers, and the Stetson Invitational Tournament in DeLand.

Chapter Four

WOMEN IN BASEBALL

"An axiom of the times was that a woman's name should appear in print but twice in a lifetime: when she married and when she died. Certainly not when she graduated from college — and positively not when she drove in a game-winning run."
— Barbara Gregorich, *Women at Play*, 1993

THE ALL-AMERICAN GIRLS PROFESSIONAL
BASEBALL LEAGUE

When women discovered baseball in the mid-1800s, they ran into a lot of prejudice and bias from those who wanted them to stay at home and leave such sports to men. Women did form teams they called the Bloomer Girls, although many of those teams included men in positions like pitcher and catcher. Some of the better teams of Bloomer Girls toured the country, including Florida, playing local male teams. At all-female colleges like Vassar (1865), Smith (1875), and Wellesley (1875), women were able to avoid the problems of mixed schools, where boys would dominate the baseball rosters, and introduce sports, like baseball, that other schools would not allow because of their reluctance to have boys and girls on the same team. Baseball offered a good alternative for female athletes who did not want to play only softball. The Depression of the 1930s forced many women's teams to disband because of the high cost of fielding teams, and Baseball Commissioner **Kenesaw Mountain Landis** ended their hopes of playing in the minors when he forbade it in 1931.

▼ A Bloomer Girls team, which usually had several male players, toured places in the South. *National Baseball Library & Archive, Cooperstown, N.Y.*

However, when World War II took away many of the male athletes in the 1940s and forced several minor league teams to fold, Chicago Cubs' owner **Philip K. Wrigley** started the All-American Girls Professional Baseball League (AAGPBL) to keep fans going to the ballpark. When the new league announced tryouts for May 1943, more than 100 women, many of them former softball players, tried out for the 60 slots available. From 1943 to 1954, teams from five Midwestern states played baseball in the AAGPBL, which provided more than a million fans with high-caliber baseball and thousands of girls with models of highly professional skills in a demanding field. The women, who played games six days a week and a doubleheader on Sunday, earned $65 to $125 a week for three months and played a 108-game, split season.

The league soon expanded to ten teams in the Midwest and attracted growing numbers of fans eager to see a different kind of baseball, at first based on softball, but gradually patterning itself after professional baseball. As the women got better, they switched from playing modified softball to regulation hardball. In 1947, the women trained in Havana, but the following spring, 200 of them traveled to Florida and began training at a decommissioned military airfield where Miami-Dade Community College's North Campus is today. They may also have come to Florida because the league's president, **Max Carey**, a former major leaguer and future Hall-of-Famer, was then living in nearby Miami Beach. He had hopes of expanding the female league from a summertime league to a winter schedule that would include Havana, Miami, and other cities in Central America and the Caribbean. Among the teams the women played in Florida was one made up of congressmen who came here each spring for some friendly competition.

The women who played in that league succeeded in keeping baseball alive during and after World War II. More importantly, however, was what they did as role models for young women. One spectator later wrote the following:

> The All-Americans were heroes for all their fans, but especially for their little-girl fans. They showed us women doing something difficult and dangerous, something that took physical courage, intelligence and a fighting spirit. Moreover, the ballplayers were doing this as a team, working hard with

▲ When the All-American Girls Professional Baseball League (AAGPBL) practiced at Opa-Locka in 1948, they had to do many calisthenics. The Fort Wayne, South Bend, Peoria, Rockford, Springfield, and Chicago teams are pictured here doing a rowing exercise. *Florida State Archives*

▼ More exercises for the six clubs. *Florida State Archives*

◀ Max Carey of Miami Beach, formerly a 24-year major leaguer, was president of the AAGPBL.
Florida State Archives

▼ Dick Bass, a former major league pitcher, gives members of the Fort Wayne club in Opa-Locka pointers on the new 10 3/8" ball which was to be used that year in the AAGP-BL. *Florida State Archives*

▲ Dottie Schroeder at bat, catcher Mary Rountree behind the plate, and umpire Norris Ward calling balls and strikes. *Florida State Archives*

▼ An inter-team practice game at Opa-Locka. *Florida State Archives*

▲ Mary Rountree, a native of Miami and a pre-med student at Florida State College for Women in Tallahassee, was in her third year with the AAGPBL in 1948. *Florida State Archives*

▲ Carl Hubbell, former pitcher for the New York Giants, umpires a game between the Sanford Girls' Team and the touring Congressional team in 1950. The batter is Representative Eugene McCarthy of Minnesota. *Florida State Archives*

▼ Representative Lowell Stockman as umpire calls Representative George Fallon out during a game with the Sanford Girls' Team in 1950.
Florida State Archives

other women to achieve something worthwhile, a game well played, and — if dedication, hard work, luck and the umpires cooperated — a victory. And they did all this with a light-heartedness that told me struggle, even combat, could be fun.

The 1948 exhibition games were played at Flamingo Park in Miami Beach and at Miami Field, now the parking lot of the Orange Bowl Stadium. One of the players for the Fort Wayne Daisies was **Mary Rountree**, a graduate of Miami Edison High School who went on to become a medical doctor after playing for six years as a catcher in the women's league. She believed that her experience in the AAGPBL helped her become a better doctor: "My ballplaying was absolutely magnificent for me. You had to meet a lot of people so you learned to get over your stage fright, your bashfulness. Because you had to do personal appearances, you overcame your inability to talk to people in a very quick amount of time. I think that it allowed me to be total-ly at home with patients. It gave you a chance to develop your personality."

Another Floridian who played for the AAGPBL was **Rossi Weeks**, a woman from Jacksonville who had played various sports in her youth. After being discharged from the Air Force in 1946, she went to Miami for a tryout with the women's league, won a position on the Racine team, trained in Cuba, and ended up as a catcher for the Rockford Peaches in the 1947 season. However, when she broke a finger on a foul tip, the team released her, and she returned to Jacksonville to play for local softball and basketball teams. In 1955, her softball team, the Gator Gals, won the state championship. Two other Florida women who played in the AAGPBL were **Margaret Berger** from Miami and **Bethany Goldsmith** from Zellwood.

The AAGPBL lasted until 1954, when televised professional (male) baseball stole the audience and caused the league to fold. More people around the country became aware of the women's league in 1988, when a permanent exhibit on the AAGPBL was unveiled in the Baseball Hall of Fame, and in 1992, when Penny Marshall's film, *A League of Their Own*, was released. One of the women in that league, **Dottie Kamenshek**, lost a chance to become the first woman to play professional baseball with men in 1950 when she declined an offer to try out from the Fort Lauderdale team in the Florida International

League, saying she preferred instead to "finish out my career with the [Rockford, Illinois] Peaches."

There was another would-be Florida experiment, which was based partly on the AAGPBL and which almost worked. It was a proposal in 1984 to have in Daytona Beach a mostly female, minor league team, the Sun Sox, sponsored by former Atlanta Braves public-relations director **Bob Hope**, as part of the Florida State League (FSL). Hope, assisted by **Jim Morris**, who was then the baseball coach at Georgia Tech, held tryouts for the team, but the other owners and farm directors of the FSL would not allow it.

The Colorado Silver Bullets

That same **Bob Hope** became president in 1994 of the Colorado Silver Bullets, a women's professional baseball team which played its first season under the experienced eye of manager **Phil Niekro**, former Atlanta Braves pitcher and minor league manager. After tryouts, in which 2,800 women applied for the team, 21 women began practicing in March and trained for six weeks, partly at Orlando's Tinker Field, before going on the road. They played men's teams, many of them over-30 men's teams, throughout the United States. Although the team finished with a poor 6–38 record, did not have a single player who hit above .220, and did not have a pitcher with an ERA below 4.50, it did attract some 300,000 fans, an average of almost 7,000 a game. Among the players who excelled were first baseman **Julie**

◄ A batter and catcher for a girls' baseball team playing in St. Petersburg in the 1960s.

St. Petersburg Museum of History

Croteau and pitcher **Lee Anne Ketcham**, who were invited to play in the Hawaiian Winter League.

In preparation for the 1995 season, the Silver Bullets came to Fort Myers to train at City of Palms Park, where the Boston Red Sox have their spring training. Fifty women were invited to the camp to try out for the 20-woman team, and each team member signed a $20,000 contract for the season.

The second year saw a much stronger group for two reasons. Many women had stayed away in the team's first year to see how it would do. Also, many women who were fast-pitch softball players, from whom the team would be expected to draw its players, had been trying out in 1994 for the 1996 Olympics team. The second-year team was so much stronger than the first-year team that four returning players were not able to make the new team, a team that was 5-3-1 in spring games against semi-pro teams from Florida.

The three-year plan (1994–96) for the Bullets, the only women's professional team which competes against men's teams, is to become good enough to compete against teams from colleges, rookie leagues, and Class A leagues and maybe to become a Class A team themselves. The team has hopes of establishing a minor league system, perhaps even a league in the Mediterranean area to allow women to develop their skills and also to provide a chance for the 30 who were cut from the main team.

Women Playing College Baseball

Two women who may have been the first and second females to play college baseball in this country both attended Doyle Baseball School in Florida. **Julie Croteau** became the first woman to play a full season of college baseball when she made the St. Mary's College team in Maryland in 1988. She had been considered, but not accepted, by Flagler College in St. Augustine. She later made the Colorado Silver Bullets. In 1990, **Jodi Haller** pitched for NAIA St. Vincent's College in Latrobe, Pennsylvania. The 5'8" 140-pound lefthander had pitched in Little League and in American Legion ball. St. Vincent's kept no statistics on Haller, but she definitely pitched in Florida when the college team played some of the state's teams on a tour. Haller pitched once in relief and once as a starter, throwing more than two innings each time. When asked why she became a pitcher, she responded:

I started pitching mainly because I'm left-handed. My father knew that when I got into upper levels of baseball I would get overwhelmed by the guys, so I concentrated more on pitching than hitting. I always had good control and that's what really helped. A lot of the guys could throw a lot harder, but it wasn't ever near the plate.

Other Women's Baseball Leagues

The idea for the American Women's Baseball Association (AWBA) began in 1988, when Illinois businesswoman **Darlene Mehrer** attended a baseball fantasy training camp, a week-long experience when older, amateur ballplayers live out their dreams of playing baseball with active and retired major leaguers. Before she died in 1990, she began a two-team women's baseball league, increasing it to three teams the next year and then to four. Another league, the All-American Women's Baseball League (AAWBL), began around 1993. Unlike the league of the 1940s, this league did not have etiquette classes for the women. The players wore traditional baseball uniforms instead of short skirts, and used regulation equipment instead of the oversized ball and shortened basepaths of the former league. The league required the women to have ten weeks of spring training in Florida.

▲ The Florida State College for Women (later Florida State University) had a women's baseball team in 1928 that played only on campus because baseball was considered unfeminine at the time.

Florida State Archives

In 1994, the four-team Women's Baseball League had teams in Apopka, Daytona Beach, Sanford, and Tavares. The Daytona team was to play its home games at Jackie Robinson Ballpark, where the Class A Daytona Cubs also played. Each team had 17 players, and the 24-game season was from October until the end of January. The Sanford team won the regular-season title of the league, while the Apopka team won the playoff championship. The Apopka team moved to Cocoa Beach for the next season and became the Brevard Diamonds. Apopka's first baseman **Sheila Bonilla**, who led in batting average (.432), hits (35), and RBIs (25), was the league MVP.

WOMEN UMPIRES

Another Florida connection with women in baseball concerned the first woman to umpire a professional baseball game. **Bernice Gera** (1931–92) was born in Ernest, Pennsylvania, and grew up playing baseball with boys. As an adult, she umpired Little League and semi-professional baseball for years, but wanted to advance to the majors. After seeing an ad in *The Sporting News* for the Florida Baseball Umpire School in West Palm Beach, she sent in her application. Officials at the school, misreading her signature as "Bernie," accepted her; once they realized that she was female, they did not change their mind, and in 1967 she became the first woman to receive a diploma from the school.

Numerous baseball organizations rejected her application for an umpiring job, citing such regulations as one that required umpires to be 5'10" tall and weigh at least 170 pounds; she was only 5'2" tall and weighed 130 pounds. She fought the regulations in court and finally won in New York State Supreme Court. On June 24, 1972, she became the first woman to umpire a professional game when she officiated in a Class A game in the New York-Pennsylvania Professional Baseball League at Geneva, New York. The players and the other umpire in that game, a man, hassled her with comments like "You should have stayed home in the kitchen peeling potatoes," but she had made a point. She quit umpiring after that game, but later worked in public relations for the New York Mets before moving in 1979 to Pembroke Pines, Florida, where she died. A Hall of Fame exhibit in Cooperstown, New York — "Women in Baseball" — honored her contributions to baseball.

Gera had paved the way for other women umpires like **Pam Postema**, who began umpiring in Sarasota of the Gulf Coast League and then went on for 13 more years in the minor leagues. Postema was in Gainesville, Florida, visiting relatives when she saw an ad mentioning the Al Somers Baseball Umpires School in Daytona Beach. When Somers rejected Postema's application, she drove to Daytona Beach and went directly to his house to ask him to accept her into the school. When she implied that she would sue him if he rejected her, he accepted her and another woman for the 1977 winter session. She described this in her book, *You've Got to Have Balls to Make It in This League.*

WOMEN TRAINERS

Another possible first for women in baseball concerned **Donna Lee Van Duzer**, who worked as the trainer for the Texas Rangers' Port Charlotte minor league team in the Class A Florida State League in 1990–91. Van Duzer was able to secure interviews by printing "D. L. Van Duzer" at the top of her resumé instead of her real name, but the Texas Rangers' **Marty Scott** was not at all concerned that she was a woman, and offered her various places to work in the Rangers' organization. Van Duzer may have been the first woman trainer to work for a full-season club.

▲ Team members on a Clearwater baseball team in 1895 dress up as women for the entertainment of fans. *Heritage Park-Pinellas County Historical Museum*

Chapter Five

AFRICAN AMERICANS IN BASEBALL

"Don't feel sorry for old Buck; I had a great life."
— John "Buck" O'Neil

SEGREGATION OF 19TH-CENTURY BASEBALL

Relatively few black players played in the majors in the 19th century, and those few who did experienced discrimination. In 1884, two African Americans, **Moses Fleetwood Walker** and his brother, **Welday**, played for Toledo in what was then a major league, the American Association, but the policies of segregation soon forced them out of the majors, and they were the last blacks to play official-ly in the majors for six decades.

A few blacks did play for white teams after the ban on their sign-ing, something the International League instituted in 1887, but usu-ally disguised as "foreigners" or "Indians" until owners of other teams revealed the ruse. Sometimes an all-black team like the Cuban Giants would try to convince audiences that they were foreigners by speak-ing an inarticulate gibberish that was supposed to be Spanish and would call themselves "Cuban" or "Spanish" or "Arabian" to disguise their race.

Occasionally, local white teams, including those in Florida, would hire a black to pitch against them in batting practice because the teams realized how good some of the black ballplayers were. For example, the white baseball team out of DeLand used to hire a local black named Dixon to pitch to them, at $1 an afternoon, because he could throw so hard. Something similar happened to **Jimmy Hill** (1918-93) of Plant City around 1937 when the Detroit Tigers hired him to pitch batting practice for them at their Lakeland spring train-ing site. Tigers like the great **Hank Greenberg** noticed the major league ability of Hill, who later went on to sign with the Albany Black Sox (1937) and then the Newark Eagles of the Negro National League (1938).

However, the collusion of major league teams against blacks in the late 19th century forced them to form their own teams, such as the Cuban Giants and the New York Gorhams, and to play in the minor leagues or to travel from town to town playing local teams, both black and white. In games against major leaguers, the black teams won some 60 percent of the time, proving that they just needed the opportunity to compete on the highest professional level.

To attract as many fans as possible to their games, the black teams injected an element of entertainment, like riding through the streets on bicycles and arriving in formal outfits with opera hats and silk umbrellas. But such antics did not mean they took their game any less seriously than their white counterparts. For example, when the Wide Awake black team from Tallahassee played another black team, the Calicoes, in 1874, the third baseman for the latter team objected so strongly to the umpire's decision on a play that the player stormed off the field. His teammates, who were comfortably ahead at that point, refused to continue the game and had to forfeit. The reporter covering the game thought their action was foolish, but it seemed to be a matter of principle to the visitors.

Baseball in 19th-century Florida, as in much of American society, was strictly segregated on the playing field and in the stands. Blacks could attend white games if they bought a ticket to the game, but they had to sit in segregated areas, usually cheap, distant bleacher seats. This practice prevailed throughout the South into the 1960s, whereas other parts of the United States had integrated their ballpark seating long before that.

Although segregation kept blacks from playing with whites, black teams attracted many fans, most of whom were black, but also whites who wanted to see baseball played well, regardless of the color of the players' skin. However, as was true of many baseball games, regardless of the players' color, because the quality of the teams was not always equal, lopsided scores sometimes resulted. For example, when the Wide Awakes from Tallahassee hosted a team from Monticello in 1874, the visitors won 86-49. Later that summer, another black club, the St. Johns of Jacksonville, also beat the Wide Awakes, 32-30, indicating that the teams were better at offense than defense.

Jacksonville and the "Southern League of Colored Base Ball"

Jacksonville, probably the strongest Florida hotbed of baseball activity in the late 1880s, had a good number of baseball teams, both black and white. One of its black teams, the Athletics, was invited by the National Colored Baseball Association to play in a tournament in Savannah, Georgia, in 1883. Three years later, Jacksonville hosted the first annual convention of the Southern League of Colored Base Ball, as well as a series of games to decide the black championship of Florida. The city's main black team was the Roman Cities, a talented group that dominated city play in the 1890s and played visiting black teams, among them the Chathams of Savannah and a team from

▲ The James P. Small Park was formerly Durkee Field in Jacksonville.
Kevin M. McCarthy

Thomasville. Other city teams that competed in the black league were the Florida Clippers, Jacksonville Athletics, and Jacksonville Macedonias.

The popularity of black baseball was so great that several leagues were established at the end of the 19th century and the beginning of the 20th. Jacksonville was later represented by the Jacksonville Red Caps in the Southern Negro League (1920) and the Negro American League (1938, 1941–42). The Red Caps' home field was Red Cap Stadium, also known as Durkee Field, Barr's Field, and Douglas Field, and was located at several sites in the city: Durkee Avenue, 1701 Myrtle Avenue, Moncrief Avenue, Davis Street, and C Street (later Hopkins Street, now West 7th Street). Built in 1937 and renamed the James P. Small Park in 1980 to honor a local black educator who coached at New Stanton Senior High School, the field is now used by local integrated teams. In the 1980s the stadium underwent more than $400,000 in repairs paid for by recreation bonds and city and federal funds.

James Weldon Johnson

One black Jacksonville youngster who did well in baseball, but who chose another profession, was **James Weldon Johnson** (1871–1938). As he related in his autobiography, *Along This Way*, a pitcher on the Cuban Giants taught him how to throw a curve ball, which he did for his own team, The Domestics, and for Jacksonville's leading black team, the Roman Cities.

Johnson pointed out that visiting black teams from Georgia drew large crowds of blacks and whites in Florida: "A good Negro team was then as great a drawing card for whites in the South as one is now for whites in the North." When a strong visiting team, such as the one from Savannah, arrived to play the Roman Cities, many shopkeepers closed their shops and headed out on the streetcars with other local citizens to attend the game.

Johnson went on to a career in teaching, law, journalism, and the foreign service instead of baseball, and became an editor and the U.S. consul to Venezuela and Nicaragua. He became a prominent songwriter, poet, and novelist, and served as executive secretary of the National Association for the Advancement of Colored People (NAACP).

African-American Teams at Flagler's Hotels

Henry Flagler, the great developer of Florida's east coast and the man who extended his Florida East Coast Railway to Key West, built several large hotels along the way in cities like St. Augustine and Palm Beach. In St. Augustine, he had **Albert Spalding** design a baseball field, which was built in 1889 and later used for spring training. That same year saw games between the African-American employees of Flagler's hotels, including members of the famous Cuban Giants. A notice in the local newspaper announced one such game:

THE COLORED EMPLOYEES OF THE HOTEL PONCE DE LEON

The colored employees of the Hotel Ponce de Leon will play a game today at the fort grounds with a picked nine from the Alcazar. As both teams possess some of the best colored baseball talent in the United States[,] being largely composed of the famous Cuban Giants, the game is likely to be an interesting one.

Further south in Palm Beach, Flagler built baseball diamonds for the entertainment of his wealthy white guests at his hotels, the Royal Poinciana and the Breakers. The black teams he fielded, the Poincianas and the Breakers, consisted of players who also worked as bellhops and waiters at the hotels when they were not playing baseball. The idea of having black teams made up of waiters and other hotel employees was also popular in Long Island, New York, where guests could see such excellent teams as the Cuban Giants, who began at Long Island's Argyle Hotel in 1885.

To run his programs in Florida, Flagler hired a former centerfielder for the Philadelphia Phillies, **George Edward "Ed" Andrews**, who is honored today by Andrews Avenue in Fort Lauderdale. Andrews (1859–1934) played eight years (1884–91) as an outfielder and second baseman in the majors, mostly for the Philadelphia Phillies of the National League, and compiled a decent .257 batting average. He eventually died in West Palm Beach after settling in southeast Florida to work with Flagler. (See Chapter One for more about Andrews.) The baseball games that people like Andrews organized were popular with spectators staying at the expensive hotels, as evidenced by what a spectator wrote in 1907:

> I went over to the baseball game and such sport I never had in my life. Both teams are colored and composed of employees of the Breakers and Poinciana hotels, who are hired because of their baseball ability and then incidentally given employment as waiters or porters. Many of them play on the Cuban Giants team during the summer so that the quality of baseball ranked with professional white teams.
>
> The greatest sport was in listening to the coaching and watching the antics of a full grandstand back of first base. Their sympathies were pretty evenly divided between the two teams, so accordingly, whenever either team would make a hit, then was the time to watch the bleachers. The crowd would yell themselves hoarse, stand up in their seats, bang each other over the head, and even the girls would go into a perfect frenzy as if they were in a Methodist camp meeting.
>
> The third baseman on the Poinciana team was a wonderful ballplayer and kept the whole crowd roaring with his horseplay and cakewalks up and down the sidelines.

▲ Two black teams at Flagler's hotels in Palm Beach: the Royal Poinciana Hotel
Team, 1915–16 (top), and the Breakers Hotel Team, 1914 (bottom).
National Baseball Library & Archive, Cooperstown, N.Y.

Andrews recruited black players from such teams as the Cuban
Giants, the Cuban X Giants, the Royal Giants, and the Leland Giants
(all of whose team names showed the popularity of the New York
Giants in those days). Among the players who entertained the
wealthy hotel guests was **John Henry "Pop" Lloyd**, an excellent
shortstop from Palatka. Also playing on those black teams were such
standouts as pitcher **Smoky Joe Williams** and home-run hitters
Oscar Charleston and **Louis Santop**. Those black teams entertained
guests at the hotels for at least the first 20 years of this century.

When a huge hurricane destroyed the Royal Poinciana in 1928, it
also wrecked the baseball bleachers there, signaling the beginning of
the end to black baseball at the resort. The great skills of the black
ballplayers may have convinced some spectators that the best of
those players could hold their own with white ballplayers, but it
would be several more decades before the color line would be broken.

▲ John Henry "Pop" Lloyd.
*National Baseball Library & Archive,
Cooperstown, N.Y.*

John Henry "Pop" Lloyd

An important black player from Florida who played for Flagler's hotel teams in Palm Beach was **John Henry "Pop" Lloyd** (1884–1965) of Palatka. His father died when Lloyd was very young, his mother remarried, and his grandmother raised him when his mother found herself unable to. He quit school before finishing the elementary grades and became a delivery boy for a local store. When he realized how skilled he was on the baseball field, he decided to play semi-professional baseball with the Jacksonville Young Receivers before going north in 1906 to play for the Cuban X Giants.

He eventually played for and managed such black teams as the Acmes of Macon (Georgia), the New York Lincoln Stars, the New York Lincoln Giants, the Chicago Leland Giants, the Chicago American Giants, the Brooklyn Royal Giants, the Columbus Buckeyes, the Atlantic City Bacharach Giants, the Philadelphia Hilldale Club, and the New York Black Yankees. Lloyd became known for his skilled playing on the field and his clean living off it; he never drank alcohol, seldom smoked, and tried to live a clean, wholesome life.

When fans compared Lloyd to the great white shortstop **Honus Wagner** (1874–1955), Wagner remarked, "They called John Henry Lloyd 'The Black Wagner,' and I was anxious to see him play. Well, one day I had an opportunity to go see him play, and after I saw him I felt honored that they would name such a great player after me." Lloyd sometimes played baseball in Cuba, where the Cubans called him *Cuchara* ("shovel") because his big hands were able to scoop up any ball hit near him. He was voted into the Baseball Hall of Fame in 1977, 12 years after he died.

Like other players in the Negro Leagues, he experienced the difficulties of segregated baseball. He spent much time traveling from town to town in order to play the games, earned little or no money, and had to stay in segregated housing facilities. Just how good Lloyd was against major league competition became clear when the Detroit Tigers, with their great star, **Ty Cobb**, went to Havana in 1910 to play a group of ballplayers, including Lloyd. According to sportswriter Al Stump, "On bases, sliding with spikes high, Cobb three times was tagged out by a fearless Lloyd. In a total of five Cuban games Cobb averaged .370. He was outshone by Lloyd, who batted .500." Even though the bigoted Cobb would not shake the hand of Lloyd, he and others had to realize just how skilled African-American players were.

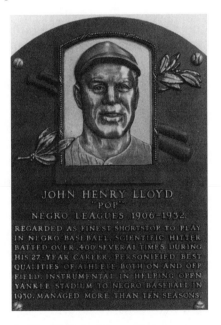

▲ Lloyd's Hall of Fame plaque.
Kevin M. McCarthy

When asked if he had been born too soon, Lloyd replied, "I do not consider that I was born at the wrong time. I felt it was the right time, for I had a chance to prove the ability of our race in this sport, and because many of us did our very best to uphold the traditions of the game and of the world of sport, we have given the Negro a greater opportunity now to be accepted into the major leagues with other Americans."

John "Buck" O'Neil

Among the Floridians who played in the Negro Leagues was **John "Buck" O'Neil**, who was born in Carrabelle, near Tallahassee, in 1911. He grew up in Sarasota and, determined to escape from low-paying jobs like picking celery, he used his skills in baseball to advance. The New York Giants had spring training at Payne Park in Sarasota, and **Connie Mack's** Philadelphia Athletics played in Fort Myers, which enabled O'Neil to see a lot of baseball players, including **Babe Ruth**, whose swing made O'Neil recall many years later: "I'd never heard a bat make a sound like that. It was something."

While in grade school, he sometimes was allowed by his teacher, Emma Booker, to miss classes to play baseball with the Sarasota Tigers, a local black team. He also saw the black teams that played for the Royal Poinciana Hotel and the Breakers Hotel in Palm Beach. Although Sarasota, like most Florida towns, did not have a high school for blacks, O'Neil won an athletic scholarship to Edward Waters College, a black college in Jacksonville that also operated a high school, and he continued to play baseball there.

After two years in high school and two years in college, he went to Miami in 1934 to play with the Miami Giants, a black semi-pro team. While he was there, the owner of the team renamed them the Ethiopian Clowns and put them in clown outfits, including straw dresses, to appeal to the crowd. So many black people objected to the "Ethiopian" name of the team that the owner eventually changed it to the Cincinnati Clowns and finally the Indianapolis Clowns.

Two years later, O'Neil went on to play first base for the Kansas City Monarchs of the Negro American League and helped them win pennants every year from 1939 to 1942. In the off-season, he returned to Sarasota, where he operated a Newtown pool hall. He served in the Navy during World War II, after which he learned with much satisfaction that the Dodgers had signed **Jackie Robinson** to become the first African American to break the color line in the modern major leagues.

When O'Neil returned to the Monarchs after the war, he won the 1946 Negro American League batting title with a .350 average — at the age of 35. He became the Monarchs' player-manager from 1948 to 1954 and prepared players like **Elston Howard** and **Ernie Banks** for careers in the majors. In 1956, O'Neil became a talent scout for

▲ "Buck" O'Neil as coach of the Kansas City Monarchs.
National Baseball Library & Archive, Cooperstown, N.Y.

the Chicago Cubs and later signed **Lou Brock** to the Cubs. When O'Neil became a coach for the Cubs in 1962, he was the first black coach in the major leagues, a fact that most white media ignored, although *Ebony* ran a feature on him entitled "First Negro Coach in Majors."

Asked if he was bitter about not having had the chance to play in the majors, O'Neil said: "If I was going to be bitter about anything, it wouldn't be about baseball but about education. I have no idea what I could have been. Suppose I could have gone to Sarasota High School, the University of Florida. All these things I'll never know, about what kind of man I could have been."

He later became chairman of the Board of the Negro League Museum in Kansas City, a member of the Baseball Hall of Fame Veterans Committee in Cooperstown, New York, and a scout for the Kansas City Royals. After Ken Burns' 1994 documentary film about baseball made the nation aware of O'Neil, he received many awards. Among the most important to him, even at age 83, was the awarding of his high school degree in March 1995 from Sarasota High School, the formerly segregated school that he had not been allowed to attend in the 1920s. That same week, officials renamed a clubhouse and four fields in east Sarasota County the Buck O'Neil Baseball Complex. The complex is at Twin Lakes Park, where Baltimore Orioles minor leaguers train.

O'Neil rightly feels that he helped bring about some of the changes in the integrated major leagues and that, having played with **Babe Ruth**, **Satchel Paige**, and **Josh Gibson**, he has played with some of the best. As he would often say to interviewers, "Don't feel sorry for old Buck; I had a great life," a point he also makes in his book, *I Was Right on Time.*

Other African Americans from Florida in the Negro Leagues

Among the other African-American ballplayers from Florida who are profiled in *The Negro Leagues Book,* edited by Dick Clark and Larry Lester, were **George Cornelius Smith** (1937–87) from St. Petersburg; **James C. "Jim" Tugerson** (1923–) from Florence Villa; and **Archie V. Ware** (1918–) of Greenville.

According to James A. Riley's work, *The Biographical Encyclopedia of the Negro Baseball Leagues*, several other native Floridians played in the Negro Leagues: **Elander Victor "Vic" Harris** (1905–78), who was born in Pensacola and played or managed for 23 years with the Homestead Grays (1925–33, 1935–48), finishing with a lifetime .299 batting average and playing in six East-West All-Star games; **Richard "Dick" Lundy** (1898–1965), who was born and died in Jacksonville

▲ "Vic" Harris (1905–78) of Pensacola played/managed for 23 years with the Homestead Grays (1925–33, 1935–48), finishing with a lifetime .299 batting average and playing in six East-West All-Star games.

National Baseball Library & Archive, Cooperstown, N.Y.

and is considered one of the greatest shortstops in black baseball history, having played for Jacksonville's Duval Giants and later for the Atlantic City Bacharach Giants; and **Theodore "Ted" "Big Florida" Trent** (1903–44), a Jacksonville native who began his professional career in St. Augustine (1924) and then pitched for the Bethune-Cookman College baseball team (1925–26), the West Palm Beach Giants (1926), the St. Louis Stars (1927–31), and the Chicago American Giants (1936–39).

Among the other black ballplayers who were born and died in Florida were **Jimmy Hill** (born in 1918 in Plant City and died in 1993 in Sarasota); and **Fred Wilson** (b. 1909, Hastings; d. ?, Miami). Among those who were born in Florida but did not die here were **Ernest "Gator" Barnwell** (b. 1910, Titusvsille), who played most of his 19-year career with semi-pro teams in Florida and also for the Ethiopian Clowns when they were based in Miami (1937); **William "Willie" Burns** (b. 1916, West Palm Beach), who played for the Miami Giants (1934); **Walter "Rev" Cannady** (b. 1904, Lake City); **Willis Crump** (b. 1890, Florida; d. 1972), who played for the Jacksonville Giants from 1907 until 1923, even after the team became the Bacharach Giants in 1916; **Napoleon "Chance" Cummings** (b. 1893, Jacksonville), who began his career in Jacksonville with the Duval Giants; **Albert "Cool Papa" Frazier** (b. 1915, Jacksonville), who played for the Jacksonville Red Caps in 1934 and 1938; **Ralph Johnson** (b. 1924, Lakeland), who began playing semi-pro baseball around 1942 with the Lakeland Tigers and also played with semi-pro clubs in Tampa and Miami; **Felix McLaurin** (b. Jacksonville), who played for the Jacksonville Red Caps in 1942; **Juanelo Mirabal** (b. 1901, Tampa); **John Reese** (b. Florida); **Henry "Flash" Turner** (b. 1913, Lloyd), who played for the St. Petersburg Stars and then for the Jacksonville Red Caps (1935–38, 1941–42); **Robert "R. T." Walker** (b. 1914, Arboa); **Archie Ware** (b. 1918, Greenville); and **Amos Watson** (b. 1926, Lake Alfred).

Among those who were born elsewhere but died in Florida were **Edmundo "Sandy" Amoros**, 1930–92 (Miami); **David "Dave" Barnhill**, 1914–83 (in Miami), who played for the Miami Giants in the Negro National Leagues (1936) and for Miami Beach (1952) and Fort Lauderdale (1953) in the Florida International League; **Jacinto "Jack" Calvo**, 1894–1965 (in Miami); **Arthur "Rube" Chambers,**

?–1928 (West Palm Beach); **John "Johnny" Davis**, 1918–82 (in Fort Lauderdale), who set the all-time league home-run record (35) in the Florida International League in 1953; **Felix "Chin" Evans**, 1911–93 (Pompano Beach), who played for the Jacksonville Red Caps in 1938; **Luther Farrell**, who died in Miami; and **Syd Pollock**, 1901–68 *No!* (Hollywood). *Owner of Clowns - not a player.*

Reporter Charles Strouse, in an article he wrote for *The Miami Herald*, "A League *apart*," described life in the Negro Leagues for several men who now live in the Miami area: **James Colzie, Leroy Cromartie, James W. Everett Sr., Eli Williams**, and **Sidney Wynn**. These players used to cruise through Miami's Overtown with a megaphone before a game, exhorting everyone to turn out for the baseball game. Each player would earn two bits (25 cents) plus whatever tips they could collect when they passed the hat during the game. The players had to stay in segregated hotels or, in those towns too small to have black hotels, in the bleachers or on the team bus. When gas stations proclaimed "No coloreds allowed" in the restrooms, the men would have to use the bushes at the side of the road.

Liberty City resident **James W. Everett Sr.**, who was inducted into the Florida Sports Hall of Fame in 1995, was from Jacksonville and starred as an athlete for Edward Waters College there and for Florida A&M University in Tallahassee in the 1930s. He later became a very successful coach at Miami's Booker T. Washington High School. He also played for such Negro League teams as the Penn Red Caps, Brooklyn Royal Giants, Harlem Clowns, Ethiopian Clowns, Jacksonville Red Caps, Miami Giants, Newark Eagles, and New York Black Yankees. The Ethiopian Clowns, who were once based in Miami, used to wear hula skirts on the field and did juggling acts before game time, but they could play an excellent game of baseball. When the teams would barnstorm through Midwestern towns, they would stay with black churchgoers.

Leroy Cromartie, whose son **Warren** recently played for the Montreal Expos, played for the Indianapolis Clowns and the Miami Giants. He recalled that restaurants would sometimes smash the plates after the African Americans had used them. **Eli Williams**, who played for the Florida Hobos in 1944, remembers playing against one of the most popular white opponents for black teams of the day, the House of David baseball team, made up of players with long, uncut hair who played excellent ball. One of the players on the House of David team was St. Augustine's **Bill Steinecke**, who also played for one year (1931) with the Pittsburgh Pirates. Black teams also would play against the team at Raiford State Prison near Starke.

BLACK TEAMS FROM FLORIDA

Florida teams like the Coconut Grove Spiders, Daytona Beach Black Cats, Miami Giants, and Palm Beach Royal Poincianas attracted thousands of fans who wanted to see good, solid baseball, even if it was segregated. The teams would pass the hat during or after a game, with the winner getting 60 percent of the take. Great visiting players like **Josh Gibson**, who hit a towering home run in Miami's Dorsey Park, played before appreciative fans long before integration opened up major league baseball to African Americans.

Even after **Branch Rickey** signed **Jackie Robinson** to play in the majors, black teams continued to play, although in time the majors signed up the best players from the Negro Leagues and it eventually faded from the scene. Even so, such teams as the Miami Giants continued on into the 1950s. Young African-American players who grew up in south Florida in the second half of the twentieth century — players like **Warren Cromartie**, **Andre Dawson**, and **Mickey Rivers** — did not have to toil in the Negro Leagues for pittance pay, but were able to prosper in the integrated majors.

Leroy "Satchel" Paige in Florida

One of the greatest players in the Negro Leagues and one who became associated with baseball in Florida was **Leroy "Satchel" Paige** (1906–82), who finally got to join the big leagues when the Cleveland Indians signed him in 1948 when he was 42. He went on that season to help the Indians win six games and lose only one on their way to the pennant.

His signing by the Indians helped precipitate the end of the Negro Leagues. More and more people preferred to see the majors, especially as the major league teams signed up the best black players from the Negro Leagues. Toward the end of his career, Paige played for the Miami Marlins in the International League (see Chapter Six for more information).

▲ Satchel Paige relaxes in an easy chair near the outfield of the Miami Marlins.
National Baseball Library & Archive, Cooperstown, N.Y.

Henry Aaron in Florida

Although not from Florida, the great **Henry "Hank" Aaron** helped break the color barrier in Jacksonville when he was one of three black players on the Jacksonville Braves of the South Atlantic League in 1953. The other two were **Horace Garner** and **Felix Mantilla**. Garner, who was later a minor league teammate of **Dick Howser**, had one of the great arms in baseball, but never made it to the big leagues because of his failure to hit a curve ball. Mantilla eventually made it to the majors, where he played for the Milwaukee Braves (1956–61), New York Mets (1962), Boston Red Sox (1963–65), and Houston Astros (1966).

Aaron reported in his autobiography, *I Had a Hammer*, that the Jacksonville Beach team in the Florida State League tried to put black players on its roster, but that the local chamber of commerce objected: "No race prejudice is involved. It's just that the patrons of the team felt they would rather have an all-white team." The Florida International League did not feel the same way and fielded three black players in 1952: **Dave Barnhill** of Miami Beach, **Claro Duany** of Tampa, and **Willie Felden** of Fort Lauderdale.

◀ Hank Aaron as a member of the Jacksonville Braves team in 1953 and depicted in a Hall of Fame display.

Kevin M. McCarthy

When Aaron joined the Braves' Class A farm club in the South Atlantic League (SALLY League) in Jacksonville in 1953, he was going to the same city that had refused to let the Royals play there because **Jackie Robinson** was on the team. When Aaron and his two black teammates played for the Jacksonville team, that may have been the first time that black players played for a Jacksonville team, although on four previous occasions blacks had played there on other visiting teams. Aaron had high praise for **Ben Geraghty**, the manager of his team: ". . . in all the years I played baseball, I never had a manager who cared more for his players or knew more about the game."

Throughout that 1953 season, so many people turned out to see Aaron and his black teammates that the team set attendance records, especially for black fans, who took great pride in the fact that black ballplayers were finally integrating the SALLY League. The ballparks were still segregated, but the excellent playing by Aaron and the other two blacks did much to acclimate people to the integration of the league.

But Aaron and the others had a difficult summer: "When the pitchers threw at us, we had to get up and swing at the next pitch. When somebody called us a nigger, we had to pretend as if we didn't hear it." The three black ballplayers spent the summer eating in the bus because restaurants would not serve them, sleeping in private homes rather than in hotels with the rest of the team, and enduring countless threats from bigots in the stands. Aaron later told **Jackie Robinson**: "We stayed at a very nice home in the Negro section [of Jacksonville], but playing in the Sally [SALLY] League was quite a bad experience for me. Some of the names I was called, I never had heard 'em in my life, before or since . . . jigaboo . . . burr-head. . . ." Despite those problems, Aaron helped his team win the pennant, led the league in many categories that year, was named the Most Valuable Player in the league, and married a Jacksonville woman. He concluded his remembrance of that summer in Jacksonville in a positive way:

> We had played a season of great baseball in the Deep South, under circumstances that nobody had experienced before and — because of us — never would again. We had shown the people of Georgia and Alabama and South Carolina and Florida that we were good ballplayers and decent human beings, and that all it took to get along together was to get a little more used to each other. We had shown them that the South wouldn't fall off the map if we played in their ballparks. At the end of the season, we still heard a few choice names being shouted at us from the stands, but not as often or as loudly as in the beginning. Little by little — one by one — the fans accepted us. Not all of them, but enough to make

a difference. That was the most gratifying part of the summer. It showed us that things were changing a little, and we were part of the reason why. And we weren't the only ones who noticed it. Dick Butler, the league president, said that we had successfully broken the color barrier in Southern baseball. A columnist for the Jacksonville *Journal* wrote that "I sincerely believe Aaron may have started Jacksonville down the road to racial understanding." I'm not sure I've ever done anything more important.

THE INTEGRATION OF MODERN MAJOR LEAGUE BASEBALL

Many fans don't know that the integration of modern major league baseball occurred in Florida. After **Moses Fleetwood Walker** and his brother, **Welday Wilberforce Walker**, and other blacks were excluded from major league baseball in the late 1880s, owners imposed a color barrier that they maintained for 50 years, a color barrier established by a "gentleman's agreement" among the owners or an outright ban. Dodger owner and general manager **Branch Rickey** broke that long-standing collusion among owners when in 1946 he signed **Jackie Robinson** (1919–72) to be the first African American to openly play baseball in modern major league history. Several owners had tried to pass off light-skinned blacks as Native Americans or foreigners, but segregationists usually foiled their attempts.

In order to prepare Robinson for the majors and to accustom the public to his presence in formerly all-white baseball, Rickey assigned Robinson to the Dodgers AAA farm team in Montreal. Robinson, who was to join the Montreal Royals in Florida for spring training in the spring of 1946, took his wife, Rachel, on the trip from Los Angeles to Florida. When they arrived in Jacksonville and found that Florida segregationist law forced them to sit in the back of the bus, even though there were empty seats in front, it was a very painful foretaste of what they could expect in Florida.

When the Robinsons arrived in Daytona Beach, they met **Johnny Wright**, a pitcher for the Homestead Grays of the Negro National League whom Rickey had signed for his Montreal team after Robinson. Both men joined the other big league hopefuls at the Dodger training camp in Sanford, a small town in central Florida that had a long history of baseball.

▲   Jackie Robinson and the owner of the Brooklyn Dodgers, Walter O'Malley.
National Baseball Library & Archive, Cooperstown, N.Y.

After an uneventful first two days of practice, Robinson and Wright had high hopes that all would be peaceful, but the Floridians made it clear that they did not want black and white players on the same field together. Because of the hostility some of the people of Sanford showed the black players, two black newspapermen from *The Pittsburgh Courier*, Wendell Smith and Billy Rowe, quickly hustled Robinson and Wright out of town the next morning and took them to Daytona. Smith had a strong interest in Robinson's safety, since Smith had been pressuring big-league baseball for the previous 12 years to end segregation and allow blacks equal opportunity to play in the majors.

Even in Daytona, the Robinsons had to stay in the black part of town, while the white ballplayers stayed in a big hotel near the ocean. The blacks also had to avoid the "white" movie houses and fraternize only with other blacks. On the practice field, Robinson was trying so hard to make a good impression on the manager and other players that he hurt his arm by throwing too hard, and Rickey had to assign him to second base and then to first base in order to save the arm. Although Robinson had been used to playing shortstop, he ended up playing first base and made his major league debut in that position.

When he made his first appearance for the Dodgers' farm team, the Montreal Royals, on March 17, 1946, against the parent team, the Brooklyn Dodgers, in Daytona Beach, he played well. The local newspaper reported that Robinson had drawn a wide round of applause from the fans when he stole second base; the paper disparagingly described him as "running like a scared rabbit," but he did well in the field and at bat. The local fans appreciated that and complimented him. The contrast between the cheering by local fans and the bad reception he had earlier experienced in Sanford greatly encouraged him, but two other experiences in Florida that spring reminded him how strong the feelings against blacks were.

Robinson and his teammates went to Jacksonville to play a game against the Jersey City Giants later that spring, but local authorities would not allow the game to begin because of the presence of Robinson and Wright on the Montreal team. What did please Robinson, in contrast to the segregationist officials, was the sight of many fans standing in line to see the game, fans who did not object to the fact that black players would be playing on the same ball field as white players.

The other incident happened in Sanford, where the Montreal team was to play against the Indianapolis Indians. In the first inning, Robinson singled, then stole second, and scored a run on another hit. At the end of the second inning, the chief of police walked onto the field and demanded that the manager remove Robinson and Wright from the ballpark, which the manager reluctantly did.

Robinson would not forget those incidents for a long time, but he eventually went to the major leagues and did well with the Dodgers. Among those who wrote of Robinson's integration of baseball in Florida, in addition to Robinson himself, are Carl Rowan, Gene

▲ The Jackie Robinson Ballpark in Daytona. *Daytona Cubs*

Schoor, and Jules Tygiel (see Bibliography).

The ballpark on Daytona's City Island west of Memorial Bridge, where Robinson made his professional debut, was renamed the Jackie Robinson Ballpark in 1988 to honor him. Outside the park's gates, officials erected a bronze statue that depicts Robinson standing with two small boys, one black and one white, both of whom represent the future. Montreal sculptor Jules LaSalle, who patterned the statue after one at Montreal's Olympic Stadium, modified the Daytona Beach statue to have Robinson wearing a Montreal Royals uniform. Behind the statue is a series of curved walls of different lengths and heights suggesting the rippling effect of a pebble dropped into a pond and symbolizing the many unforeseen benefits that came from Robinson's integration of modern baseball.

At the 1990 dedication ceremonies of the statue, **Bill White** of Lakewood, Florida, a former major league ballplayer and president of the National League who had also experienced segregation in Florida, noted how much Robinson had meant to him: "To me, Jackie represents perseverance. He succeeded despite a lot of obstacles, and I think that's important for any kid to learn. I know I wouldn't be where I'm at now if it hadn't been for Jackie."

In his major league career, Robinson had a batting average of .311, set three fielding records for the National League (most double plays for a rookie first baseman — 144 in 1947; most double plays in a season for a second baseman — 133 in 1950 and 137 in 1951), won the first Rookie of the Year Award and his league's Most Valuable Player Award in 1949, and was elected to the Baseball Hall of Fame in 1962, his first year of eligibility.

The Reverend Jesse Jackson noted at Robinson's funeral how much the man had done for baseball and for African Americans everywhere. He pointed out that Jackie's tombstone would record the years of birth and death, "1919 dash 1972, but on that dash is where we live. And for everyone there is a dash of possibility, to choose the high road or the low road, to make things better or worse. On that dash, he snapped the barbed wire of prejudice." (For more details, see John Carter, Steve Moore, and Jackie Robinson in the Bibliography.)

Jackie Robinson wrote a book entitled *Baseball Has Done It*, in which he included interviews with other black ballplayers. Several described the bad conditions they found in Florida. Among the comments about the state are the following:

Roy Campanella: "Mr. Rickey said there'd be no segregation at Vero Beach. But if you leave out Dodgertown, we were segregated everywhere."

Monte Irvin: "We complained about discrimination in St. Petersburg the year we trained there. We had to stay at a boardinghouse with one toilet. White players had individual hotel rooms, individual toilets; they ordered dinner from a full menu card. We ate whatever was shoved before us. They had but one idea — to make the team. We had to worry about our rest, our diet, how to get to the ball park, where to relax after games, which store door to open as we walked down the main street."

Billy Bruton: "There were beaches everywhere in Florida, but none where she [his wife] could go with other wives. And for many springs I had to eat in the kitchens of roadside restaurants while the club was traveling by bus from town to town. In towns where we played exhibition games I had to wait for a Negro cabdriver to come along and tell me where I could get a meal."

Frank Robinson: "It was watch my step every time I went on the street [in Tampa]. Negroes couldn't go out to the jai alai fronton. At the dog track I had to go downstairs and sit so far away that the dogs looked like rabbits and the rabbits like fleas. No movies, no bowling, nothing to take your mind off a bad arm and what you'd done wrong at practice sessions or in exhibition games. Conditions haven't changed in Tampa to this day [1964]. It's downright cruel to send rookies to places like that."

Dodgertown and the Integration of Baseball

When **Branch Rickey** established a training camp in Vero Beach in 1948 for the entire Dodger organization (see Chapter Seven), he may have been motivated by the desire to integrate major league baseball as painlessly as possible or at least to shield his black ballplayers from the racism prevalent in Florida. The isolation of Dodgertown allowed black players to get away from the Jim Crow segregation found at other spring training sites in this state, even though, according to one writer, Vero Beach was full of prejudice, and local blacks who did not play baseball for the Dodgers had to live "huddled together in the tiny adjoining town of Gifford, which consisted of a movie house, a drugstore, a barber shop, and a pool hall." Despite the confinement of Dodgertown, local racists continued to cause trouble. They spread an unfounded rumor that **Don Newcombe**, the great Dodger pitcher, had attacked a white man and therefore ought to be lynched. Newcombe later said to Jackie Robinson: "I got a taste of how Negroes get into nasty scrapes down South that couldn't happen to white men." The matter died down when Rickey decided to go to the mayor and apologize for any trouble Newcombe might have caused. Rickey's experiment at Dodgertown worked in that its relative isolation from the public allowed the coaches and players to concentrate on baseball and prepare for the coming season.

SEGREGATION IN SPRING TRAINING

Even though **Rickey** was able to desegregate major league baseball with the signing of **Jackie Robinson** in 1946, spring training facilities in Florida remained segregated until the mid-1960s. Cities and towns that were very enthusiastic about attracting major league teams and their followers — and their cash — were reluctant to integrate hotels, restaurants, movie theaters, and public beaches. The restrictions imposed by Florida segregationists in the 1950s and 1960s

▲ Bill White as a St. Louis Cardinal.

Bill White

persuaded several teams to relocate to Arizona, but they found similar conditions there. Florida native **Bill White**, first baseman for the St. Louis Cardinals who went on to become president of the National League, expressed the frustration of many black players when he stated in 1961, "This thing keeps gnawing at my heart. When will we be made to feel like humans?"

Florida officials, following the lead of other Southern leaders, made statements like "We're doing the best we can to accommodate everyone" or "We need to let the courts decide these matters," but integration came slowly. Owners knew that their black players played a major role in the success of their teams, but, as historian Jack Davis points out in "Baseball's Reluctant Challenge: Desegregating Major League Spring Training Sites, 1961–1964," they were reluctant to try to change 100 years of segregation in the South. And local communities did not want to antagonize thousands of white visitors by giving in to a minority of black players.

Some blacks argued that they should not challenge the local authorities, but instead should work quietly behind the scenes to change the segregation practices. Some felt that their jobs would be in jeopardy if they openly challenged their white superiors in baseball.

When the NAACP joined the fight to integrate Florida's facilities by drawing national attention to the problem, matters came to a head. The Yankees requested integrated facilities for their players, but backed down when the hotel they had been staying at refused to give in. The White Sox and their president, **Bill Veeck**, however, canceled reservations at a Miami hotel in March 1961 after its management refused to integrate the facilities. Players on the Braves objected to the segregation in Bradenton, which led to the blacks' being allowed to stay at the team hotel. Still, they had to sit behind partitions in the dining room during meals.

Curt Flood, **Bob Gibson**, and **Bill White** of the St. Louis Cardinals in the early 1960s pointed out the injustice of segregation practices in St. Petersburg, where both the Cardinals and the Yankees trained, and the city finally dropped its restrictions. The motel where the Cardinals trained attracted its share of sightseers. "A major highway ran right by the motel, and there, in an otherwise segregated Florida, locals and tourists alike could see the rarest of sights: white and black children swimming in the motel pool together, and white and black players, with their wives, at desegregated cookouts. That helped bring the team together."

The early 1960s were difficult times for the black ballplayers. The great **Bob Gibson**, for example, was appalled at conditions in Florida as he took his family to spring training: "We drove from Omaha to St. Petersburg, but everything in between was disgusting and degrading. We could not eat because most of the restaurants would not serve us. We could not stop for the night when we were tired because most of the motels would not accommodate us."

Conditions throughout America slowly began to change in the 1960s, and with them conditions in baseball. The growing economic benefits of spring training to Florida and other states were simply too great to continue that segregation. Florida towns and cities finally desegregated their facilities after the Civil Rights Act of 1964 was passed. Whether major league baseball hastened those changes or simply reflected them, the social fabric of this country officially became less prejudiced. Players could be judged on and off the field, less by their color than by their skill.

▲ Segregated section of Al Lang Field about 1953 in St. Petersburg.
Heritage Park-Pinellas County Historical Museum

All-Black Little League Teams

The exclusion of blacks from major league baseball was mirrored in the lower levels of baseball. In fact, youth baseball remained segregated until only recently. Key Largo, for example, had an all-black Little League team that in 1967 played "without gloves, real baseballs, or even shoes." Before Key Largo's Coral Shores High School was integrated and before black teams were allowed to play white teams, the African-American children would show up at their lot to play the game they loved, determined to play even with inferior equipment. In 1968, an all-white women's group, the OK Club, donated $200 to equip the 16 children for the games. With their new uniforms and equipment, the children on the newly named Newport Sluggers team went on to win the 1968 league championship. The former coach of that team, **Lawrence Johnson**, is today trying to establish at mile marker 101 in the Florida Keys a baseball diamond and other sports facilities for all children.

Chapter Six

THE MINOR LEAGUES

"The new owner [Sam Wolfson] promised the fans that he would do his utmost to have a new ballpark ready for the 1955 season. The new stadium will have a seating capacity of approximately 13,000 and parking facilities for a minimum of 5,000 cars."

—Joe Livingston, *"How Sam Wolfson Saved the Jacksonville Braves."*

DIFFERENT USES OF THE MINORS

In the past, the majors have used the minors for two purposes: to farm out their new players to a place where experienced coaches and former big leaguers can teach them the nuances of the game, and to allow players on their way down one more chance to prove their aging skills or recuperate from injuries.

Today, however, all that is changing. In the callous world of the "bottom line," players today last in the minors for only as long as they are prospects for the majors. Gone are the days when a player could spend his whole career — 15, even 20 years — in the minors. Managers, on the other hand, can still spend all or most of their careers in the minors. **Stan Wasiak**, for example, who spent part of his career coaching at Class A Vero Beach, became the winningest manager in minor league history. When he retired after the 1986 season, he had 2,530 wins in 37 straight seasons of managing in the minors, both all-time records.

Florida has several examples of former big leaguers spending their twilight years helping a Florida State League team. **Spud Chandler**, who spent 11 years with the New York Yankees (1937–47) and accumulated a good pitching record (109–43, 2.84 ERA), helped the Yankees in 1943 win their sixth World Series championship in eight years and was named the league's Most Valuable Player. He then

▲ The 1922 St. Petersburg Saints were champions of the Florida State League.
St. Petersburg Museum of History

served in World War II and returned for a good year in 1946 (20–8, 2.10 ERA), but he needed surgery on his arm and was released by the Yankees in 1948. Six years later, he went to north Florida to manage the Jacksonville Beach Sea Birds of the Florida State League (FSL).

1954 was Jacksonville Beach's third and last year in the FSL as it competed with teams from Cocoa, Daytona Beach, DeLand, Lakeland, and Orlando. Chandler led the Sea Birds to the championship of the first half of the season of the FSL and taught the younger players on their way up through the ranks. Before he died in South Pasadena, Florida, in 1990, Chandler spent another 30 years as a scout and manager for the Indians, Yankees, Kansas City Athletics, and Minnesota Twins, finally retiring in 1985 after a lifetime in the game he loved.

Another example of a former big leaguer who managed a baseball team in Florida is **Ben Geraghty** (1912–63). After playing for the Brooklyn Dodgers (1936) and the Boston Braves (1943–44) of the National League, he managed the Jacksonville Braves from 1951 to 1956, when they were with the South Atlantic League (SALLY), and again from 1962 to 1963, when they became the Jacksonville Suns of the International League. Twice he was named the nation's minor league Manager of the Year, first at Wichita (1957) and then at Jacksonville (1962). In 14 seasons, he had six second-place teams and six pennant winners, three of them at the Triple-A level. A plaque honoring Geraghty, who was inducted into the Florida Sports Hall of Fame in Lake City in 1975, is on the wall near one of the entrances to the stands inside Jacksonville's Wolfson Park.

Even minor leaguer **Pat Jordan**, who had very negative thoughts about his Florida baseball experiences, had only good things to say about Geraghty: "His players spoke of him with an awe and reverence one associates not with a minor league manager who had enriched their careers, but with a man who had enriched their lives in a way that had nothing to do with baseball."

UNIQUE CHARACTER OF THE FLORIDA MINORS

The minors in Florida have facilities and fan loyalty that distinguish the teams from minor league teams elsewhere. While the 14 teams of the Florida State League offer their players a chance to play

▲ Members of the Tampa Smokers minor league team.
Tampa-Hillsborough County Public Library

in major league spring training facilities and experience only short bus trips for away games, Florida fans, satiated with major league spring training and excellent college baseball, do not turn out in the numbers they do in other states. While he agrees with that assessment, Ernest Green, in *The Diamonds of Dixie*, did find throughout the South that minor league games attracted the whole family and provided a closeness to the field missing in the majors. The Vero Beach Dodgers, for example, have been known to print the name of a season-ticket owner on an oversized bumper sticker and plaster it to the person's chair. Part of that mutual feeling of affection between minor leaguers and townspeople is the extra effort they make to have contact. The former may go into the public schools, as the Brevard Manatees do, to encourage reading; the townspeople may take the ballplayers out for a fishing trip on off-days.

The type of fan attending a minor league game is different from the one attending spring training. In the summer, the crowds attending the Florida State League games are more often families and young people looking for a cheap evening's entertainment. Almost everyone in the stands roots for the home team, although watching a favorite player advancing up the ladder of the minors is probably more fun than having the home team win. Fans at spring training games, on the other hand, are often snowbirds (people from the North who winter in Florida) or corporate types, and fan loyalties are divided between the two teams playing.

Minor league personnel also have an attachment to their local communities not usually found at the major-league level. Typical of that local involvement is **Peter D. "Pedro" Bragan Jr.**, vice-president and general manager of the Jacksonville Suns. For several years, he has gone into Duval County's schools in complete baseball uniform and recited **Ernest Lawrence Thayer's** famous poem "Casey at the Bat" to inspire the schoolchildren to read more. Bragan would give any student who could recite the 13 stanzas of the poem a Suns' baseball glove, bat, ball, or replica jersey. The Solomon Schechter Day School in Mandarin, for example, had 10 students who could recite the poem about the Mudville Nine, and the R. L. Brown Sixth Grade Center in Jacksonville had 43. Such outreach programs may indeed encourage the reading habits of the children.

(In February 1995, that same manager Bragan married the former Dwana Guinn at home plate of Wolfson Park, the home field of the Suns, an appropriate place since the two had met there several years ago after one of Bragan's over-30 hardball games.)

A newspaper clipping ▶
about a 29-inning game
in 1964.
St. Petersburg Museum of History

Problems with the Minors

One problem with the minors is that the majors have sometimes depleted their ranks with little notice and not given managers much time to develop their players. The resulting rapid change in the roster and therefore in the fortunes of a team can greatly hinder its support by fans. For example, the Jacksonville Suns had won the International League pennant in 1962, the team's first year in Triple-A, just below the majors, but then the Cleveland Indians and St. Louis Cardinals terminated their contracts with the Suns, who then affiliated with the (at that time) lowly New York Mets. The Mets proceeded to call up so many players from the Suns that season that the Jacksonville team struggled to keep an intact team and a roster that did not change from week to week. The International League was so annoyed at the wholesale raiding of the Suns by the Mets that its president wrote to the president of the minor leagues, pleading for a stop to the Mets' indiscriminate recalls.

The Alabama-Florida League

Among the leagues established after World War I was the Alabama-Florida League, which began in 1926. Ken Brooks wrote about it in *The Last Rebel Yell: The Zany but True Misadventures of Baseball's Forgotten Alabama-Florida League*. **Paul Hemphill** wrote about players in the league after he had played one game for the Graceville Oilers before being released in 1954. Hemphill wrote a short story in *Life* magazine, which he included in an anthology (*The Good Old Boys*) and expanded into a novel (*Long Gone*), which became a 1987 movie of the same name. He finally concluded, "When you can't make it with the Graceville Oilers — the smallest town in baseball, in one of the worst leagues, at the bottom of the line — the message is clear."

That league consisted of teams in Class D baseball, a designation that the National Association of Professional Baseball Leagues dropped after the 1962 season. Although it was the lowest level of professional baseball, Class D gave such future stars as **Pat Dobson** (who in 1971 started the first night game in World Series history), **Mike Marshall** (the only Cy Young Award–winner [1974] from the league), **Phil Niekro**, **Tony Perez**, **Lou Piniella**, and **Pete Rose** the opportunity to begin their careers. The Florida cities which had teams in that league were Crestview (1954–56), Fort Walton Beach

(1953–62), Graceville (1952–58), Panama City (1936–39, 1951–61), Pensacola (1957–62), and Tallahassee (1939, 1951).

The Georgia–Florida League

Another league established after World War I was the Georgia–Florida League, founded in 1935 as a Class D circuit and lasting until 1958. One of the players in that league was future New York Governor **Mario Cuomo**, who hit .244 for the Brunswick Pirates in 1952 before deciding that a life in politics was preferable to that of a baseball player. The Florida cities in that league were Panama City (1935) and Tallahassee (1935–42, 1946–50). Pensacola tried to join the six-team circuit, but had to bow out when an eighth team could not be found to round out the teams. The league struggled in the beginning, but did much better after a three-year layoff during World War II, especially when it added night games to attract more fans.

The Panama City Pilots played in a site somewhat distant from the other five clubs (Tallahassee in Florida and Albany, Americus, Moultrie, and Thomasville in Georgia) and could not attract enough paying fans to continue in the league. The Tallahassee Capitals, who became the Pirates when they joined the Pittsburgh Pirates organization in 1946, played at Centennial Field, where the seating capacity of 6,000 was the largest in the league. Among the 70-plus players from the league who made it to the majors were **Ace Adams** (Giants, 1941–46), **Gene Bearden** (Indians, 1947–50; Senators, 1950–51; Tigers, 1951; St. Louis Browns, 1952; White Sox, 1953), **Johnny Beazley** (Cardinals, 1941–42, 1946; Boston Braves, 1947–49), and Hall-of-Famer **Red Schoendiens**t (Cardinals, 1945–56, 1962–63; Giants, 1956–57; Milwaukee Braves, 1958–60).

A "might-have-been" concerning that league involved the great **Babe Ruth** in 1935. When the Yankees released him that year and the Boston Braves hired him as a player-coach until June, he still had thoughts of managing in the big leagues. After the Braves released him, Ruth received an offer from Tallahassee Mayor Leonard Wesson to manage the Capitals in the Georgia–Florida League. The mayor might have been hoping that managing the Capitals would be appealing to Ruth, and that the Yankee slugger would remember the state's temperate climate, fishing, and pleasant living conditions he had experienced in spring training. Ruth, however, wanted to manage only in the majors and turned down Tallahassee's offer, despite Wesson's lure that what the team lacked in salary they would make up for in fishing, golf, and other attractions.

THE MINORS IN WORLD WAR II

When the major leagues had to restrict their travel during World War II to save fuel, they did not make their annual trek south, opting for places closer to their home sites for spring training. To make up for the lack of spring training, Floridians flocked to local games, intent on using baseball to help them forget tedious jobs and war restrictions. The people of Tampa, for example, turned out in numbers that averaged several thousand a week for games of the Inter-Social League, made up of four teams, primarily of Latin players living in West Tampa and Ybor City. Wes Singletary, in "The Inter-Social League: 1943 Season," pointed out how good some of the players were, including the fathers of major leaguers **David Magadan** and **Lou Piniella**.

For a city-by-city listing of Florida entries in the minor leagues, see Appendix C.

The Minor Leagues Use Gimmicks to Attract Fans

By 1974, with attendance at minor league games continuing to plummet, team owners began using gimmicks to attract the public again and make the games fun for the whole family. Some of the gimmicks — like Easter egg hunts, soak-the-roach contests, or racing a person dressed up as a mustard bottle around the bases — might seem silly, but they did attract more fans. Other tinkering with the system also paid off. For example, general manager **Mal Fichman** stocked his Miami Marlins of the Class A Florida State League in 1985 with as many former big leaguers (seven) as the rules allowed. Not only did it give those ballplayers another chance to work up to the majors and enable them to teach the younger players, but it also gave families a chance to see former big leaguers for a very low admission price.

Attendance figures began rising in the 1980s when about 40 new ballparks were built and many old ones were renovated. Attendance, which had hovered around the 10 million to 11 million mark in the 1960s and early 1970s, grew rapidly in the late 1970s and topped 20

▲ Tony Cucinello, manager of the Tampa Smokers in 1947, smoking a cigar, a practice that the minor leagues discourage these days.
Florida State Archives

million in 1987 for the first time since 1953 and then 27 million in 1992 and 35 million in 1994.

Movies like *Bull Durham* (1988), basketball superstar **Michael Jordan**'s baseball debut with the Birmingham Barons, and the 1994 major league strike have also helped attendance at minor league games, as have free parking, cheap seats, and proximity to the players. During the strike, many people, disgusted at what they perceived as avarice in the majors, came out to watch a minor league game, some for the first time.

An example of the informality and fan-centered nature of the Florida State League was the use by the Fort Myers Miracle of a golden retriever to greet fans at the front gate; before he died in 1995, Jericho the Miracle Dog also chased foul balls at the Lee County Sports Complex, carried a wicker basket in his mouth to deliver cold drinks to the umpires, and stood at attention while holding a tiny flag in his mouth during the playing of the national anthem.

THE ECONOMICS OF OWNING A MINOR LEAGUE TEAM

Owning a minor league team has become profitable in the last decade, which has induced celebrities like Jimmy Buffett and Robert Wagner to buy teams. That profitability has increased the cost of buying a typical A-team franchise, a cost which used to consist of merely taking over the outstanding debts in the early 1970s and which rose to more than $1 million in the 1990s. A Triple-A team franchise can cost around $5 million, up from $300,000 15 years ago. A team like the El Paso Diablos, which the owner bought in 1974 for $1,000, was worth $5 million in 1994. Entrepreneurs realize that having a minor league team can help the economy of the local town considerably, sometimes bringing in an extra $7 million, and local businesses like to advertise on outfield billboards and in the program.

Just how much a minor league team can mean to a city was clear in 1963 when the Jacksonville Suns of the Triple-A International League were close to extinction. In 1963, when the team had finished in a miserable 10th place, the local population determined to save it: 4,300 fans bought stock in the Suns for $10 a share. Jacksonville cardiologist Roy Baker led Community Baseball of Jacksonville, Inc., and secured a working agreement with the St. Louis Cardinals whereby the major league team would fill the minor league team with players and in turn could raid the team for promising stars in the National League pennant race. Although Jacksonville manager **Harry "The Hat" Walker** used 47 different players that year, the team still managed to become the 1964 champions of the International League. How the community rallied behind their Suns was a tribute to just how strongly the people felt about their team. One of the player-coaches on that team, **Joe "Mumsie" Morgan**, went on to become the very successful manager of the Boston Red Sox in 1988.

THE MAJORS TAKE PRECEDENCE OVER THE MINORS

The pecking order of the leagues became clear when the 1994–95 major league strike ended and the regular players showed up in April 1995 to have a shortened spring training. The 12 teams of the Florida State League that had the same playing sites as the major league teams had to give way to the senior league. For example, the FSL

▲ The front of Al Lang Stadium in St. Petersburg.
Kevin M. McCarthy

Phillies and Blue Jays had to give up their clubhouses and move several miles to new headquarters. The situation was very bad at West Palm Beach Municipal Stadium because the major league Braves and Expos share the facilities, which are also the home for the FSL's Expos. The only FSL clubs that did not play at major league spring training sites were the Daytona Cubs and the Tampa Yankees; the other teams were asking visiting teams to arrive at the ballpark in uniform and were using auxiliary clubhouses. All were looking forward to the regular major league season getting back to normal.

Likewise, the minors realize that once the majors decide to expand, as happened in 1991 and 1995, it is at the expense of the minors. For example, the St. Petersburg Cardinals, the minor league team in St. Petersburg from 1920 to 1927 and from 1955 to the present, will have to move from Al Lang Stadium when the major league Tampa Bay Devil Rays start up in the area in 1998, since the Cardinals cannot compete with the majors.

The Florida State League

In 1994, the Florida State League (FSL) celebrated its 75th year, although several gaps have interrupted its history. It began when several individuals met to form an organized league of baseball teams in central Florida composed of the following six charter member cities: Bartow, Bradenton, Lakeland, Orlando, Sanford, and Tampa. That "D" league ran until after the 1927 season and was reorganized in

1936 for five more years (through the 1941 season) to include Daytona Beach, DeLand, Gainesville, Palatka, Sanford, and St. Augustine.

◆

STAN MUSIAL IN DAYTONA BEACH

One of the players for the Daytona Beach Islanders in 1940 was the great **Stan Musial**, who pitched for a while until he was switched to the outfield, which changed his entire career and led to Hall-of-Fame statistics with the St. Louis Cardinals (1941–63). His manager at Daytona was **Dickie Kerr**, who had pitched for the Chicago White Sox (1919–21, 1925), including the "Black Sox" scandal, but had not been in on the fixing of the 1919 World Series and had in fact won two games in that Series.

After a hiatus during World War II (1942–45), the league began again in 1946 with eight teams: Daytona Beach, DeLand, Gainesville, Leesburg, Orlando, Palatka, Sanford, and St. Augustine. In the 1940s, Orlando, St. Augustine, and Gainesville dominated the eight-team league, but in the 1960s Fort Lauderdale, Miami (which had joined the FSL from the International League in 1962), Tampa, and St. Petersburg dominated. In the 1970s, Cocoa, Daytona Beach, Dunedin, Fort Lauderdale, Fort Myers, Key West, Lakeland, Miami, Orlando, Pompano Beach, St. Petersburg, Tampa, West Palm Beach, and Winter Haven played in the FSL, although not all at the same time.

◆

A DOUBLE NO-NO

Two FSL pitchers in 1992 achieved a very rare feat: both starting pitchers threw complete-game no-hitters. The Clearwater Phillies, led by pitcher **Andy Carter**, scored one run in the seventh inning with two walks and two sacrifice bunts to beat the Winter Haven Red Sox, led by pitcher **Scott Bakkum**.

▲ The Daytona Cubs play at Jackie Robinson Ballpark.
Daytona Cubs

The 14 teams in 1995 and the major league teams that owned each were:

Eastern Division
Brevard County Manatees (Marlins)
Daytona Cubs (Cubs)
Kissimmee Cobras (Astros)
St. Lucie Mets (Mets)
Vero Beach Dodgers (Dodgers)
West Palm Beach Expos (Expos)

Western Division
Charlotte Rangers (Rangers)
Clearwater Phillies (Phillies)
Dunedin Blue Jays (Blue Jays)
Fort Myers Miracle (Twins)
Lakeland Tigers (Tigers)
St. Petersburg Cardinals (Cardinals)
Sarasota Red Sox (Red Sox)
Tampa Yankees (Yankees)

Among the longest-running, current minor league affiliations are three from Florida:

CLUB	PARENT	SINCE	RANK
St. Petersburg	Cardinals	1966	tied for 4th
Lakeland	Tigers	1967	tied for 8th
West Palm Beach	Expos	1969	tied for 10th

▲ The inside of Al Lang Stadium.
Kevin M. McCarthy

The FSL attracted a little over one million fans in 1994, a decent number considering the fact that the state now has a major league team and spring training. Teams change cities from time to time, as the Yankees did recently, moving from Fort Lauderdale to Tampa. Teams even change their name, as in 1994, when the Osceola Astros, who were named for the Florida county, became the Kissimmee Cobras, honoring the city where they play.

The place where a minor league team plays can make the team look good, at least on paper. The Tampa Yankees broke the FSL record for homers in 1994 when they played temporarily at Red McEwen Field at the University of South Florida, but that field was much smaller than other teams' fields. The new stadium that the Tampa Yankees will move into in 1996 will be a state-of-the-art facility with the identical dimensions of Yankee Stadium, which should familiarize the new Yankees with what it will be like playing in the New York stadium.

◆

SOCKO THE GREEN MONSTER

In 1995, the Sarasota Red Sox completed what may have been the first trade of a team mascot in pro ball. In exchange for the vague "future considerations" common in trade negotiations, the Red Sox obtained "Socko the Green Monster" from the Lynchburg Hillcats after that team switched affiliations from the Red Sox to the Pirates. The 7-foot-tall, 230-pound Socko was to replace "Perky the Pelican," who was retiring from the Red Sox after five years.

FSL Players in the Hall of Fame

Many players in the FSL have gone on to the major leagues, and eight have been inducted into the Baseball Hall of Fame:

PLAYER	TEAM	WHEN HE PLAYED
Al Lopez	Tampa Tarpons	1925–26
Early Wynn	Sanford Lookouts	1937
Stan Musial	Daytona Beach Islanders	1940
Ferguson Jenkins	Miami Marlins	1962–63
Rod Carew	Orlando Twins	1965
Rollie Fingers	Leesburg Athletics	1965
Johnny Bench	Tampa Tarpons	1967
Jim Palmer	Miami Marlins	1967–68

Another Hall-of-Famer who lived in Miami, **Jimmie Foxx**, worked as a part-time coach for the Triple-A Miami Marlins (1956) and for the University of Miami (1956–57).

ROOKIE AND INSTRUCTIONAL LEAGUES IN FLORIDA

Several rookie leagues, which combined instruction and competitive league play for beginning minor leaguers, were established in

Florida: the Florida East Coast League (1940–42, 1972), the Cocoa Rookie League (1964), and the Sarasota Rookie League (1964). The latter was succeeded by the Florida Rookie League (1965), which in turn was succeeded by the Gulf Coast League (1966–).

The rookie leagues usually had four teams, and all of the games were played in one or two cities. The 1964 Cocoa Rookie League, for instance, had the Cocoa Colts, the Cocoa Tigers, the Florida Mets, and the Melbourne Twins, and they played their 52-game schedules in Cocoa.

The Gulf Coast League was established by three men deeply involved with baseball in the state: **George Brophy**, farm director of the Minnesota Twins; **George MacDonald Sr.**, president of the Florida State League; and **Glenn Miller**, farm director of the Chicago White Sox. These men wanted a place to assign first-year players just out of high school and college so they could start playing baseball immediately after graduation, instead of having to wait until the following spring when minor league clubs began spring training. Four clubs — the Atlanta Braves, Chicago White Sox, Minnesota Twins, and St. Louis Cardinals — were the first members of the Gulf Coast League. Since then, 17 different major league teams have participated, with the highest number at one time (15) in 1992.

Some of the major league teams also established instructional leagues, two-month-long teaching camps in the fall that emphasize fundamentals with promising prospects out of the glare and intensity of the minors. These leagues also enable the majors to nurse injured players back to full strength. They began in 1957, when the Cardinals, Phillies, Tigers, and Yankees sent teams to Tampa. Even the Japanese have taken advantage of such teaching, sending the best prospects of the Hiroshima Toyo Carp of the Japanese pro league to the Florida Instructional League (FIL).

Many ballplayers who play in the Florida Instructional League, which operates after the regular season and before winter ball begins, look on the experience as more of a tune-up than an overhaul. The instructional leagues expanded and retracted over the years, depending on the economy and the owners of the teams, but the basic principle remained: teach the basics to prospects (or recuperating major leaguers) who show good promise.

Stars like **Tony Conigliaro** of the Red Sox, **Carlos May** of the

White Sox, **Al Oliver** of the Pirates, **Jim Palmer** of the Orioles, and **Chris Short** of the Phillies, as well as countless others, did well enough in the FIL to rejoin the majors and make an immediate impact. The FIL sometimes had as many as 16 teams from the majors and one from Mexico, all living, practicing, and playing within a 40-mile radius of St. Petersburg. Each team cost its parent team in the majors about $40,000 a year, although none paid salaries — only $15 a day for living expenses. Detroit general manager **Jim Campbell** summed up the feelings of many:

> There is no doubt that the money we spend here [in the FIL] is one of our very best investments. Because of the time players spend in military service and getting themselves through school, the days they get to spend down here become very productive. Players have excellent coaching, and the pressure on them is at an absolute minimum. They learn the little extra things they need to make the majors.

The Life of a Minor Leaguer

A day in the life of a minor leaguer during the season is highly regimented. Teams in the Florida State League play a 140-game schedule during a five-month season, April through August. Unlike years ago, when minor league players had to take long bus trips for away games, the league's 14 teams are near enough to each other that they spend only 27 nights in hotels. The average salary for a Class A player is $1,500 a month plus $15 per diem on road trips. Because most games begin at 7 P.M., players can sleep until noon. They arrive at the ball park for a 3:45 P.M. practice, which involves 30 minutes of stretching exercises and calisthenics, 15 minutes of warming up their arms, 60 minutes of batting practice, a short break, and then infield practice before the game starts.

▲ Emblem of the Vero Beach Dodgers.
Vero Beach Dodgers

The daily coaching is something the players would not receive if they had entered college. They also get to experience the difficulties of an everyday schedule, the extensive traveling from city to city, the problems of being away from home, and the pressure from the media and fans — all of which they will experience if they make the majors.

The contracts of many minor leaguers stipulate that the player will be given a scholarship if he decides to attend college during or up to two years after his professional baseball career. Such an option means today's players can avoid the difficult decision former players faced: do they attend college and give up their chance to play professional baseball for some time or do they enter the minors and give up a scholarship to college? To show local youngsters that going to college is important and that the minors value colleges, the Vero Beach Dodgers started a scholarship program in 1995 that other teams around the country may emulate; the Dodgers will award two $1,000 college scholarships to current or former Indian River County high school students who work for the Dodgers in Dodgertown.

Very few players in the minor leagues ever reach the majors; the 6,000 minor leaguers are vying for just 700 roster spots in the majors. Playing in the minors can be a very difficult experience for players, most of whom were stars on their high school teams but who are now competing with others of similar or better ability and are experiencing failure for the first time in their lives. Because most of the players have such great baseball skills, those who make it to the Show (only about 10.6 percent of minor leaguers) are the ones who are consistently good, have a mental edge, and can stay away from mental highs and lows.

Hating the Minors

Not every ballplayer has liked his experience in the Florida minor leagues. **Pat Jordan**, a pitcher with great potential, signed with the Milwaukee Braves, but was sent down to the minors and spent two months playing for the Palatka Azaleas in 1962. As he described in his book, *A False Spring*, he hated the town and the baseball facilities: "Palatka was a suffocating place, claustrophobic, and everything in it emitted an overwhelming sense of decay." He wrote about the vines in the ballpark that tripped players, of the segregated stands, and the time when the umpire called time-out when a snake slithered onto

▲ Pat Jordan played at Azalea Field in Palatka.
Kevin M. McCarthy

the field and one of the players beat it to death with a baseball bat. Much of that bitterness may have been due to Jordan's realization that he would not make it in the majors and that all his minor league experiences were for naught.

Miami and the Minors

The fortunes of Miami may not be typical of American cities nationwide, but they point out the ups and downs of baseball. The city attracted its first minor league team when the Miami Magicians joined the Class D East Florida State League in 1912 and lasted until the start of World War I. The city, which made a commitment to the sport when it built the 9,000-seat Miami Stadium in 1949, had its first Marlins team when the Triple-A franchise Marlins of the International League moved from Syracuse to Miami in 1956. That year, **Bill Veeck**, former owner of the American League's St. Louis Browns and now a member of the Baseball Hall of Fame, took over the Marlins and made plans to increase its popularity, according to Bill O'Neal in *The International League*. Always the showman, but also a keen observer of baseball talent, Veeck immediately sought out and signed **Satchel Paige** for $15,000 and a percentage of the gate receipts.

After having spent his early career in the Negro Leagues, Paige (1906–82) had signed on with the Cleveland Indians in 1948 and had gone on to win six games against only one loss in their winning of the pennant. Out of the major leagues since 1953, the 50-year-old was eager to join the Miami Marlins and show that he still had his skills. By that time, the great pitcher was showing his age, but he could still attract large crowds. The manager of the Marlins, **Don Osborn**, did not think Paige could last against good hitting and did not want to use him in anything other than an exhibition game. However, once Paige retired Osborne's best nine hitters, the manager agreed to put the ageless pitcher in his rotation at the appropriate time.

That time took awhile to arrive. On opening day, Osborne had a helicopter deliver Paige to the ball field, but not as the starting pitcher, just in the bullpen. When he finally got a chance to pitch, he threw a complete game, allowed only four hits, and won 3–0. The great pitcher had a record of 5–2 in a few weeks, ending the season with an 11–4 record and a league-best 1.86 ERA.

Promoter Veeck, eager to take advantage of the popularity of Paige, planned to have his star pitcher break the single-game minor league attendance mark of 56,391 set in 1941. Veeck rented Miami's 70,000-seat Orange Bowl for an August 7 game against the Yankees' Columbus team and drummed up interest by having musicians Cab Calloway, Al Hibbler, Ginny Simms, and Margaret Whiting perform in what author Mark Ribowsky called "possibly the largest jazz café known to man." "Satch" pitched his usual good game and even hit a three-run double to secure the 6–2 victory, but the attendance, 51,713, did not break the record.

At the end of that profitable season, Veeck helped the owners sell the Marlins for a tidy profit and then exited the game once more. Paige remained with the Marlins for two more seasons and continued pitching well and amazing his critics. A typical Paige story: during a distance-throwing contest before a night game, Paige walked out to the outfield and, without even warming up, threw the ball sidearm 400 feet on a straight line to home plate. **Whitey Herzog** pointed out in his autobiography, *White Rat: A Life in Baseball*, that his own best experience playing for the Marlins in 1957 was playing with Paige, a man who "had the greatest control of any pitcher I've ever seen, regardless of age." Satchel would lay a gum wrapper on the ground some 60 feet 6 inches from where he would begin pitching and then throw the ball nine times out of ten right over the wrapper. In his final two years with the Marlins, without Veeck to look after his interests, Paige did not get along well with the new owners. He commented in his autobiography that "I wasn't running out on baseball. It just looked like that maybe baseball was running out on Ol' Satch, the way nobody seemed to be wanting me." After Paige left the Marlins and when the team could not attract enough paying fans, it moved to San Juan, Puerto Rico, after the 1960 season.

Jacksonville and the Minors

This city has had a long association with the minors. It began in 1904, when **King Kelly** managed the city's first minor league team, the Jacksonville Jays, in the newly formed South Atlantic League, a Class-A circuit nicknamed the SALLY. Except for 15 years (1918–20, 1923–25, 1931–35, 1943–45, 1969), Jacksonville has had such a team since 1904:

YEAR	TEAM	LEAGUE
1904–07	Jacksonville Jays	SALLY
1908–10	Jacksonville Scouts	SALLY
1911–17	Jacksonville Tarpons	SALLY
1921	Jacksonville Scouts	Florida State League
1922	Jacksonville Indians	Florida State League
1926–30	Jacksonville Tars	Southeastern League
1936–42	Jacksonville Tars	SALLY
1946–50	Jacksonville Tars	SALLY
1951–61	Jacksonville Braves	SALLY
1962–68	Jacksonville Suns	International League
1970–84	Jacksonville Suns	Southern League
1985–90	Jacksonville Expos	Southern League
1991–	Jacksonville Suns	Southern League

Two of the players on the Tars who went on to the majors were pitcher **Sheldon Jones**, who had an eight-year career (54-57 record) with the Giants (1946-51), Braves (1952), and Cubs (1953); and **Don Mueller**, who had a 12-year career (.296 average, with three consecu-

▲ At minor league games like this one in Jacksonville, the fans are close to the players and the field.

Jacksonville Suns

tive years above .300, once hitting as high as .342) with the Giants (1948-57) and White Sox (1958-59). Before the team moved to its new stadium in 1955, it played in Durkee Field off Myrtle Avenue. In 1964, the new stadium was named in honor of philanthropist and sportsman **Samuel W. Wolfson**, the one-time president of the Jacksonville Braves who was instrumental in generating interest in the local team.

Leaders in Florida Minor League Play

The annual overall minor league pitching percentage leaders from Florida teams, according to John Thorn's *Total Baseball,* were:

Year	Player	Team	League	Record
1927	Ben Cantwell	Jacksonville	Southeastern	25–5
1958	Art Henriksen	St. Petersburg	Florida State	17–3
1977	Mike Chris	Lakeland	Florida State	18–5
1980	Gene Nelson	Ft. Lauderdale	Florida State	20–3
1989	Walt Trice	Osceola	Florida State	16–4
1990	Randy Marshall	Lakeland	Florida State	7–2
1993	John Dettmer	Charlotte	Florida State	16–3

The annual overall minor league batting leader included three from Florida teams:

Year	Player	Team	League	Percentage
1954	Neal Cobb	Crestview	Alabama–Fla.	.432
1958	Neb Wilson	Ft. Walton Bch. Pensacola	Alabama–Fla.	.396
1959	Tom Hamilton	St. Petersburg	Florida State	.387

Among the players who had outstanding seasons in the minor leagues in Florida was **Juan Pizarro**, a left-handed pitcher from Puerto Rico in his first professional season (1956) playing for the Jacksonville club in the single-A South Atlantic League. With a record of 23–6 and a low ERA of 1.77, he led the league in games started (31), wins (23), complete games (27), innings pitched (274), bases on balls allowed (149), and strikeouts (318). The 19-year-old went on to an 18-year career in the majors, winning 131 games and playing for the Milwaukee Braves (1957–60), Chicago White Sox (1961–66), Pittsburgh Pirates (1967–68, 1974), Boston Red Sox (1968–69), Cleveland Indians (1969), Oakland Athletics (1969), Chicago Cubs (1970–73), and Houston Astros (1973).

Florida Teams in the Southern League

The two Florida teams in the Class AA Southern League are the Jacksonville Suns (affiliated in 1995 with the Detroit Tigers) and the Orlando Cubs (affiliated with the Chicago Cubs). The two teams struggled in 1994, finishing at the bottom of the standings, but they drew well. Jacksonville attracted 240,580 fans, or 3,759 fans a game, while Orlando attracted 195,270, or 3,150 fans a game.

▲ The Jacksonville Suns play the Orlando Cubs, both teams in the Southern League. *Jacksonville Suns*

The Suns play in Wolfson Park, which was built in 1955 and has a capacity of 8,200. Among the local team's former standouts who went on to the majors were **Phil Niekro** (1959), **Nolan Ryan** (1967), **Bret Saberhagen** (1983), **Tom Seaver** (1966), **Larry Walker** (1987), **Frank White** (1972), and **Willie Wilson** (1976); the Hall-of-Famers who played on the team were **Hank Aaron** (1953), **Tommy John** (1962), and **Hoyt Wilhelm** (1948–49).

The Cubs play at Tinker Field, which was built in 1936 and has a capacity of 6,000. The team's former standouts include **Gary Gaetti** (1981), manager **Tom Kelly** (1981–82), **Chuck Knoblauch** (1990), **Pat Mahomes** (1991), **Denny Neagle** (1990), **Ryne Sandberg** (1993), and **Frank Viola** (1981).

The Southern League did well in drawing fans in 1994, primarily because of the presence of **Michael Jordan**, the National Basketball Association star who tried baseball with the Birmingham Barons for a while before returning to the NBA in 1995. Among the marketing ideas generated by the Southern League was a hall of fame to honor its best players and a national radio network to broadcast a game each Sunday night.

Umpires in the Minors

Florida plays a role in the training of umpires in the minor leagues. At baseball's 1964 winter meetings in Houston, Texas, officials established Baseball Umpire Development (B.U.D.) to organize, supervise, evaluate, and eventually promote minor league umpires. This represented a step forward from the sometimes less-than-professional hiring and promoting of umpires in the minor leagues. One of the first evaluators of umpires was **Bill Lee**, formerly a football coach at Sarasota High School.

In the late 1970s, B.U.D. established its headquarters with the National Association of Professional Baseball Leagues next to Al Lang Stadium in St. Petersburg. Today, B.U.D. trains and promotes all 200-plus minor league umpires, many of whom will end up umpiring in the majors. The three surviving umpire schools, beneficiaries of several different schools over the years, are all in Florida: the Harry Wendelstedt School for Umpires (Daytona Beach), the Brinkman-Froemming Umpire School (Cocoa), and Jim Evans Academy of Professional Umpiring (Kissimmee).

▲ Joe DiMaggio practices being an umpire at the former McGowan Umpire School in West Palm Beach in 1948.

Florida State Archives

Chapter Seven

SPRING TRAINING

"I ain't going out there anymore. There're alligators out there."
— Babe Ruth, 1925, about spring training
in St. Petersburg

SPRING TRAINING DIFFERS FROM THE REGULAR SEASON

Florida means different things to different people. To vacationers, it means Disney World and sandy beaches and spring break. To science buffs, it means Cape Kennedy and marine fisheries. To litterateurs, it means Ernest Hemingway, Marjorie Kinnan Rawlings, Zora Neale Hurston, and John D. MacDonald. To baseball fans, it means spring training, or *camp d'entrainement,* as the Expos say in West Palm Beach, and the start of another season. William Zinsser wrote in *Spring Training* that "Of all the romantic datelines in the newspapers of my boyhood — the *New York Herald Tribune,* the *New York Times* and the baseball-obsessed *New York Sun* — none sent as strong a message as those towns in the 'Grapefruit League' that annually came out of hibernation. To every baseball fan stuck in the frozen North they shouted the good news: the long freeze is over."

The six to seven weeks of spring training used to be a time to get the winter kinks out of muscles, to get physically and psychologically ready for the long regular season ahead, and to work rookies and newly acquired players into the lineup. Today, however, physical reconditioning is less necessary, since the high salaries of players have

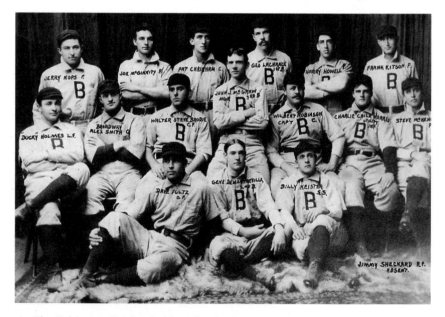

▲ The Baltimore Orioles, led by John McGraw (center), stopped in Gainesville in 1899. *Florida State Archives*

allowed them to skip off-season jobs and to stay in shape on their own. As Ken Coleman noted in *Grapefruit League Road Trip*, "Spring training isn't for the players. It's for the fans, which is to your advantage. Most players agree they don't need six weeks to get into playing shape. Today's players, in fact, are rarely out of shape."

Baseball has changed a lot this century, and that includes spring training. The players today often come out of college with skills more developed than in the past. They are bigger, faster, better trained, and more conscious of the benefits of proper nutrition and regular exercise. In addition, pitchers often have a repertoire of the split-finger, fastball, sinker, changeup, and slider that it used to take several seasons to develop. And the teams themselves are more evenly matched, with few if any walk-ons — undrafted, unsigned players who show up wanting a chance to try out for and make the team.

Despite the crowds and slowly increasing ticket prices, spring training is still a pleasant time for fans: they can have good seats close to the field or dugouts, chat with ballplayers or managers, and relax in a setting far more comfortable than the cavernous major league stadiums. Those attending spring training games usually don't really care that much who wins. No organ music tries to induce spectators to cheer. No electronic scoreboard tells them the scores of other games or even when to "do the wave." Pennant races seem far off, as does end-of-the-season competition among players for most home runs or most steals. Authors like Donald Hall describe the almost-playful atmosphere of spring training. In *Playing Around: The Million-Dollar Infield Goes to Florida*, Hall shows how several professionals in other fields (a doctor, poet, lawyer, and journalist) fared in a small stint with the Pittsburgh Pirates in Bradenton during spring training — to the entertainment of the fans and the amusement of the ballplayers.

Because the players' salaries do not begin until the regular season starts, teams compensate the players during spring training, paying them allowances of approximately $190 per week and a weekly supplement of $34 if they do not live at the team's hotel. Players also receive $53.50 a day for meal money, compared to regular-season meal money of $60.50 in 1994. During the 1995 strike, that low pay provided no incentive to show up for spring training and risk the wrath of players on strike.

Historian Trent Frayne has pointed out that spring training records are often meaningless in the regular season, that players who did well in March often did poorly the rest of the season, while players who did poorly in the Grapefruit or Cactus leagues often did very well in the majors. Spring training does, however, give managers time to assemble the best team possible. Before the season begins, each team can have 40 players on the roster; former team members returning from the armed services are not counted against the total. By the beginning of the season in April, each squad has to pare down to 28 players and a month later to 25 players. During the last month of the regular season, a team can have more than the 25 in order to examine prospects from the minor leagues.

Discussing spring training in Florida, Roger Angell in 1989 asked the questions on the minds of many writers and fans: How do today's players compare with those of the past? How has the game changed? How much difference do the high salaries make to the players? He wrote:

> Spring training isn't what it used to be — the games are sold out, the concession lines are endless, the traffic is dismaying, the newer parks are too big and overfenced, the players are farther away, the sweetness is thinned — but still . . . Driving to a spring ballpark early in the day, down some straight-line Florida back-country pike, or with the morning shadows still darkening one side of the nearest mesa, is good for a man's soul.

What spring training does offer fans is the chance to see the future stars of the game, baseball played on grassy fields in the sunshine rather than in domed stadiums with Astroturf, and professional ballplayers up close.

EARLY SPRING TRAINING IN THE SOUTH

Spring training began in the late 19th century when a few teams ventured south to prepare for the upcoming season. The barnstorming trips that baseball teams had made as early as the 1860s, playing local teams and searching for new talent before the days of minor league farm clubs, increased interest in major league baseball among fans and allowed players to get back into shape.

In 1870, the Chicago White Stockings and the Cincinnati Red

Stockings established spring training camps in New Orleans and then traveled throughout the South playing exhibition games. Other teams established camps in Savannah, Georgia; Washington, D.C.; Charleston, South Carolina; and Hot Springs, Arkansas. The players did not like the idea of training away from home, but the regular-season success of teams that did train in the South convinced other owners to do likewise.

Early Spring Training in Florida

Florida had its first spring training team in 1888, when the Washington Capitals (also called the Statesmen, Senators, and Nationals) of the National League arrived in Jacksonville to train for three weeks. When the team finally located lodgings, a difficult task for manager **Ted Sullivan**, the hotel clerk insisted that the ballplayers not eat in the same dining room with the other guests, not mingle with them, and not even mention their profession to the guests. He shared the opinion of many Americans of the time that ballplayers were unsavory, coarse, and poorly educated individuals. The Jacksonville hotel, which consisted of two shacks near the ballpark on the outskirts of the city, charged the Washington team a dollar a day for three meals and a bed for each player. The income generated from that first experience would later mushroom into a multimillion-dollar-a-year business for the state.

Because many people considered baseball players boorish and ill-mannered, the players had a poor reception that first spring, including an uncooperative hotel clerk and inadequate playing conditions: the ball field was in a poor section of town and full of weeds and brush. It became the site of the first preseason exhibition game in Florida when the Capitals played the New York Giants, also of the National League, on March 22, 1888. Some 1,200 people attended the game and saw the Giants win, 10–2. The fact that the Washington Capitals finished last in the 1888 season, 37 ½ games out of first place, may have discouraged them from returning to Florida the following spring, but it did give vaudevillians a new quip: "Washington is first in war, first in peace, and always last in the National League."

The poor conditions the Capitals encountered did not discourage all players, however. The team's young second-string catcher, **Connie Mack** (paternal grandfather of Connie Mack III, Florida's representative and senator in the 1980s and 1990s), reveled in the weather and his rising status as a ballplayer. His biography explained: "As he [Mack] basked in the semitropical sun, listened to the raucous cries of angry mockingbirds, the croaks of frogs — even of distant alligators — he knew he was living, seeing his country and the world. And again he chuckled that he was being paid good money for all this." After Mack became the successful manager of the Philadelphia Athletics, he brought his own team to Jacksonville in 1903. Conditions had improved over the 1888 dollar-a-day price tag for three squares and a bed, but not by much. The A's stayed in the Casino, a former gambling hall, but had to settle for cots instead of beds in the barnlike structure.

A baseball misadventure occurred in the spring of 1903 in Jacksonville when future Hall-of-Famer **Rube Waddell** fell in love with a local brunette. When she rebuffed his advances, he resolved to kill himself by jumping into the St. Johns River. Fortunately for base-ball, he decided to jump into the river at low tide, which permitted his concerned teammates to rescue the muddy ballplayer. At another time, Waddell wrestled a live alligator while staying in Jacksonville, but suffered no serious harm.

Other teams chose Jacksonville for spring training: the Athletics (1903, 1914–18), the Cincinnati Reds (1905), the Boston Braves (1906), the Brooklyn Dodgers (1907–09, 1919–20, 1922), the

▲ The Cincinnati Reds, who held spring training in Jacksonville (1905), Miami (1920), Orlando (1923–30), Tampa (1931–42, 1946–87), and Plant City (1988–), stopped at Stetson University in DeLand in 1923.
Florida State Archives

Pittsburgh Pirates (1918), and the New York Yankees (1919–20). But only in 1914 did more than two teams have spring training in Florida at the same time: the St. Louis Cardinals in St. Augustine, the Philadelphia Athletics in Jacksonville, the Chicago Cubs in Tampa, and the St. Louis Browns in St. Petersburg.

When Jacksonville officials realized how important such training could be to the economic base of their city, they built Southside Park across the river from the downtown area. When the Dodgers left the city in 1922, however, Jacksonville could not lure another team for spring training. Instead, major league teams who came there headed further south to places like Clearwater, St. Petersburg, Bradenton, and Miami, where the weather was warmer and the facilities newer.

Spring training began to boom in 1918, when the Pirates and Athletics trained in Jacksonville, the Philadelphia Phillies in St. Petersburg, and the Braves in Miami. One Florida activity that attracted some ballplayers in the 1920s was the buying and selling of local real estate. Among those who devoted more and more time to the real-estate boom were **Joe Tinker** (of the Tinker-to-Evers-to-Chance double-play fame), who had become president and manager of the Orlando team in the Florida State League; **Bill Doak**, **Jacques Fournier**, and **Milton Stock** of the Brooklyn Dodgers; and **John J. McGraw**, manager of the New York Giants, who took out several large advertisements in *The Sporting News* about the benefits of investing in Florida land.

St. Petersburg and Spring Training

The concentrated efforts of dedicated people also served to attract major league teams to places like St. Petersburg. One such man, the one who probably did the most to convince teams to have their spring training in Florida, was **Albert "Al" Lang**, a former laundry owner in Pittsburgh, Pennsylvania, who had moved to St. Petersburg around 1910 for his health. As business manager at a ballpark in St. Petersburg, he was determined to make better use of its facilities and help the sagging tourism industry by attracting a major league team for spring training. He first tried to lure his favorite team, the Pittsburgh Pirates, but was rebuffed by owner **Barney Dreyfuss**, who wrote to Lang: "Al Lang, you must think I'm a damn fool, suggesting I train in a little one-tank town that's not even a dot on the map."

▲ Spectators watch a spring training game between the St. Louis Browns and Philadelphia Phillies in 1915 near Coffee Pot Bayou in St. Petersburg.
St. Petersburg Museum of History

Lang may also have made a mistake in touting to Dreyfuss the recreational facilities that St. Petersburg offered; Dreyfuss was more interested in his players training hard than in their enjoying the fishing and swimming in Florida. Lang did convince the Chicago Cubs to move away from New Orleans, but they wound up choosing Tampa over St. Petersburg.

Lang then decided to work on American League teams, and in 1914 convinced the St. Louis Browns (who would later become the Baltimore Orioles), under manager **Branch Rickey**, to move to St. Petersburg. According to longtime newspaper columnist D. B. McKay, a baseball committee, formed to attract a major league team to the city, raised $20,000 in a stock issue to buy a large tract of land for a ballpark. The committee apparently agreed to pay the expenses of a team training in the city plus the expenses of five newspapermen who would cover the team for hometown newspapers. Later, Lang and public officials would say that they never really agreed to pay all the expenses of the Browns.

The committee chose for its field Coffee Pot Bayou because it cost nothing the first year and they could buy it cheaply at the end of that year. Near the bayou, where the players could swim, fish, or boat when they weren't playing ball, the committee built a 2,000-seat grandstand.

When the Browns arrived, they settled into their new quarters, but Rickey immediately imposed several rules that cramped their style. He did not allow liquor or cigarettes or poker in camp (he argued that card-playing would keep the players up late), but did encourage the playing of handball (he believed it would make them better baseball players). At meals he would not allow the players to have seconds, probably to have them maintain a good playing weight. The reporters following the team were supposed to be under the same eating rules, but they protested so loudly that they were exempted from the no-seconds rule. The players did not like the fact that the movie houses in St. Petersburg closed at 9:30 P.M. and the city had only one dance a week — and even that closed at 10:30 P.M. Worst of all was the "dry" status of the city. The Elks Club served liquor, but only one player was a member of that group.

The first intersquad game, between the Browns and the Chicago Cubs, who were training in nearby Tampa, attracted 4,000 fans to the park. The mayor had declared a half-holiday for the game, which promoters called the first game between major league teams in the state; schools closed and businesses locked up so that everyone could attend the game. Later that spring training season, merchants would close their doors on Monday and Wednesday afternoons to allow employees and customers to attend the games.

The Browns did well that year, jumping from last place in 1913 to fifth place in 1914. One would have thought that the team, if they were as superstitious as most teams have been, would have returned to St. Petersburg the following year, but instead they moved on, probably because Lang and other public officials, who claimed that they had never agreed to pay all the expenses of the Browns' group of 50 people, refused to pay any of the $6,500 bill. The Philadelphia Phillies replaced the Browns in St. Petersburg the following year, 1915.

THE GRAPEFRUIT LEAGUE IS ESTABLISHED

In 1914, officials established the Grapefruit League, in which teams played a five-week schedule of exhibition games. One of those teams, the Phillies, went from sixth place in 1914 to win the National League pennant in 1915 and, reluctant to change spring training sites due to superstition, returned to St. Petersburg through 1918. In 1920, "Sunshine Al" Lang convinced 20 local residents to each contribute $1,000 to build a new ballpark, Waterfront Park, a little north of today's Al Lang Field, the ballpark built in 1947 and named in honor of the great baseball promoter.

Lang lured the Boston Braves to the city in 1922, and then the New York Yankees in 1925. He convinced Yankees owner **Jake Ruppert**

▲ The Boston Braves play at Waterfront Field in St. Petersburg in 1923.
St. Petersburg Museum of History

that the "minds of the players would be more on baseball and less on wine and wild women" in the little town of St. Petersburg than in such places as New Orleans. It probably did not hurt that Yankees manager **Miller Huggins** had recently bought a home in St. Petersburg.

When the Yankees arrived, so did players like **Babe Ruth**, who attracted many sightseers. He enjoyed the city immensely, partly because he took advantage of the golfing and fishing readily available. Historian Raymond Arsenault pointed out that Ruth's popularity and carousing gave to the city an image of one that "flirted with decadence" through its bootleggers and speakeasies during the Depression.

That first spring training for the Yankees in St. Petersburg went well until they headed back to New York to begin the season. On the train ride north, Ruth collapsed in North Carolina, reportedly from overindulging his appetite for large quantities of food. The "stomachache heard round the world" caused him to miss the first month of the baseball season and eventually to be suspended in August for poor performance.

The Braves stayed in St. Petersburg for spring training until 1937 and the Yankees until 1942 with two more stretches in 1946–50 and 1952–61. The fact that the Yankees, under the ownership of Colonel **Jacob Ruppert**, signed a three-year contract to stay at the Don CeSar Hotel in the early 1930s is said to have saved the place from financial ruin. The team, family members, and the sportswriters who covered the Yankees filled 125 rooms of the hotel for the season. They also filled the hotel restaurant, where the ballplayers were to have steak every morning for breakfast and unlimited amounts of milk. While most of the Yankees stayed there, **Babe Ruth** and **Lou Gehrig** stayed at the Flori-de-Leon at 130 Fourth Avenue North.

Lang was so successful in luring teams to the city and so well liked that voters elected him mayor in 1916 and 1918. Yankees manager **Casey Stengel** once said that "Al Lang certainly had the betterment of baseball and St. Petersburg on his mind daytime and nighttime; he knew baseball was great advertisement for city and state and he carried that thought through to the fullest."

St. Petersburg was also greatly aided in attracting baseball to the city by columnist **Fred G. Lieb**, who wrote over a dozen books about the sport as well as a "Hot Stove League" column for *The St. Petersburg Times*. Lang's success with baseball teams convinced more than a dozen Florida sites to lure major and minor league teams in a process that has continued to this day.

Casey Stengel and Spring Training

Spring training was a time for fans and players alike to enjoy the game before the serious play started. During the pre-season in Daytona in 1915, a funny incident involved **Wilbert Robinson**, manager of the Brooklyn Dodgers and a former major league catcher (1886–1902). Pioneer aviator Ruth Law took a Dodger player for a ride in her plane, a player who was to drop a baseball for Robinson to catch on the ground. Either because he forgot the baseball or decided a baseball dropped from a plane would be too dangerous for someone on the ground, the player substituted a grapefruit without telling Robinson. The dropped grapefruit fell at a high rate of speed and, careening off Robinson's outstretched mitt, split open on his chest. The force of the grapefruit threw him to the ground and splattered him with the grapefruit juice, at which point the manager cried out, "Jesus, I'm killed! I'm dead! My chest's split open! I'm covered with blood!" When he found his teammates roaring with laughter at the hoax, he swore at all of them and particularly blamed **Casey Stengel**, one of his players and someone he suspected of such pranks.

That same year, Daytona was the scene of another not-so-humorous incident in Stengel's early life as a Brooklyn Dodgers outfielder. At that time, Daytona Beach on the Atlantic and Daytona on the mainland were joined by a trestle bridge. One night, George Underwood, a writer for the New York *Press*, was driving back to Daytona Beach when he came upon Stengel in the middle of the bridge, trying to work up his courage to jump to his death in the water below. Casey was in a hitting slump, felt the manager did not like him, and feared he may have contracted venereal disease. One author concluded that "Underwood persuaded him to get into the car instead of jumping, and so perhaps saved Casey for posterity." Creamer's biography also repeats this story, but notes that Casey's problem may have been typhoid.

▲ "Stan the Man" Musial of the St. Louis Cardinals and promoter Al Lang prepare the infield in St. Petersburg in the mid-1940s.
St. Petersburg Museum of History

Babe Ruth and Spring Training in Florida

One of the big draws in attracting visitors to spring training games was **Babe Ruth**, who played in exhibition games in several Florida sites, including Miami, Palatka, Palm Beach, and Sarasota. On April 4, 1919, when Ruth was in Tampa for spring training for the Boston Red Sox, in a pre-season game against the New York Giants he hit what many consider his longest home run: 587 feet. The feat is commemorated on a plaque at Tampa's Plant Field on the campus of the University of Tampa. Historian James Covington wrote that it "was the longest home run that Ruth ever hit and probably longer than any other man had hit at that time." Ruth noted in *The Babe Ruth Story* that writers covering that game began to speculate how many home runs he would hit if the Braves switched him from the pitcher's mound to the outfield. When **John McGraw**, manager of the New York Giants, heard that speculation, he said, "If [Ruth] plays every day, the bum will hit into a hundred double plays before the season is over." From then on, whenever Ruth would get a long hit off of one of McGraw's pitchers, the Bambino would yell over to McGraw, "How's that for a double-play ball, Mac?"

▲ Babe Ruth played in Miami in 1920.
Florida State Archives

After the New York Yankees first acquired Ruth in 1920, he joined them for their spring training in Jacksonville, where an irate fan almost did him in. Ruth had started off slowly, striking out many times and failing to hit the long balls expected of him. One day a particularly obnoxious fan in the stands started in on Ruth, making disparaging remarks, until Ruth finally ran to the stands, jumped over the bleacher fence, and climbed up the steps after his heckler. Instead of running, the little man pulled a long knife on Ruth, but a Yankees official prevented him from doing any damage to the big slugger. For some reason, whether the taunting of the fan or finally getting used to the Yankees' system, Ruth then began hitting the long ball and was on his way to the successful career he had with the New York club.

Ruth had another bad experience in Florida that spring, after Prohibition had become the law. When the Yankees went to Miami for two exhibition games, they discovered the vast amount of liquor smuggling and partying that made Miami famous. Ruth had apparently imbibed so much of the imported stuff that, when the Yankees played in Palm Beach on their way north from Miami, he collided with a large tree in the outfield and knocked himself out. He soon regained consciousness, but not before speculators wondered if the Yankees had made a mistake in luring the big man from Boston. That trip to Miami and Palm Beach became such a sore point for Yankees' owner Colonel Ruppert that he never again booked the team in Miami.

That trip also annoyed Ruth for another reason. Sportswriter **Damon Runyon**, who was accompanying the Yankees north from spring training, had bought an alligator named Alice and seemed to prefer to write about it rather than the players. Ruth got so annoyed at being upstaged by an alligator in Runyon's daily columns that he finally asked the writer, "Hey, Damon, who are you covering on this trip, me or an alligator?" To which the writer replied, "I can't keep writing about your lousy home runs every day." Only when Alice died in Washington, D.C., did Ruth return to Runyon's columns more regularly.

Ruth spent many springs in Florida, most of which brought good publicity for the state, but one early one did not. On the first day of spring training in 1925, the New York Yankees were getting ready for their first training camp at a new ballpark at Crescent Lake Field in St.

▲ Yankee greats Lou Gehrig and Babe Ruth with local baseball booster Dick Mayes of Brooksville as the Yankees train in St. Petersburg in 1934.

Florida State Archives

Petersburg. They had hopes of returning to their winning ways: they had won the American League pennant in 1921, 1922, and 1923, and the World Series in 1923, and in 1924 had finished second to Washington, the winner of the pennant and World Series. After Ruth had been shagging fly balls for a short time in the outfield, which bordered Crescent Lake, he suddenly gave up and walked to the dugout. Yankees manager **Miller Huggins** asked him what the problem was. Ruth responded, "I ain't going out there anymore. There're alligators out there." Indeed, alligators had come out of the lake to see what was going on in the new ballpark. They were quickly shooed away, and, fortunately, northern reporters accompanying the team did not use a headline like "Gators Chase Ruth." Officials later renamed Crescent Lake Field to honor Yankees manager Huggins and years after that added to the field the name of **Casey Stengel**, one of his most famous successors.

Several years later in Tampa, Ruth had the kind of experience that would happen throughout his career. Right before one of the Yankees–Reds exhibition games was to start, a car drove up to the right-field foul line and parked, allowing the man and his very sick son to watch the game from a good vantage point. After the game, when the players jogged past the car to their bus, Ruth called out, "Hi'ya, Kid," to the sick youngster in the car. At that greeting from his idol, the boy struggled to his feet and called out something to the Babe. The boy's father was overwhelmed at the sight of his son upright and kept repeating, "My boy stood up. My boy stood up. This is the first time in two years that my boy has stood up." Many such boys were moved by the great Yankee in his lifetime.

When the Boston Braves of the National League acquired Ruth from the Yankees in 1935, toward the end of his career, he joined them in St. Petersburg, where they sometimes played the Yankees and Cardinals in spring training games. In *The Babe Ruth Story,* Ruth wrote that he enjoyed pointing out that he, "the Boston Brave, drew more at the old Waterfront Park one day than he ever had drawn as a member of the famous Yankees." One day, in fact, his team attracted more than 6,000 paying fans in a park built for 2,500. It would be his last spring training as an active player, the 22nd season in a most remarkable career.

HOW SPRING TRAINING HAS CHANGED

The concept of spring training has changed over the years. In the beginning, overweight and out-of-shape players headed south to get back in shape and work off the excess pounds accumulated during the winter months. Coaches took time to look over rookies and non-roster players who were invited to the camps, although they usually knew ahead of time what their rosters would be like. The camps often attracted walk-ons, especially during the Depression of the early 1930s, when many young men came to Florida, hoping to make a roster or at least to have some good meals while the camps lasted. As time went on and the players were more often recruited out of college instead of high school, they were usually in good physical shape. This allowed managers and assistant coaches to spend more time teaching the fundamentals of the game, especially as sliding pits, batting cages, and pitching machines improved the techniques of the players.

The teams might schedule games with local amateur teams and generally put up with whatever the local communities supplied in terms of facilities. They usually did not make many demands. As cities began competing with each other to lure teams (and their large payrolls and trailing fans), officials built new stadiums with permanent bleachers and state-of-the-art training equipment. In cities like Clearwater, Fort Myers, Miami, and St. Petersburg, newer ball fields replaced the early makeshift fields and often matched the well-designed and carefully maintained facilities in the teams' home ball fields. The newer high-tech machines and sophisticated training equipment also convinced managers to have the players concentrate more on honing skills and on weight training rather than on just enjoying themselves as they had in the past.

WHY FLORIDA FOR SPRING TRAINING

By 1929, ten of the 16 major league teams had moved their spring training to Florida, partly because it was closer to most major league cities in the Northeast and Midwest than other warm-weather states like Arizona. St. Petersburg, in particular, continued to attract teams: the St. Louis Browns (1914), the Philadelphia Phillies (1915–18), the Boston Braves (1922–37), the New York Yankees (1925–42, 1946–50, 1952–61), the St. Louis Cardinals (1938–42, 1946–), the New York Giants (1951), and the New York Mets (1962–87).

▲ Some Washington Senators take a break from spring training to sample local oranges in 1925.

Tampa-Hillsborough County Public Library

During World War II, especially 1943–45, travel restrictions would not allow the major league teams to head south to warmer climes, and that hurt Florida's economy. In 1951, the Giants and Yankees traded spring training bases, which meant the Giants went to St. Petersburg and the Yankees went to Arizona. Major league teams also went for spring training to other Florida sites, especially along the lower east coast. (See Appendix D, Part II.)

In the 1920s and 1930s, major league teams shopped around for the best location, often spending a year here and a year there, trying to determine what was best from baseball and financial points of view. The Detroit Tigers, for example, shifted from San Antonio, Texas, to Lakeland, Florida, in 1934. Tigers' president **Frank Navin** had liked the warm, dry weather of Texas, but the facilities at Tech Field were not good enough, especially with the uncomfortable seats and very short right-field fence. The move to Lakeland began one of the longest spring training locations in the major leagues: 59 years (1934–42, 1946–).

The relocation of the Tigers to Lakeland as well as that of other teams to nearby Florida cities cut down on travel costs and travel time during spring training and brought more tourists to Bradenton, St. Petersburg, Tampa, and Winter Haven. Other Florida sites added more teams: Fort Myers (Athletics), Miami Beach (New York Giants), Orlando (Brooklyn Dodgers), Sarasota (Red Sox), and West Palm Beach (St. Louis Browns).

Lakeland knew from first-hand experience how much a major league team could help the local economy, especially during the Great Depression, when building and expansion were greatly curtailed. The Cleveland Indians had trained in Lakeland from 1923 to 1927 after the city paid $100,000 to buy land and build a facility for them. The fact that the Tigers went on in 1934 to win their first American League pennant since 1909 attracted even more visitors to Lakeland the next spring, fans who wanted to see the team's stars like

▲ Detroit Tigers in 1955: L-R: pitcher Billy Hoeft, manager Bucky Harris, and outfielder/infielder Harvey Kuenn.

Special Collections Room, Lakeland Public Library

player-manager **Mickey Cochrane**, second baseman **Charlie Gehringer**, first baseman **Hank Greenberg**, and outfielder **Leon "Goose" Goslin**.

A local high school student, **Sidney "Burrhead" Howell**, caddied for Cochrane at the Cleveland Heights Golf Course in 1934 and so impressed the Detroit player-manager that he was hired to be the spring training batboy. Howell took full advantage of the opportunity, joined the Tigers whenever possible in fielding and batting practice, and progressed so rapidly in his skills that he signed a contract at the end of spring training to play for Detroit's farm team in Pennsylvania.

Thirty-five different Florida sites have had spring training sites: Avon Park, Baseball City, Bradenton, Clearwater, Cocoa, Cocoa Beach, Daytona Beach, DeLand, Dunedin, Fort Lauderdale, Fort Myers, Fort Pierce, Gainesville, Jacksonville, Kissimmee, Lakeland,

▲ The Washington Senators/Twins, shown here in DeLand in 1923, held spring training in Tampa and later in Orlando.

Florida State Archives

Leesburg, Melbourne, Miami, Miami Beach, Orlando, Pensacola, Plant City, Pompano Beach, Port Charlotte, Port St. Lucie, St. Augustine, St. Petersburg, Sanford, Sarasota, Tampa, Tarpon Springs, Vero Beach, West Palm Beach, and Winter Haven. All but five (Angels, Brewers/Pilots, Mariners, Padres, Rockies) of today's major league teams have trained in Florida. The Florida cities with the most years of spring training are St. Petersburg (139 years), West Palm Beach (78 years), Tampa (75 years), Sarasota (68 years), Clearwater (66 years), Lakeland (64 years), Orlando (62 years), Fort Myers (55 years), Vero Beach (47 years), Winter Haven (42 years), and Miami (41 years).

The teams that have stayed the longest in one Florida site, although not necessarily in one unbroken stretch, are the Tigers in Lakeland (59 years), the Cardinals in St. Petersburg (55 years), the Reds in Tampa (53 years), the Senators/Twins in Orlando (52 years), the Phillies in Clearwater (49 years), and the Dodgers in Vero Beach (47 years). (For a more complete list, see Appendix D, Part III.)

The New York Giants at Sanford

The New York Giants decided in 1948 to consolidate their different training camps in one place. They had their 700 players come togeth-

▲ A Congressional baseball team stops at the Giants' training camp in Sanford in 1950. *Florida State Archives*

er at the former Sanford Naval Air Base in 1948, where workers built eight full-size diamonds on the former airstrip, enabling eight games to go on at the same time. Using spring training as a time to train all their players in the same way added a consistency to Giants' teams and reduced the expense of having far-flung training camps in different states.

The Giants also had a tryout school before the regular players assembled, which allowed coaches to examine previously undiscovered talent. Teaching their own new-found talent allowed the organization to avoid the expensive practice of buying star players on the open market.

One other connection with the New York Giants is in St. Augustine's Amphitheatre, site of the annual summer play, *Cross and Sword*: the open-air facility's seats are from the New York Polo Grounds and still bear the Giants' logo.

Branch Rickey Establishes Dodgertown

If having all of their players in one place could help the Giants, maybe it could help the Dodgers, too. When Brooklyn Trust, the company that owned the Dodgers, sold them in the mid-1940s to a triumvirate of partners, **Walter O'Malley**, **Branch Rickey**, and **John L. Smith**, the team entered a new age of prosperity. Rickey had come to the Dodgers from the St. Louis Cardinals and had already pioneered the farm system, scouts, and modern spring training camps.

To bring together all the players associated with the Dodgers, whether minor league or major league, and find a compatible site for spring training, Rickey assembled his 600 ballplayers first in central Florida. He then moved them in 1948 to a former naval air station in Vero Beach that had 109 acres and two large barracks that could accommodate 500 to 600 athletes at a time. After he bought the property, he installed pitching machines, seven batting cages, parallel base paths for rundowns and base-stealing lessons, a swimming pool, basketball and tennis courts, and even an artificial lake full of trout and bass.

At first the living facilities were rudimentary. One reporter wrote: "Wicker furniture, February dankness persisting through March twilights, plasterboard walls and suites like hutches were the Dodgertown barracks at Vero Beach." Soon, however, the Dodgers were pouring money into the facilities to make them as modern as possible. One writer praised the facility in glowing terms in 1956: "There is nothing in all baseball that matches the factory the Brooklyn Dodgers operate at this training base here on Florida's East Coast."

The site's main playing field was Holman Stadium, where 5,000 fans could watch the Dodgers in spring training and then the Class A Vero Beach Dodgers in their home games. The facility cost the Dodgers $250,000 a year, but exhibition games, a summer camp for boys on the site, and the sale of players developed there offset the cost. Players trained in Dodgertown became known for their consistently good skill in baseball fundamentals. Whenever the Dodgers won the pennant or the World Series, the prestige of the training camp grew.

Dodgertown facilitated Rickey's system, in which coaches could evaluate all of their players at one camp and teach them the same fundamentals of the game. Rickey would begin each morning at Dodgertown with a lecture to the 500 players on such topics as "The Cure Is Sweat" and "Leisure Time Is the Anathema of Youth." Afterwards, the great baseball innovator would watch his players at the different diamonds working with his pitching machines, sliding pits, and hanging rectangles of string (for pitchers to aim at in a strike-zone). Dodgertown also allowed the Dodgers to avoid the discrimination toward African Americans prevalent in the South for decades (see Chapter Five). They could relax and become more of a family.

When Rickey established Dodgertown in Vero Beach, the city had a population of 3,500 and was the smallest one in America to host a major league team for spring training. Because the community was so small and because the Dodgers set up a year-round facility there, a closeness developed between the team and the town that other sites envy. The wholesome family atmosphere existing at the ballparks of Dodgertown brought out many members of the community day after day. The fact that town residents could see the ballplayers in the restaurants and stores established a special bond between them and the team. Today Vero Beach, a town of 17,000 in a county of 90,000, may still be the country's smallest community to support a full-season professional baseball team.

When Walter O'Malley ousted Rickey from managing the Dodgers in 1950 and moved them to Los Angeles eight years later, some wondered if O'Malley would sell Dodgertown and move the team's spring training facilities to the west coast. After all, his hated rival, Rickey, had built the Vero Beach facility and had the Dodgers play in Florida's Grapefruit League rather than the closer Cactus League of Arizona. That was not cost-effective, and O'Malley was always looking for ways to save money. For some reason, perhaps to try to attract the former fans of the Dodgers from Brooklyn, who might be expected to make a vacation trip to Florida rather than to the more-distant Arizona, he kept the team's spring training camp at Vero Beach.

Even so, General Manager **Buzzy Bavasi** struggled to keep the team financially strong. He and O'Malley had an agreement whereby the owner would not cut down on the farm system as long as Bavasi could sell enough players each year to pay for Dodgertown. Over the years, many Brooklyn fans have remained loyal and continue to visit Vero Beach in the spring to see the Dodgers train. Street names like Roy Campanella Avenue and Sandy Koufax Lane are reminders of the skilled players the Dodgers have had over the years.

Dodgertown's 450 acres included some ten Dodger-owned businesses operating year-round, employing over 200 people on a payroll of more than $1 million. The businesses included a restaurant, a 45-unit residential development, a 70-acre citrus grove, and two golf

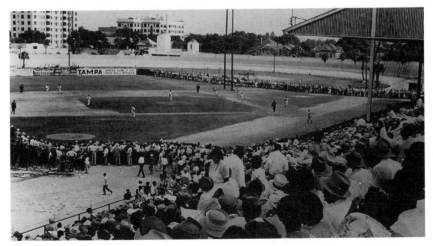

▲ The Dodgers traveled from Dodgertown to Plant Field in Tampa in 1954 to play the White Sox in spring training. *Tampa-Hillsborough County Public Library*

courses. The site has played host to 300 annual business meetings and a professional football team, as well as its own minor league team. Most baseball teams rent their facilities, usually from the local city, but the Dodgers own their facilities in Vero Beach and pay more than $100,000 annually in property taxes.

FREE PUBLICITY FOR FLORIDA SITES

Florida has dominated the spring training business for the past 50 years, although it took a few decades after the first team came here before others followed suit in large numbers. Now 20 of the 28 major league teams come to Florida at the beginning of March to compete in the Grapefruit League. This means free positive publicity and a great influx of cash to the state. The glowing reports of the weather and ocean swimming and fishing that hometown reporters send back to their northern readers, many of whom are just beginning to thaw out, entice visitors to head south to take advantage of Florida's March and April benefits and to take in some ballgames.

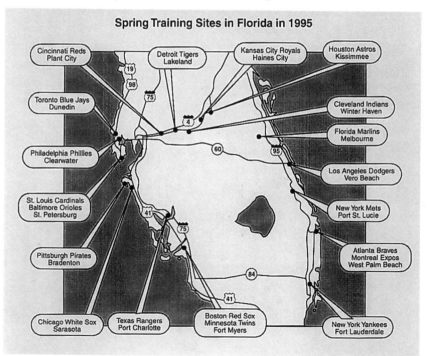

▲ Map of spring training sites in 1995.

The reporters, columnists, and feature writers often send back glowing reports about the teams and the Florida site. In spring training, all teams are "contenders," and hopeful news from reporters could stimulate ticket sales for the season. Some teams even televise their spring training games to the fans back home, allowing fans in freezing New England, for example, to see their Red Sox basking in the Fort Myers sun near beautiful palm trees. It is wonderful, free publicity for the area.

FINANCIAL ASPECTS OF SPRING TRAINING

The financial benefits of spring training to the local economy have been considerable. J. Roy Stockton, in "Spring Training in Florida," estimates that the 12 clubs training in Florida in 1960 pumped half a million dollars into Florida; this did not include spending by 700 ballplayers, wives, officials, and visiting friends. In the 1990s, that total rose to about $300 million a year. Of that total, about $3.4 million is spent on tickets, souvenirs, and food at the parks; $12 million on food, housing, and transportation by the teams themselves; and $283 million for food, lodging, and other amenities by the fans and their families in the local communities. The Grapefruit League generates some 300 full-time jobs and 3,500 part-time jobs, a small but significant part of the state's annual $16 billion sports industry. A community could earn as much as $17 million hosting a spring training team.

Because that money is the main source of tourism dollars for several Florida sites, the competition among cities to land and keep a spring training site is intense. Florida cities have tried, in some cases successfully, to lure teams from the Cactus League in Arizona, a state that is also courting Florida-based teams. The eight teams that play in the Cactus League are based on the West Coast or in the Midwest: the California Angels, Chicago Cubs, Colorado Rockies, Milwaukee Brewers, Oakland Athletics, San Diego Padres, San Francisco Giants, and Seattle Mariners. They are reluctant to move further east to Florida, and also have some long-term loyalty to Arizona. The competition between the two states to lure more teams made it to the front page of *The Sporting News* (November 6, 1957) with a sketch of a soggy player standing ankle deep in a Florida downpour looking longingly at the bright sunshine of Arizona. The negative image of

Florida in that widely circulated newspaper caused much consterna-tion in the state and a fear that Florida-based teams would head west. Florida officials, however, could recently gloat that no Cactus League club finished the regular season above .500 in 1994.

Florida cities are also trying to lure teams from other Florida cities. Such intra-state competition pits city against city for the most lucra-tive incentives. The professional teams take advantage of the intra-state fighting to obtain the best possible deal for themselves, espe-cially when most major league teams are losing around $250,000 each year on their spring training and are looking for any means to reduce their losses and even make a profit. As a result, the Houston Astros left Cocoa Beach for a new $5.5 million stadium in Kissimmee in 1985, the Texas Rangers left Pompano Beach for Port Charlotte in 1987, the Kansas City Royals left Fort Myers for Baseball City in Davenport in 1988, the Minnesota Twins left Orlando for Fort Myers in 1991, and the Boston Red Sox left Winter Haven for Fort Myers in 1993.

The result is that the teams spend very little money of their own to move and build new facilities, but the local communities have to spend millions to entice teams. It takes $8 million to $10 million to build a modern baseball facility on 70 to 100 acres, plus thousands more per year to maintain the grounds and buildings. The cost of building a new facility has risen substantially from the time in 1987 when Charlotte County spent $5.6 million on a new stadium to lure the Rangers from Pompano Beach. Four years later, Lee County in southwest Florida spent $15 million to build a new stadium to lure the Twins from Orlando, and Fort Myers spent a whopping $25 mil-lion on its new City of Palms Park to lure the Red Sox there after 27 years in Winter Haven.

The raiding that Florida cities engage in, whether to lure teams from Arizona's Cactus League or to convince a Grapefruit League team to switch to another Florida city, is increasing. Tampa, for exam-ple, convinced the Yankees to move there from their spring training home in Fort Lauderdale beginning in the 1995 season. Fort Lauderdale had originally enticed the Yankees to move from St. Petersburg in 1962 with a modern, 8,300-seat stadium, although it probably did not hurt that Yankees owner **Dan Topping** docked his boat in Fort Lauderdale. Hillsborough County commissioners voted

4–2 in 1994 to build a $17 million ballpark and training facility for the Yankees after being without a team since the Cincinnati Reds ended 53 years of training there in 1987. Tampa, hoping to land a major league team in an expansion or move, razed Al Lopez Field in 1989, but will have to settle for a spring training team (the Yankees) for now and hope that the team will bring in some $55 million annually, as consultants told them it would.

Towns can build impressive, state-of-the art stadiums with a tourist or resort tax, but they have to be sure it is worth the expense, especially since the team may choose to go elsewhere or even threaten to move when its lease expires, usually before the stadium is paid for.

Just how much conditions have changed became evident when the state's new franchise, the Florida Marlins, instead of waiting for prospective spring training sites to contact them, sent out a ten-page proposal to various cities around the state. The proposal, as reported in *Florida Trend*, indicated exactly what the Marlins expected from the city that would win their contract: "the facility's budget ($8.5 million to $15 million, excluding land cost) right down to the type of sod on the field ('Pro-turf' with Bermuda 419 grass)."

The Pitfalls of Building a New Stadium

Sometimes a city will spend millions on building a new facility or refurbishing an old one, only to find that circumstances beyond their control will help decide a situation. For example, Homestead, an agricultural town of 25,000 residents, spent $22 million in 1991 building a state-of-the-art complex for the Cleveland Indians, only to have Hurricane Andrew come through in 1992 and severely damage it — to the tune of $8 million. Even after the city made extensive repairs to the facility, the Indians and other teams were unwilling to relocate there, either for fear that another hurricane might come through again or because the site, 30 miles south of Miami, was too far away from the other Grapefruit League teams. The town has rehabilitated the facility, and it has been used by local college teams, the U.S. Olympic baseball team, the Florida Marlins for a few exhibition games, and free agents hoping to sign on with new teams at the start of the 1995 season. Still, the town needs a spring tenant to be able to recoup its losses.

Florida cities depending on tourism dollars from baseball fans attending spring training games have been badly hurt by labor disputes. The 1990 lockout by owners and the 1995 strike by players effectively wiped out spring training and caused much hardship for the state. According to a study by the U.S. Conference of Mayors, Florida loses $580,000 for every canceled game of spring training. In Fort Myers, St. Petersburg, and West Palm Beach, the loss of income due to a baseball strike is doubly bad since those cities host two teams apiece.

SPRING TRAINING STADIUMS

Among the better-known baseball stadiums in Florida are several that honor men long associated with the sport in the state. Al Lang Stadium in St. Petersburg memorializes the two-term mayor (1916–20) responsible for bringing spring training to the state in 1914. In the same city, the Mets trained at Huggins-Stengel Field, named after both **Miller Huggins**, the manager of the St. Louis Cardinals (1913–17) and New York Yankees (1918–29), and **Casey Stengel**, the manager of the Brooklyn Dodgers (1934–36), Boston Braves (1938–43), New York Yankees (1949–60), and New York Mets (1962–65). Al Lopez Field in Tampa honors the Baseball Hall-of-Famer and native son who spent 19 years catching in the majors (1928, 1930–47) and then 17 years managing (1951–65, 1968–69).

▲ Manager Casey Stengel sends the New York Mets onto their spring training field in St. Petersburg in 1962. *St. Petersburg Museum of History*

▲ Miller Huggins Field plaque. *St. Petersburg Museum of History*

Lakeland's Joker Marchant Stadium memorializes **Marcus "Joker" Marchant**, who was in charge of the city's parks and recreation department from the 1950s to the 1970s. Bradenton's McKechnie Field honors the late **William "Bill" McKechnie**, the Hall-of-Fame manager of Newark in the Federal League (1915) and the Pittsburgh Pirates (1922–26), St. Louis Cardinals (1928–29), Boston Braves (1930–37), and Cincinnati Reds (1938–46) in a 25-year managerial career.

Clearwater's Jack Russell Stadium honors **Jack Russell**, a major league pitcher with the Boston Red Sox (1926–32, 1936), Cleveland Indians (1932), Washington Senators (1933–36), Detroit Tigers (1937), Chicago Cubs (1938–39), and St. Louis Cardinals (1940). Russell was a local city commissioner in the 1950s who led the effort to build the facility. Sarasota's Payne Park honors **Calvin Payne**, an oil businessman who arrived in Sarasota in 1917 and eventually bought the land on which the ballpark is located.

Today's spring training games in Florida attract an average of 4,400 fans a game. The Grapefruit League's approximately 250 games in 1987 drew some 1.1 million fans, who paid $2 to $9 a seat. In 1994, the number of fans increased to 1.66 million, with this breakdown:

City	Team	Attendance	Games Played	Av.
Bradenton	Pittsburgh Pirates	68,975	14	4,927
Clearwater	Philadelphia Phillies	98,811	14	7,058
Davenport	Kansas City Royals	67,770	15	4,518
Dunedin	Toronto Blue Jays	80,178	13	6,168
Fort Lauderdale	New York Yankees	122,379	16	7,649
Fort Myers	Boston Red Sox	103,077	16	6,442
Fort Myers	Minnesota Twins	97,053	17	5,709
Kissimmee	Houston Astros	59,237	15	3,949
Lakeland	Detroit Tigers	87,832	14	6,274
Plant City	Cincinnati Reds	72,895	14	5,207
Port Charlotte	Texas Rangers	61,585	14	4,399
Port St. Lucie	New York Mets	79,405	16	4,963
Sarasota	Chicago White Sox	115,366	16	7,210
St. Petersburg	St. Louis Cardinals	70,974	15	4,732
St. Petersburg	Baltimore Orioles	64,358	15	4,291
Vero Beach	Los Angeles Dodgers	69,269	12	5,772
Viera	Florida Marlins	105,183	15	7,012
West Palm Beach	Atlanta Braves	90,004	14	6,429
West Palm Beach	Montreal Expos	62,858	16	3,929
Winter Haven	Cleveland Indians	80,000	15	5,333

DANGERS IN SPRING TRAINING

Spring training in Florida has many advantages, but it also has certain dangers inherent to the state, dangers such as lightning, boat accidents, and hurricanes. **Brian Foster**, a pitching prospect for the Twins in 1991, learned how serious lightning can be when he was struck by it in Fort Myers while talking on the telephone during a thunderstorm; he survived, despite the fact that the muscles in his left side had been charred.

The worst boating accident was the 1993 tragedy when three Cleveland Indians' players, out boating on Lake Nelly near Clermont, plowed into an unlighted dock at a high rate of speed; **Steve Olin** and **Tim Crews** were killed, and **Bob Ojeda** was seriously injured.

And hurricanes, while they do not usually occur during spring training, can affect it, as when Hurricane Andrew caused extensive damage in 1992 to the Cleveland Indians' new $22 million spring training complex in Homestead, Florida. Other near-tragedies include the times players out fishing in the Gulf or the Atlantic found themselves capsized or caught in a storm.

Chapter Eight

THE MAJOR LEAGUES

"I actually feel kind of sad today because I lost two long-time animal friends of mine: the white elephant down at the Dome and that 10,000-pound gorilla that's been on my back."

— Rick Dodge, St. Petersburg City Administrator

MAJOR LEAGUE TEAMS BARNSTORMED IN FLORIDA

In the early 1900s, Florida's location on the way to warm winter ballparks in the Caribbean attracted teams like the New York Giants, recent losers in the 1911 World Series who stopped off in north Florida on their way to Cuba, where they would play during the winter months. A Florida team of amateurs and professionals from the South Atlantic League beat the National League champs in Jacksonville that November and did much to bolster local spirits in that off-season. Playing in Florida also may have helped major leaguers appreciate the benefits of having spring training in the Sunshine State.

Also in Jacksonville in 1912 was a ballplayer from nearby Georgia, the great **Ty Cobb**. Instead of playing baseball, however, Cobb was performing as the male lead in a drama, *The College Widow*, at the Duval Theatre at Main and Monroe streets. Georgia critics had praised the performance of Cobb as he played the role of a halfback on a football team, and many people in Jacksonville turned out to see him. Also in the audience were the Giants, who applauded loudly, perhaps worried that the Georgia Peach would storm into the audience at the first catcall. Cobb soon tired of theatrical life and returned to baseball, where he hit an impressive .412 the next season.

Reluctance to Locate a Team in the South

For many decades, owners of major league teams refused to move their teams to the South, arguing that the oppressive heat and humidity would sap the energies of their ballplayers and hurt the chances of their teams' reaching post-season play. That might have been true in the days before air-conditioning and night games and when players wore heavy uniforms, but the move of the Milwaukee Braves to Atlanta in 1966 showed how well a southern team could do with the help of modern technology. And once air travel made road trips to distant cities feasible, owners began considering moving their franchises south. Two other factors encouraged them: colleges in the southern half of the United States, especially in Arizona, Arkansas, Florida, and Texas, have had consistently good baseball teams, and minor league and industrial-league teams there had done well over the years.

EXPANSION

Although all 16 major league teams were located in the North in 1950, the move of the Dodgers and Giants to California after the 1957 season, the expansion to 26 teams, and the population shift west and south made locating a team in Florida more of a possibility. Demographics in the 1980s indicated that Florida should have had a team. As the fourth most populous state behind California (which had five major league baseball teams), New York (two teams), and Texas (two teams), Florida deserved at least one team.

A 1983 report by *Florida Trend* writer Barry Stavro indicated that landing a major league team at that time might cost as much as $75 million, including building a new stadium ($50 million) and buying a team ($25 million), and then $2 million to $3 million a year in losses for the first decade. The report added, however, that those deficits would be partly offset by staging 50 or 60 non-baseball events in the stadium; for example, soccer, basketball, boxing, and music concerts. And having a team in a community could also add $25 million to $50 million a year through money spent in hotels, restaurants, other tourist sites, publications, and construction, plus the ripple effect of such spending by teams and fans, as for example when hotels, restaurants, and other businesses have to hire more staff to accommodate the baseball people.

▲ Major leaguers like Dizzy Dean, Babe Ruth, and Rabbit Maranville, here judging a race at a dog track in Florida, spent much time in the state before and after the regular season. *St. Petersburg Museum of History*

▲ Babe Ruth and a local woman, Jenny Worden, in St. Petersburg about 1934. He was a favorite with fans of all ages.

Heritage Park-Pinellas County Historical Museum

Granted that Florida should have a team. Where should it be? The three main contenders in the 1980s were Miami, Tampa Bay, and Orlando. Miami supporters could point to the presence of many Hispanics in the area, many of whom might be expected to support baseball, and could claim status as the gateway to Latin America, a hotbed of baseball fervor. Tampa Bay supporters could point out that five million people live within 100 miles of the area, that St. Petersburg has a long history of baseball support, and that the success of Tampa's professional football team, the Tampa Bay Buccaneers, in attracting fans despite very poor seasons was a good sign of a strong sports base. Orlando could point out that its popular theme parks like Disney World and Sea World were annually attracting thousands of visitors, many of whom might be expected to attend major league baseball games in the area.

Tampa Bay Pursues a Major League Team

A 1984 report by Greg Larson (see Bibliography) stated that an expansion franchise at either Tampa or St. Petersburg would draw 1,486,350 paying spectators in its first season, or about 18,350 per game for 81 games. If the two major cities of the Tampa Bay area, Tampa and St. Petersburg, had cooperated in attracting a team, that might have helped land one there more quickly, but they competed instead and hurt each other's chances. St. Petersburg, upset that the area's major airport, pro-football stadium, and major theme park (Busch Gardens) were in Tampa, wanted a team located on its side of the bay, and decided to build a domed stadium as a lure for a major league team willing to move south. Tampa businessmen moved more cautiously. They claimed they had a 75-year lease on land near the football stadium and enough money in escrow to build a 45,000-seat, privately financed, domed stadium, but they did not want to begin building the facility until they received a team franchise. The Tampa group also claimed their city had a younger population base compared to the "retirement village" across the bay, so that a team would do better establishing itself in Tampa.

In 1983, the Tampa Bay Baseball Group (TBBG), led by businessman **Frank Morsani**, contacted Minnesota Twins' owner **Calvin Griffith** about selling the team and moving it to Tampa. The TBBG bought 42.14 percent of the Twins from a minority owner and began

▲ An example of how Florida businesses used the popularity of Babe Ruth: a Babe Ruth look-alike contest endorses a local oil company in 1937.
Tampa-Hillsborough County Public Library

making plans for moving the team. However, after Minnesota banker **Carl Pohlad** bought Griffith's stock in order to keep the team in Minnesota, the Tampa group backed off and sold its stock in the team to Pohlad, winning praise from then-commissioner **Bowie Kuhn** and a vague commitment to receive favorable treatment in the next relocation or expansion.

In 1985, the TBBG approached the owners of the Oakland A's and thought they had an agreement to buy the team for some $38 million, but team officials used that potential move to convince Oakland officials to give the team a loan and a new stadium lease.

St. Petersburg decided to go a different route; they would build a domed stadium as a lure to attract a team, even though Baseball Commissioner **Peter Ueberroth** and major league baseball tried to discourage them from doing so. However, instead of letting the voters decide in a referendum whether to build the stadium, the city council decided on its own to go ahead with the project and impose a heavy financial burden on the taxpayers, something resented by many in the community. Local lawmakers approved spending $85 million of public funds for the 43,000-seat stadium. The cost soon increased to $138 million, but no team was yet in sight. Local officials

▲ Tampa Bay spent much time promoting baseball and trying to lure teams to the area. Here a float of the Mets and Cardinals in a Festival of States parade in 1966. *St. Petersburg Museum of History*

▼ The ThunderDome in St. Petersburg will be the home of the Tampa Bay Devil Rays.
Kevin M. McCarthy

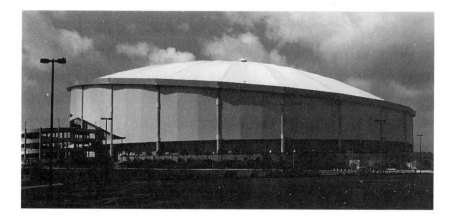

pointed out that 20,000 fans pledged $50 toward season tickets, but the stadium became a bone of contention between officials and the public. When the city fully repays its bonds by the year 2016, it will have paid about $300 million in principal and interest for the Dome. Some characterized the city's philosophy as "Build a field (or dome) of dreams, and the team will come," but it would be five years from when it opened in 1990 before that dream came true.

Three years later, St. Petersburg officials thought they were about to lure the Chicago White Sox to their new ThunderDome, but team owners used that potential move to convince Illinois legislators to approve funding for a new Comiskey Park, at one point stopping the clock to prevent it from reaching the deadline hour of midnight, at which time the legislative session was to have ended. That same year, the TBBG almost bought the Texas Rangers, with the chance of moving it to Tampa Bay, but Commissioner **Ueberroth** arranged for **George W. Bush**, the son of then-President George Bush, to buy the team and keep it in Texas. In 1991, Tampa Bay was again in the running for an expansion franchise, but **H. Wayne Huizenga** beat them out for a Miami team. The next year, the Seattle Mariners were up for sale, possibly to a group from Tampa Bay, but a group led by the Japanese founder of Nintendo bought the team and kept it in Seattle. In 1992, **Vince Naimoli** of Tampa thought he was going to buy the San Francisco Giants for $115 million. When the impending move of the Giants to St. Petersburg was announced, Florida Marlins owner **Wayne Huizenga** congratulated the city, but some thought he did not like it and that he worked behind the scenes to kill the deal in order not to have any Florida competition for his Marlins. In the end, National League President **Bill White** convinced a local California group to buy the Giants and keep the team there.

Those failed attempts to lure major league teams to the Tampa Bay area soured many investors and fans there, but only urged others on. One reporter thought that past failures might help Tampa-St. Pete land a professional team: "First, because the area has been rebuffed so many times, it will have the sentimental support of some major league owners. And experience with the financial difficulties encountered by previous investment groups has made Tampa-area boosters savvy." One could wonder if coming in second so many times would make them try harder or just give up the fight.

The Florida Marlins

The competition to have one of the two new National League expansion teams was very intense in the early 1990s, especially since major league baseball had not added any new teams since the American League added Toronto and Seattle in 1977.

In the early 1990s, efforts to establish a major league baseball team in Florida shifted from Tampa Bay to Dade County, where Miami officials had some strong arguments for giving them one of the new teams. First, in 1985 the Miami-Fort Lauderdale area was ranked the nation's 13th-largest television market. South Florida had a high percentage of households with cable television, an important point because baseball owners could sell their games through cable or pay-cable networks and increase revenues. The argument that teams could not play in Florida's heat and humidity without a domed stadium was offset by the fact that the Marlins planned to play the large majority of their home games at night. Finally, the area's proximity to baseball-crazy Central America and the Caribbean, with the possibility of televising the games there, increased Miami's chances.

Some believed having a professional baseball team would take some of the media spotlight off such problems as the city's high crime rate, and would give the citizens something to rally around, to cheer for. It might also attract new corporate clients. Baseball could offer another entertainment option for visitors and residents. On the negative side was the fact that Floridians tend to spend more time outdoors than residents of other parts of the country and therefore would not watch as much TV. *Sports Illustrated*'s columnist Steve Wulf wrote that no Florida city had been able to support a Triple-A franchise since 1968 and that support for spring training was weak in Florida.

A man who labored long and hard before his death to bring baseball to south Florida was **Joe Robbie**, owner of the Miami Dolphins of the National Football League. He had built Joe Robbie Stadium for the Dolphins to play ten home games, but needed more use of the facility to pay for it. Baseball, with its 81 home games, would help solve his problem, but he would not see it in his lifetime. After he died, his successors convinced Blockbuster Entertainment Corporation's **H. Wayne Huizenga** to buy a half-interest in Joe Robbie Stadium from the Miami Dolphins for $30 million, at which point professional-baseball supporters in the area felt renewed hope. The fact that one person, Huizenga, would be in charge of the new Florida baseball team, if there were to be one in the Miami area, had greatly strengthened his bid for one of the new teams.

After months of hard work on the part of Huizenga and his staff, the 26 owners of major league teams voted unanimously on July 5, 1991, to admit the Florida Marlins and the Colorado Rockies to the National League, to begin play in 1993. "Now, champagne for everyone," Huizenga announced in celebrating the prize. In that first major league expansion in 14 years, he became the only person in the United States to own major portions of three sports franchises: the Florida Marlins, the Florida Panthers hockey team, and the Miami Dolphins football team. David Whitford, in *Playing Hardball*, described the many obstacles Huizenga overcame to land himself a baseball franchise, but also all the work that went into fielding the team's first players, from signing up scouts and fanning out across the country, and across Japan and South America as well, compiling lists of desired players, and finally entering its first draft.

In a name-the-team contest sponsored by the new National League franchise, fans sent in 17,439 entries; of the 3,500 different names, the most popular name was Manatees, with Marlins coming in second. Other suggested names were the Sun Devils, Renegades, Miami Marlins, and South Florida Marlins. Naming the new team the Florida Marlins instead of the Miami or South Florida Marlins indicated Huizenga's desire to make the whole state his domain. "When we picked out that name [Florida Marlins], we figured we and Tampa Bay or we and Orlando would share the state of Florida," Huizenga said. "Now that we're the only one, it makes sense for everyone to reach out and make everyone in the state of Florida our fans."

Many fans in the Tampa Bay area would never consider the Marlins their team, since they felt that they deserved their own professional baseball team. One could see signs in Bradenton, for example, during a 1993 spring training game with the Marlins that read "Tampa Bay hates Wayne and his Miami Marlins" and "My two favorite teams are the Pirates and any team that beats the Marlins."

The new team would play in the East Division of the National League and would call Joe Robbie Stadium home. For team president, Huizenga hired **Carl Barger**, president of the Pittsburgh Pirates, and for general manager, **Dave Dombrowski** of the Montreal Expos. The team logo has a black, aqua, white, and gray marlin leaping through a gray life raft, which resembles a baseball and bears the "FLORIDA MARLINS" name. Huizenga liked the marlin as team symbol because the fish "is agile, proud, powerful, sleek, alert, a fierce fighter, and an adversary that can test one's mettle and can also shake itself loose just when you think it's in trouble."

The cost of the Marlins and Rockies franchises ($95 million apiece) was so high, compared with the paltry $7 million for a new team in 1977, that American League owners successfully fought to receive some of that franchise money — in exchange for giving up some of their players to the new teams. After Huizenga spent $95 million for the franchise, he spent another $35 million in start-up costs. He also looked at the history of other teams and resolved to avoid the mistakes they had made. For example, he was determined to create a front office that resembled south Florida in its racial mixture. Among the Marlins' 145 employees in the front office and on the field, excluding players, 45 people or 30% were non-whites, well above the major league average of 17%. Two African Americans were in high-ranking positions: **Jonathan Mariner**, the team's chief financial officer, and **John Young**, major league scout in the West and the president of major league baseball's Reviving Baseball in Inner Cities (RBI) program, which promotes inner-city baseball (see Chapter Two). At a time when Cincinnati Reds owner **Marge Schott** was being criticized for racist remarks and the Reverend **Jesse Jackson** was calling on owners to hire more non-whites in front-office positions, the Marlins were well on their way to creating more racial balance in their operations.

The Marlins staff did a good job of making the team appealing to south Florida, selling (at up to $1,215 a seat) more than 21,000 season tickets, which is more than 50 percent of the stadium capacity and one of the highest totals in the majors. The marketing staff, pointing out that Miami is close to Latin America, hoped for many paying fans from that area and maybe loyalty from future major leaguers. According to one writer, "where America began [Latin America] is now known for a quintessentially American product: the baseball player." To make the team more appealing to Latin America, which sends more than 2 million tourists to the Miami area each year, the team, calling itself *Equipo de las Americas* (Team of the Americas), signed popular players like **Orestes Destrade** of Cuba and **Benito Santiago** of Puerto Rico, made **Nigel Wilson** of Trinidad its number-one pick in the expansion draft, made Cuban-born **Cookie Rojas** its third-base coach, and hired former all-star **Tony Perez** of Cuba as its director of international relations and ambassador to Latin America.

In February of the first year, several Marlins' executives and players went on a quick road trip to the Dominican Republic, Puerto Rico, and Venezuela, spreading Marlins' souvenirs and goodwill. Future plans called for playing exhibition games in Latin America, broadcasting the games in Puerto Rico and the Dominican Republic, and having Perez write a column for a Spanish-language newspaper. The team arranged with travel agents and tour operators in many Latin American countries to sell Marlins tickets as part of their tour packages.

Attracting more tourists during the summer season, usually a slow time compared to the high winter season, was important to the Miami economy. The team spent over $1 million to sell the Marlins as the "Team of the Americas" to Central and South America. As part of that appeal, the concession stands at Joe Robbie sell, in addition to soda and hot dogs, *media noche* (a Cuban cheese-and-pork sandwich) and *arepa* (fried mozzarella on cornmeal pancakes).

When the Marlins played their first game on April 5, 1993, Yankee great **Joe DiMaggio**, who lives in south Florida and contributes much to the Joe DiMaggio Children's Hospital there, threw out the first ball in Joe Robbie Stadium. For his starting pitcher, manager **René Lachemann** chose **Charlie Hough**, a former draft pick by the Dodgers out of high school in 1966 and a third-baseman-converted-to-pitcher who had hurt his arm so badly that his major league career seemed over before it began. Determined not to quit, he learned how to throw a knuckleball and went on to pitch for the next 20 years for the Dodgers, the Texas Rangers, the Chicago White Sox, and finally the Florida Marlins. With a fierce competitive attitude ("I'd rather pitch hurt than let someone else pitch"), vast experience (the only pitcher ever to work at least 375 games as a starter and 375 in relief), and a sense of humor, he was expected to help the young Marlins weather their first season. When the Marlins defeated the Dodgers 6–3 in that first game, Hough got the first win of the team and the Marlins were undefeated.

In the first season of play (1993), some 41,000 fans turned out for each Marlins' home game, a respectable number that belied doomsayers who predicted that Miami's humidity, heat, and mosquitoes would keep the fans away. The team had an above-average (64–98) record the first year, followed by a 51–64 season in 1994 before the strike ended their hopes of a good year. Fans with a knowledge of history will have to be patient if they want a winning team, since the average win-loss record for new teams is 60–102 in their first year. The New York Mets were the only one of 12 expansion teams since 1960 to win a World Series during its first ten years. Only two others have won their division in that time span: the Kansas City Royals (once) and the Toronto Blue Jays (three times).

The Devil Rays

Meanwhile, back on Florida's west coast, baseball fever was simmering. It had taken almost nine years and $138 million to build the multipurpose ThunderDome, but it still did not have a major league tenant. Supporters had endured years of jokes, and some had lost hope, but a few stalwarts like County Commissioner **Bob Stewart** kept pushing for a team. Then, in March 1995, the hopes of baseball fans in the area seemed to come to fruition when the owners of major league baseball voted unanimously to add two expansion teams: one in Arizona and one in Tampa Bay. "I think this is the greatest day in the history of Tampa Bay," team owner **Vince Naimoli** said.

For baseball proponents in St. Petersburg, that announcement was sweet music. After 18 years of courting potential teams away from their northern or western cities or trying to start a new team, Naimoli and his band of patient, persistent wooers won. St. Petersburg City Administrator **Rick Dodge**, who had labored for years to bring a major league team to the area, said after the announcement of the new franchise: "I actually feel kind of sad today because I lost two longtime animal friends of mine: the white elephant down at the Dome and that 10,000-pound gorilla that's been on my back."

The price for having a new team would be a hefty $130 million, which could rise to $150 million with payment schedules and interest charges, but few thought about that in the euphoria of the moment, nor did it seem to matter that professional ballplayers were on strike in the early part of 1995. Owners would decide later which league the two teams would be in. If they put one club in each league, that would force major league baseball to have interleague play, something they had resisted for decades.

Some 7,000 fans made suggestions for naming the new team, names that ranged from Barracudas to Pelicans. Naimoli and many others wanted a nautical name like the Stingrays, but Maui of the Hawaiian Winter League would not part with the name. The final name for the new team, Devil Rays, caused some consternation for the superstitious who wanted nothing to do with the devil, but most people would end up calling the team the Rays. Naimoli also said that he did not want to name the team after a creature that caused harm; the devil ray or manta ray seemed to be a good choice because the creature is gentle and prefers a simple cuisine of plankton. With its huge black fins extended, the ray looks like a large floating blanket and can jump out of the water and sail some 20 feet in the air. The name of that gentle, peaceful creature would be in marked contrast to names of other sports teams in the state: the Florida Gators, the Miami Hurricanes, the Miami Heat, and the Tampa Bay Storm. Because so many people expressed dismay at the Devil Rays' name, owner Naimoli allowed fans to vote on whether it would be Devil Rays or Manta Rays. Some 50,000 fans voted for or against the name, and in the end, because the votes were split, Naimoli decided to keep the name, commenting that people kept telling him, "'The name grows on you. Don't change it.'"

Why Tampa Bay finally secured its long-anticipated major league team in 1995 was probably due to several factors. Arizona, the other site selected for a team, had a deadline of securing a franchise by April 1, 1995, in order to get a stadium built there, and professional baseball has tended to establish new teams in pairs. Major league baseball also might have been worried about congressional efforts to eliminate baseball's antitrust exemption; two members of the Florida delegation, Senator Connie Mack (the grandson and namesake of the great Philadelphia Athletics owner) and St. Petersburg area Representative C. W. Bill Young, backed off their support of those congressional efforts when they found out the area would land a baseball team; some pundits might have changed the "Field of Dreams" maxim to "If you sue them, they will come." That antitrust exemption, which dated back to 1922, has allowed major league baseball to essentially

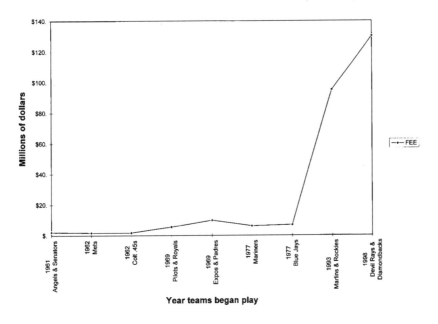

The chart shows "Millions of dollars" on the y-axis ($, $20., $40., $60., $80., $100., $120., $140.) and "Year teams began play" on the x-axis with the labels: 1961 Angels & Senators; 1962 Mets; 1962 Colt .45s; 1969 Pilots & Royals; 1969 Expos & Padres; 1977 Mariners; 1977 Blue Jays; 1993 Marlins & Rockies; 1998 Devil Rays & Diamondbacks. Legend: —◆—FEE

▲ Fee for Expansion Baseball Teams.

act as a cartel. Finally, Florida Marlins' owner **H. Wayne Huizenga** and New York Yankees' owner (and Tampa resident) **George Steinbrenner** supported the efforts of Tampa Bay to lure a team. Everyone, even dermatologists, could finally "Catch the Rays!"

Having a major league team in the Tampa Bay area was appropriate for many reasons. St. Petersburg had long been associated with professional baseball from the early days of spring training. Area schools had produced such well-known baseball figures as **Wade Boggs, Steve Garvey, Dwight Gooden, Tony La Russa, Al Lopez, Dave Magadan, Fred McGriff, Lou Piniella,** and **Gary Sheffield.** The baseball tradition continues with the likes of teams like North Brandon, which won the Senior League World Series in 1994; the University of Tampa, which won the Division II College World Series for the second time in 1993; and Hillsborough Community College, which won the national junior college championship in 1988. From an economic point of view, Greater Tampa Bay is the 23rd-largest metro area in the United States, hosts ten million tourists a year, and is the nation's 10th-largest cable TV market. And it was the most populous area not served by major league baseball.

How much the new team will mean to the Tampa Bay area is difficult to determine. While some economists predict a $100 million influx into the area and others see the new team as evidence that Tampa Bay is thriving and large enough to support professional teams in football, hockey, and baseball, still others say that the new team will siphon away money that would have been spent on other attractions such as concerts and theme parks.

OFF-SEASON DECISIONS IN FLORIDA

Florida in the off-season has also played a part in several important decisions of major league baseball. In 1966, after a resounding defeat by the players having spring training in Arizona in his attempt to become executive director of the Major League Baseball Players Association, **Marvin Miller** won enough votes among the players having spring training in Florida to win the post and began his very effective leadership of the players, a leadership that eventually gave them much power and high salaries. In 1969, at a meeting in Bal Harbour, major league owners selected **Bowie Kuhn** (who later retired to north Florida) to be the fifth commissioner of baseball and then in Tampa in 1984 selected **Peter Ueberroth** as his replacement.

If the 1994–95 baseball strike had continued into the regular season, Florida would have had a chance to host some major league games. With permission from the American League, the Toronto Blue Jays would have used Grant Field, the Dunedin Blue Jays' stadium, because Ontario law would not allow replacement players in Toronto's SkyDome. The strike was called off just before the regular season began, so the Blue Jays played their home games in Canada and not in Dunedin.

MAJOR LEAGUERS FROM FLORIDA

Among the major leaguers from Florida (see Appendix E for a complete list) one deserves special mention: Hall-of-Famer **Alfonso "Al" Ramon Lopez** (1908–), who entered the Hall of Fame in 1977 after establishing three records as a player: 465 put-outs in 1930, the most for any rookie; 1,861 games as a catcher in the National League, a record not yet broken; and 1,918 games as a catcher in the major leagues, a record not broken until 1988. He also established two records as a manager: the most wins in one season (111 in 1954 with the Cleveland Indians of the American League, a record not yet broken), and a winning percentage in one season (.721 in 1954, also as yet unbroken). As a manager for 17 years, he had two first-place finishes and ten second-place finishes. In 1992, his native Tampa erected a statue of him and renamed Horizon Park the Al Lopez Park at Himes Avenue and Dr. Martin Luther King Jr. Boulevard. Al Lopez Field, which the Reds had used for many spring trainings, was razed in 1989 when the Reds moved to Plant City.

▲ Photo of Hall of Fame plaque of Al Lopez. *Kevin M. McCarthy*

The Florida cities that have produced the most major leaguers are Tampa (37), Miami (23), Jacksonville (15), Pensacola (13), West Palm Beach (11), St. Petersburg (8), Orlando (7), Sarasota (7), Tallahassee (5), Brooksville (4), and Fort Lauderdale (4). The fact that Tampa leads the state's cities in number of major leaguers is a testament to how strong baseball is in the Tampa Bay area.

THE MAJORS TODAY

Major league baseball has changed in the last decade. Owners have added more teams, allowed others to consider moving to better sites, divided the two leagues into three divisions, added "wild card" teams to an extra round of post-season play, and endured a potentially crippling strike in 1994–95. Owners faced the real possibility that Congress would end its antitrust exemption and the probability that many fans would not return or would return begrudgingly to a sport that some see as bloated with greed. The fact that the average salary of major league players in 1995 was $1.2 million and the average median salary was $410,000 gave some fans the idea that the bottom line was the most important statistic in today's game for both owners and players.

Chapter Nine

OTHER BASEBALL LEAGUES
AND PLAYERS

"Tallahassee honored Red with a camellia garden in
the city's McCarthy Park. It's a fitting memorial to a
man who told the world of Tallahassee's beauty."
— Bob Edwards

EARLY CONGRESSIONAL BASEBALL IN FLORIDA

Among the teams that have played in Florida over the years was one made up of Congressmen on a yearly swing through Florida when Congress was not in session. To get into shape each year and to have a baseball vacation, members of Congress would sometimes head south to engage in their own version of spring training, often playing in Daytona Beach for a week or ten days because the Daytona Beach Chamber of Commerce would pay their expenses. Proceeds from the exhibition games would go to charities like the Damon Runyon Cancer Fund. Among the players in the mid-1950s were Representative **Eugene McCarthy** of Minnesota and Senator **John F. Kennedy** of Massachusetts.

▲ Former New York Giants pitcher Carl Hubbell shows a group of Congressional baseball players in Sanford in 1950 how he held the ball for his famous screwball pitch.
Florida State Archives

THE SENIOR PROFESSIONAL BASEBALL ASSOCIATION

In an attempt to take advantage of fans' interest in baseball during the off-season, to pattern a league after the successful Senior Professional Golfers Association, and to enable fans to see former stars play once again, Colorado real-estate developer and former minor league outfielder **Jim Morley** established the Florida-based Senior Professional Baseball Association (SPBA) in 1989 for former major leaguers in their 30s and 40s. Morley explained his idea in 1,250 postcards sent to former major leaguers and received 730 positive replies for the 192 roster spots. Most players had to be at least 35

▲ Representative Eugene McCarthy signs a baseball for a fan in Sanford in 1950.

Florida State Archives

years old; catchers could be 32, supposedly because the position is more difficult. The ballplayers, some of whom still had hopes of returning to the majors, would earn between $2,000 and $15,000 a month and get a chance to return to the sport they had participated in with some success.

Among the former major league greats who expressed interest and eventually played in the league were **Paul Blair**, **Vida Blue**, **Rollie Fingers**, **Dennis Leonard**, **Amos Otis**, and **Louis Tiant**. Former Cardinals outfielder **Curt Flood** became the league's commissioner.

Morley based the SPBA in Florida because the state had the warm weather to attract tourists from November through January and already had spring training facilities that were available after baseball season. The short season would run from November 1 to the end of January. This is the time between the World Series and spring training when baseball addicts cannot find much to substitute for the Show, but it is also a time when there is competition from live and televised football, basketball, and hockey. Owners of the eight charter teams, encouraged that a Denver-based television network agreed to televise 30 of the games to some 18 million U.S. homes, hoped that big-name players from baseball's past would attract paying fans to the ballpark and that high-caliber play would keep the fans returning. To survive financially, the league had to attract an average of 1,500 to 2,000 fans to each of the 72 scheduled games, fans who were willing to pay $6 to $11 for a ticket.

The SPBA had its share of jokes: "where the crack of the bat meets the creak of the bone," "every day is an old-timers' day," "pitchers vied for the Cy Old Award," and "the Show is now the Late Show." The SPBA played its first and only season, which the St. Petersburg Pelicans won, in 1989–90, but in the end the league could not attract enough paying fans to make it financially feasible. At least the players had enjoyed it: "The money was nice," said Pelican infielder **Todd Cruz**, "and I could really use it. But most of all, playing in this league, playing baseball, was the thrill of a lifetime for most of us. I'll come back next season if they do it, and I think most of the players will, too. We loved the idea of this league."

Similar leagues have been planned for Florida from time to time, but usually don't succeed, possibly because fans in the state are used to top-quality play, whether from the many colleges and universities in Florida, minor leagues, spring training, or the Florida Marlins. One planned league, the Sunshine Baseball League in south Florida, designed for players out of baseball or undrafted collegians, was to play a 56-game schedule in 1992, but never got off the ground. A new organization, founded in 1995 and headquartered in Deerfield Beach, is the American Association of Professional Baseball Players. Founded by former Pirates' star **Rennie Stennett**, this major league alumni group planned on having exhibition games and clinics in various states. It had on its honorary advisory committee such former players as **Ernie Banks, Rollie Fingers, Ken Griffey Sr., Ferguson Jenkins, Al Oliver, Dave Parker, Gaylord Perry, Mickey Rivers, Willie Stargell**, and **Roy White**.

MEN'S ADULT BASEBALL LEAGUES

The state has two baseball leagues that cater to men who want to play ball past the age of 18: Men's Adult Baseball League (MABL) for men 18 and older; and Men's Senior Baseball League (MSBL) for men 30 and older. These national organizations, as described in official publications and their own *Hardball Magazine*, have over 150 local affiliates, 1,500 teams, and more than 20,000 members. Such well-organized leagues allow athletes who have been playing hardball to continue competing at the local level as well as in state and regional tournaments. Rather than trying to accommodate aspiring pros, these leagues are geared to serious amateurs who want to play baseball for as long as possible and to compete with players their own age.

Florida teams have done well in recent years. In the MSBL Fall Classic Championship Games, 1991–93, the St. Petersburg Hurricanes beat both the Rhode Island team (1991) and the Orlando Twins (1992), and the St. Petersburg All Stars won the following year (1993) after beating the St. Petersburg Hurricanes in semifinal action. In the 30+ national group, the Fort Lauderdale All Stars (1991) and the Clearwater Tigers (1992) both came in second. In the 40+ national group, the St. Petersburg 39ers won (1992), and in the following year (1993) the Tampa Pirates came in second.

The Florida sites and the number of Men's Senior Baseball League (MSBL) teams in each in 1995 were Miami (18), Clearwater (16), Orlando (16), Tampa (16), Jacksonville (8), Coral Springs (6), Manasota (6), and Martin County (6). The Florida sites and the number of Men's Adult Baseball League (MABL) teams in each in 1995 were Tampa (20), Orlando (12), Tallahassee (12), Miami (10), Daytona (8), Gainesville (8), St. Petersburg (8), Winter Haven (8), Fort Lauderdale (6), Manasota (4), and Treasure Coast (4). The MABL has a Fall Classic in Florida each November that attracts teams from around the country.

SEMIPRO LEAGUES

Baseball teams from Florida have been involved in various semipro leagues for years. One of them, the National Baseball Congress (NBC), founded in 1931 and headquartered in Wichita, Kansas, sponsors summer amateur baseball. Among the Florida players who did well in the NBC's national tournaments was **Bob Seltzer** of Tampa (1960); more recently, **Dave Montiel** of the Miami Hooligans won the Bauldie Moschetti Award for Most Inspirational Player (1993). In the national tournaments, the Army Air Base team from Orlando was runner-up in 1945. The NBC alumni from Florida who made it to the majors are **Ed Shoakes** of Sanford (1940); **Tom Fine** of Orlando (1945); **Dennis Aust** and **Hal Lanier**, both of Tampa (1960); and **Alex**

Fernandez of Miami (1993). Winter Springs hosted a recent qualifying tournament, and three other sites in the state have had leagues: Miami, North Miami Beach, and Orlando.

BILL WHITE

Among the most important major league players/officials from Florida was **Bill White**, who was born in 1934 in Lakewood, a very small town in the northwest corner of the state about three miles from the Alabama border. When he and his family moved to Ohio, he decided to become a baseball player rather than a medical doctor and went on to excel in the majors and later in broadcasting and baseball administration.

▲ Bill White. *Bill White Museum*

After breaking into the National League with a home run in his first at-bat, he proceeded to play first base for 13 seasons, including six All-Star games. While playing for the New York Mets (1956), the San Francisco Giants (1958), the St. Louis Cardinals (1959–65, 1969), and the Philadelphia Phillies (1966–68), he amassed impressive statistics: a .286 batting average, 202 home runs, 870 RBIs, and seven Gold Gloves.

Florida played another role in his career, when, in 1960, he was in St. Petersburg for spring training with his fellow St. Louis Cardinals. When he saw the segregation being practiced there, he objected to the fact that black players could not stay in all-white hotels with the other players but had to stay with black families. The ensuing publicity encouraged the team's management to threaten to leave the city if the situation was not rectified. The next year, local officials relented and allowed all the Cardinals to stay in the same hotel. *New York Times* sportswriter Claire Smith pointed out that the 1960 Cardinals' training camp "actually became a tourist attraction of sorts, with people driving out of their way to stop and gawk at the remarkable sight of integration in a state where Jim Crow laws lingered into the 1970s." She went on to imply that the integration achieved in part by Bill White's efforts led to better relations among the players, a stronger team by 1963, and the world championship in 1964.

After retiring from the playing field, White became the first African American to secure a major announcing job when he became a New York Yankees' broadcaster in 1971, a position he kept for 18 years. In 1989, 42 years after **Jackie Robinson** broke the modern color line in the majors, White became president of the National League, succeeding **A. Bartlett Giamatti**, the new baseball commissioner. At that time White, a unanimous selection by the owners, was the only African American to head a major national professional sports organization. He retired from that position in 1994.

RED BARBER

Broadcaster **Walter Lanier "Red" Barber** (1908–92) was born in Mississippi, but grew up in Sanford, Florida, after his father secured a railroad job with the Atlantic Coast Line when Red was ten years old. There Red played baseball for his high school team, the Celery-Feds, before going to the University of Florida in Gainesville, where he began working on the school radio station.

▲ "Red" Barber in Tallahassee prepares for his weekly National Public Radio program in 1987. *Florida State Archives*

After a long broadcasting career with the Cincinnati Reds, Brooklyn Dodgers, and New York Yankees, he spent his final years in Tallahassee, where he did a very popular weekly commentary on National Public Radio for 12 years, much of which is chronicled by Bob Edwards in *Fridays with Red*. In between his eloquent descriptions of the camellias in his garden and the fact that the sun rises even after disastrous sporting events, he taught a generation of listeners, many of whom knew little or nothing about baseball, what it was like growing up during the golden age of radio when he covered the Dodgers and Yankees. The microphone that Barber used at the University of Florida is in a special exhibit at the National Baseball Hall of Fame in Cooperstown, N.Y., where Barber is a member of the broadcasters' wing. He also received the Ford C. Frick Award for his distinguished career in broadcasting.

RETIRED MAJOR LEAGUERS IN FLORIDA

Over the years, thousands of ballplayers became familiar with the good lifestyle that the Sunshine State provides its residents. After having experienced the pleasures of living in the state during their minor league and/or spring training days, many former major leaguers retired to Florida to take up new careers or enjoy the investments they had made as ballplayers. One baseball celebrity who spent much time in the state was **Babe Ruth**, who retired from the game he loved in 1935 and returned to Florida, where he had gone through so many spring trainings. Ruth attended the Yankees' games in St. Petersburg, where he was called on to stand up and wave his cap to the fans, and taught at Ray Doan's baseball school in Palatka in the 1940s, but he had a hard time adjusting to an inactive life.

Other ballplayers came to Florida to recover from injuries, some of them not related to baseball. For example, when a disturbed woman shot Phillies infielder **Eddie Waitkus** in 1949, the owner of the Phillies, **Bob Carpenter**, paid for him and the team trainer to spend the winter in Florida recuperating. He returned to the majors the following season and played for another six years. When St. Petersburg began having an old-timers' game in the 1950s to raise money for the March of Dimes, officials found some 200 former big leaguers living in the state. Among the Florida retirees that Chuck and Pat Wills wrote about in *Beyond Home Plate* were **Earl Battey**, **Bruce Dal**

▲ Fred Merkle had a fishing float business in Daytona Beach in 1949.
Florida State Archives

Canton, **Monte Irvin**, **Ron LeFlore**, and **Bob Watson**, all of whom live or work, or both, in Florida.

One famous (or infamous) major leaguer who made Daytona Beach his home was **Fred Merkle** (1888–1956), who lived at 616 South Palmetto Avenue and worked in a business that manufactured fishing floats. Although a skilled first baseman for **John J. McGraw**'s New York Giants, he became best known for failing to continue running from first to second base when his teammate hit what Merkle thought was the winning hit in a 1908 game with the Chicago Cubs. When a Cubs' infielder noticed that Merkle had headed for the clubhouse without touching second base to avoid the crowd streaming onto the field, the infielder retrieved the ball, touched second base to make an out on Merkle, and then convinced the umpires, who had left the field, about what had happened. The senior umpire ruled that Merkle was the third out and the game ended in a tie, especially since the umps could not clear the field for extra innings. The game had to be played over to decide the pennant winner; the Cubs won and went on to the World Series. Merkle was forever known after that as "bonehead," despite a good 16-year career in which he batted .273.

Two others who retired in Florida also deserve mention. **Ray Dandridge**, who played in the Negro Leagues (1933–49) for such teams as the Detroit Stars, Nashville Elite Giants, Newark Dodgers, Newark Eagles, and New York Cubans, lived in Palm Bay before his death in 1994 at age 79. He was inducted into the Hall of Fame in 1987. **Ted Williams**, who spent much time in the Keys fly-fishing but left there when they became too crowded, eventually settled in Citrus County near a museum that honors him.

The Ted Williams Museum and Hitters' Hall of Fame

The Ted Williams Museum and Hitters' Hall of Fame opened on February 9, 1994, in Citrus Hills, near where the former Boston Red Sox player lives. The museum has game footage of "The Splendid Splinter"; commentary from **Joe DiMaggio**, **Bob Feller**, and **Stan Musial**; memorabilia from Williams' careers in baseball, fishing, and piloting in World War II and the Korean conflict; and other displays about baseball. Williams was the last batter to hit over .400 in one season (1941) and won two Triple Crowns (1942 and 1947), six batting titles, and two MVP awards. The museum is at 2455 North Citrus Hills Boulevard in Hernando; phone: 352-527-6566; hours: 10–4; closed Easter, Thanksgiving, and Christmas. At Williams's insistence, it features a very low admission: adults $1, children 50 cents.

◀ The Ted Williams Museum near Inverness.

Kevin M. McCarthy

▼ The Florida Sports Hall of Fame in Lake City.

Kevin M. McCarthy

THE FLORIDA SPORTS HALL OF FAME

Lake City is the home of the Florida Sports Hall of Fame, founded in 1958 to honor Floridians who have excelled in sports. The baseball honorees include major league players **Steve Carlton, Andre Dawson, Steve Garvey, Hal McRae, Lou Piniella, John "Boog" Powell, Tim Raines, Al Rosen, Herb Score, Truett "Rip" Sewell, Don Sutton, Paul Waner,** and **Early Wynn; James W. Everett Sr.** of the Negro Leagues; coaches **Ron Fraser** of the University of Miami and **Hal Smeltzly** of Florida Southern College; managers **Ben Geraghty, Dick Howser, Fred Hutchinson, Al Lopez,** and **Zack Taylor;** owner **George Steinbrenner** of the New York Yankees, who lives in Tampa and has done much to support college baseball in the state; broadcaster **Red Barber;** and promoter **Al Lang.** The displays give a small glimpse of the rich tradition of baseball at all levels in Florida. The Hall is open 8–5, seven days a week; phone: 904-758-1310.

FLORIDA'S BASEBALL CAPITAL

If any city deserved a major league franchise and the moniker of The Baseball City in the state, St. Petersburg surely would be it. It has hosted seven major league teams for spring training over the years and has what may be the oldest old-timers' baseball game in the nation. Many Hall-of-Famers have played in the game; for example, in 1990, ten Hall-of-Famers played during the first convention of the Major League Baseball Players Alumni Association (MLBPA), which

◀ E. C. Robinson, chairman of the Baseball Committee of the Florida Chamber of Commerce, and Yogi Berra of the New York Yankees and Mets in St. Petersburg. *St. Petersburg Museum of History*

later announced that it was moving its headquarters to St. Petersburg. Today, the 11-member board of directors of the MLBPA, which was established in 1982 by former major leaguers living in the Baltimore-Washington area, directs efforts to establish pension and supplemental insurance programs for its members, put on clinics and exhibition games, and raise money for charities.

The governing body for all organized professional minor league baseball in the United States, Canada, Mexico, and the Dominican Republic — the National Association of Professional Baseball Leagues — has had its headquarters in St. Petersburg since 1973.

The city has been the headquarters for the Southern Region of the Little League since 1966 and has sometimes hosted the annual Florida Governor's Baseball Dinner, which salutes baseball. At the 1987 Governor's Baseball Dinner, the St. Petersburg Chamber of Commerce Baseball Committee founded and sponsored the Dick Howser Memorial Award to honor the nation's best college baseball player. (See Chapter Three for the list of winners.)

The city was also home for many years to one of the game's great writers: **Fred Lieb**, author of histories of the Detroit Tigers, Boston Red Sox, Pittsburgh Pirates, Baltimore Orioles, and Philadelphia Phillies, and a man who once wrote of St. Petersburg that "I cannot think of a better place for a baseball writer to make his home." His home at 136 Seventh Avenue Northeast hosted many baseball greats, including **Connie Mack** (who showed up one day to get Lieb to record Mack's voice for posterity) and **Babe Ruth** (who needed Lieb to verify Ruth's great skill as a pitcher for the Red Sox). Since 1931, St. Petersburg has had the Kids and Kubs, also known as the Three-Quarter Century Softball Club, an exclusive athletic club that requires its members to be at least 75 years old.

Governor's Baseball Dinner

The Governor's Baseball Dinner, which is open to the public with the purchase of a ticket, is an annual salute to spring training in Florida and to minor league teams that play in the state year round. Cities such as St. Petersburg, Orlando, and Lakeland have all played host to the dinner, which has been held for 47 years, although not in 1995 because of the baseball strike. Invitees/attendees have included league presidents, major league owners, managers, executives, current and former players, Hall-of-Famers, and other baseball personalities. The Old-Timers' Game was played in conjunction with the dinner for several years. The dinner is put on by the Florida Sports Foundation (phone: 904-922-0482), a public/private partner of the Florida Department of Commerce, in conjunction with the governor's office.

▲ Governor Farris Bryant addresses the annual baseball dinner in 1963.
St. Petersburg Museum of History

BASEBALL SCHOOLS/CLINICS

One of the early baseball camps was begun by Yankee second baseman **George "Snuffy" Stirnweiss**, who teamed up with **Bob Doty**, a recreational director, to open a baseball school in Bartow in the 1940s. Armed with a ten-year lease on an old army airfield four miles from the town center, they built three baseball fields, two batting ranges, a dozen pitching rubbers, sliding pits, dormitories, a gym, a recreation room, and a theater. They then convinced 130 students to learn the fundamentals of baseball from such major leaguers as **Tommy Henrich, Charley Keller, Phil Rizzuto, Rip Sewell**, and **Mickey Vernon**. So successful was the school that 56 of its first 130 students went into organized baseball one year, and 88 of 170 students another year.

Among the baseball clinics held statewide is the Fred Waters Baseball Clinic in Pensacola, named in honor of Pensacola native **Fred Waters** (1927–89), who pitched for the Pittsburgh Pirates (1955–56) and later scouted for the Minnesota Twins. Baseball camps include the All Pro Baseball Camp in Spring Hill; Athletes in Action Baseball Fantasy Camp and Enrichment Conference in Kissimmee; Athletes in Action Baseball School in Orlando and Tampa; the Babbitt Baseball Camp in Sarasota; Bucky Dent's Baseball School in Delray Beach; Chet Lemon's School of Baseball in Lake Mary; Doyle Baseball

◀ Phil Rizzuto of the New York Yankees teaches prospective major leaguers how to bunt at a baseball school in Bartow in 1948.

Florida State Archives

▲ Tommy Henrich, New York Yankees batting star, shows a group of boys the proper hand-grip on the bat at a baseball school in Bartow in 1948.
Florida State Archives

School in Winter Haven; the Harry Wendelstedt School for Umpires in Ormond Beach; the Hollywood Legends Baseball Experience in Orlando; the Jim Evans Academy of Professional Umpiring in Kissimmee; the Playball Baseball Academy in Fort Lauderdale; and the Ulti-Met Week in Port St. Lucie.

The Doyle Baseball School deserves more mention, since it has become so important to many different levels of baseball. Founded in 1978 by former major leaguers **Denny**, **Brian**, and **Blake Doyle**, the school has since benefited more than 300,000 participants. Denny Doyle played second base for the Phillies (1970–73), Angels (1974–75), and Red Sox (1975–77); Brian played for the Rangers, Yankees, A's, Indians, and Blue Jays; Blake played in the Orioles and Reds organizations. Broadcaster **Tony Kubek**'s comments during the 1978 World Series about unlikely hero Brian Doyle's new baseball school filled first-year programs, but continued quality training has attracted hundreds of thousands of youngsters and coaches since then.

Today, Doyle Baseball reaches approximately 40,000 players and coaches annually. The organization offers full-week sessions in Florida, Arizona, and Canada, with weekend and full-week programs conducted throughout the United States and Canada. The serious baseball instruction imparted by Doyle Baseball also helped give rise to college baseball schools across the nation. Among the major leaguers who have attended the Doyle Baseball School are **Derek Bell**, **Steve Karsay**, **Dave Martinez**, **Joe Oliver**, **Manny Ramirez**, **Jody Reed**, **Robby Thompson**, and **Walt Weiss**. Being finalized in 1995 was Doyle's most exciting new venture, the American Baseball Centers, indoor training center franchises for baseball and softball. Another undertaking is the International Baseball Institute, a non-profit (pending) organization seeking to improve instruction and safety, boost international competition, expand inner-city outreach, and undertake activities focused on re-establishing baseball as the world's pre-eminent sport.

The Kansas City Royals Baseball Academy

Among the promising developments in baseball in the early 1970s was the concept of a school to develop ballplayers. Situated near Exit 37 of Interstate 75 on Clark Road southeast of Sarasota, the Kansas City Royals Baseball Academy opened in August 1970 on 121 acres. Unlike the fall instructional leagues, which took promising prospects from the major league teams and gave them intensive instruction (an idea begun by Yankees' manager **Casey Stengel** in the early 1950s), the Baseball Academy was to be year-round and would train players with little or no baseball experience.

The Royals' owner, **Ewing Kauffman**, appointed as director of the academy **Syd Thrift**, the Royals' East Coast scouting supervisor and a man who later described the academy and its innovations in *The Game According to Syd*. After the academy opened, the players took classes at nearby Manatee Junior College in the morning and played baseball in the afternoon in a program that was to last 16 months.

The program, which produced major leaguers like **Luis Salazar**, **Ron Washington**, **U. L. Washington**, and **Frank White**, had five full fields, nine pitching machines, many batting cages, and buildings housing a weight room, cafeteria, offices, classrooms, and motel-style rooms.

Some 28,000 players attended tryout camps for the academy over the four years it was in business, but the recession of the 1970s made it too expensive to operate. Kauffman closed it in 1974 and donated the property to the YMCA, which later sold it to Sarasota County. The Royals used the facilities for their minor league training camps, the Gulf Coast League, and instructional-league teams before they all moved to the Boardwalk and Baseball complex in 1988.

Boardwalk and Baseball

Another idea that did not work was Boardwalk and Baseball near Orlando. Officials built a baseball theme park on the remains of Circus World in 1987 and enticed the Kansas City Royals into leaving their spring training site in Fort Myers and bringing their Class A minor league team to train in the 7,000-seat stadium there. The 135-acre amusement park/baseball complex that publisher Harcourt Brace Jovanovich owned and which the Kansas City Royals moved into did not draw enough paying fans to make a profit, so it had to close in 1990. One problem was its location, a little too far out of the Disney/Sea World area to attract enough customers. Another problem was that the park's parent company, Harcourt Brace Jovanovich, had to lay off staff members because of the company's massive debt; in 1987, the parent company endured a $3 billion recapitalization in order to defeat efforts by British publisher Robert Maxwell to take over HBJ for $1.73 billion.

Next to Boardwalk and Baseball is Baseball City Stadium, a major league-quality facility with an 8,000-seat capacity. Serving as the spring training home of the Kansas City Royals, the facility has 5H fields which also host hundreds of amateur games and the regular-season games of the Royals' Florida State, Gulf Coast, and instructional-league teams each year.

BASEBALL IN THE ARMED SERVICES

The numerous armed services camps and training fields around Florida often had their own teams, especially during wartime, when thousands of men were training in the state. For example, the Naval Air Station at Pensacola during World War II had such major leaguers as **Ben Chapman**, **Bob Kennedy**, **Ray Stoviak**, **Nick Tremark**, and **Ted Williams**. The latter, having interrupted a promising career with the Boston Red Sox because of World War II, played in Pensacola on the Bronson Field Bombers baseball team in 1944. Although he once wrote that "I didn't have my heart in it at all and I played lousy," in fact he did well, hitting some towering line drives, one of which carried some 600 feet. Williams' exposure to Florida weather and fishing helped influence him to retire to central Florida when his career was over.

▲ The Coast Defense Station baseball team in Key West won the YMCA championship in 1918. *Florida State Archives*

BASEBALL NOVELS AND MOVIES SET IN FLORIDA

Several baseball movies have been set in Florida, although some take place in fictitious towns. *The New Klondike* (1926), which takes place in fictitious Beach Haven, is about a minor league pitcher in spring training who sells the use of his name to a local real-estate developer. Filmed just before the real-estate collapse and severe hurricanes in south Florida, the movie did not do well financially and reminded potential investors about the insecurities of get-rich-quick schemes.

Slide, Kelly, Slide (1927), which featured real-life Yankees **Tony Lazzeri** and **Bob Meusel**, takes place in a spring training camp in the fictitious Delano, but has an improbable, sentimental ending at the World Series. The main character is patterned after 19th-century star baseball player **Michael "King" Kelly**. *Take Me Out to the Ballgame* (1949), a movie about a spring training camp in Sarasota in 1906, stars Frank Sinatra, Esther Williams, and Gene Kelly. *Kill the Umpire* (1950) is about a baseball fanatic from St. Petersburg who hates umpires, but eventually becomes one.

Big Leaguer (1953) stars Edward G. Robinson as a scout in charge of a training camp of the New York Giants in Melbourne. *Safe at Home* (1962) stars **Mickey Mantle** and **Roger Maris** and was filmed at Fort Lauderdale Stadium. It is about a young boy who fibs about being friends with the two stars and then hitches a ride to the Yankees' spring training camp, where the two men reprimand him for not telling the truth.

Bang the Drum Slowly (1973), often rated one of the best baseball movies, was filmed partly at the Fort Harrison Hotel in Clearwater, now owned by the Church of Scientology and used by them as a training center. *Blue Skies Again* (1983) is about a young woman who travels to the Fort Lauderdale winter training camp of an all-male baseball team to try to become the first female second baseman in the majors; the movie was filmed at Fort Lauderdale Stadium.

Long Gone (1987), based on a novel of the same name by Paul Hemphill, takes place in a fictional place, Tampico, in 1957, and concerns a Class D minor league team and its manager, who is tempted to lose a game to bettors; the film was made at Tampa's William Field. *Trading Hearts* (1988), set in Florida in 1957, is about a former big leaguer who finds a job with a Cuban baseball team training in the Everglades.

Major League (1989) is partly about Florida: The Cleveland Indians will move to Miami if they do so badly they can't attract enough fans; the city of Miami promises the new owner a new stadium, a Boca Raton mansion, and membership in the Palm Beach Polo and Country Club if she will move the team. Finally, two Manatees players, **Lou Lucca** and **Scott Samuels**, appear as extras in Disney's 1994 summer movie, *Angels in the Outfield*.

Among the Florida novels with baseball in them are Connie May Fowler's *Sugar Cage*, which features an annual Free Men and Prisoners

Baseball game in an unnamed prison; and David Everson's *Suicide Squeeze*, a mystery set partly in Gainesville and Micanopy. Michael Shaara's *For Love of the Game* is a baseball novel, although not set specifically in Florida, by the late Pulitzer Prize–winning author from Florida State University.

Modern spring training was the site for one of the more entertaining fictional hoaxes in modern baseball history. In an article for *Sports Illustrated* on April 1, 1985 (a date that should have alerted readers) and in a book entitled *The Curious Case of Sidd Finch*, George Plimpton claimed that the New York Mets had at their St. Petersburg camp a young man, **Sidd Finch**, who could throw a fastball 168 miles per hour. Although revealed in subsequent issues of the magazine (April 8, 1985, p. 27, and April 15, 1985, p. 4) as an April's Fool hoax, the story generated an enormous amount of hope, especially among Mets fans, that such a pitcher might exist in the Himalayas or St. Petersburg. **Casey Stengel** certainly would have enjoyed that one.

APPENDIX A

STATE HIGH SCHOOL BASEBALL CHAMPIONS

YEAR	CLASS	CHAMPION	RUNNER-UP	SCORE
1922		Bartow	Williston	9–0
1923		Williston	Bartow	5–0
1924		Bartow	Inverness	5–2
1925		Bradenton	Orlando	7–5
1926		Miami Senior	Bradenton	13–6
1927		Orlando	Cocoa	4–2
1928		Orlando	Miami Senior	3–2
1929		Palatka	Orlando	7–5
1930		Lakeland	Palatka	5–2
1931		Bradenton	Ocala	16–7
1932		Bradenton	St. Augustine	8–2
1933		Monticello	Mulberry	4–1
1934		Gainesville	Mulberry	3–2
1935		Hillsborough	Jackson (Jacksonville)	6–0
1936		Lakeland	Jackson (Jacksonville)	3–2
1937		Hillsborough	New Smyrna Beach	12–3
1938		West Palm Beach	Jackson (Jacksonville)	11–2
1939		West Palm Beach	Hillsborough	9–2
1940		Leon (Tallahassee)	Bartow	13–6
1941		Miami Edison	Miami Senior	8–5
1942		Bradenton	Orlando	5–2
1943		Orlando	Leon (Tallahassee)	3–2
1944		Leon (Tallahassee)	Miami Senior	4–2
1945		Lee (Jacksonville)	Lakeland	10–1
1946		Lakeland	Avon Park	9–8
1947		Ft. Lauderdale	Avon Park	9–3
1948		Avon Park	Jackson (Jacksonville)	1–0
1949	A	Jackson (Jacksonville)	Orlando	3–2
	B	Sebring	Winter Haven	6–3
1950	A	Lakeland	Palm Beach	2–0
	B	Ft. Pierce	DeLand	11–4

Year	Class	Champion	Runner-Up	Score
1951	AA	Leon (Tallahassee)	Lee (Jacksonville)	4–0
	A	Mulberry	DeLand	5–4
1952	AA	Miami Edison	Orlando	15–2
	A	Lake Worth	Cocoa	3–2
1953	AA	Palm Beach	Winter Haven	5–0
	A	Key West	Tate (Pensacola)	7–3
1954	AA	St. Petersburg	Key West	9–5
	A	St. Augustine	Gainesville	6–2
1955	AA	Key West	Jackson (Jacksonville)	3–2
	A	Avon Park	Paxon (Jacksonville)	10–1
1956	AA	Key West	Jackson (Jacksonville)	8–3
	A	Ft. Pierce	Gainesville	8–7
1957	AA	Sarasota	Boone (Orlando)	7–2
	A	Dade City	Winter Park	3–1
1958	AA	Miami Senior	Palm Beach	2–1
	A	Key West	Avon Park	1–0
1959	AA	Lakeland	Lee (Jacksonville)	3–2
	A	Key West	Milton	3–2
1960	AA	Coral Gables	Jackson (Jacksonville)	3–0
	A	Mulberry	Cocoa	3–1
1961	AA	Lee (Jacksonville)	Boca Ciega (St. Petersburg)	2–1
	A	DeLand	Avon Park	3–1
1962	AA	Northeast (St. Petersburg)	Pensacola Senior	2–0
	A	Tate (Gonzalez)	Forest Hill (West Palm Beach)	3–1
1963	AA	Manatee (Bradenton)	Pensacola Senior	7–5
	A	Palatka	Dunedin	4–3
1964	AA	North Miami	Forest Hill (West Palm Beach)	5–4
	A	Dunedin	Tate (Gonzalez)	2–1
	B	Avon Park	Boca Raton	9–0
1965	AA	Escambia (Pensacola)	Forest Hill (West Palm Beach)	3–0
	A	Palatka	Plant City	14–0
	B	Boca Raton	Taylor (Pierson)	9–0
1966	AA	Escambia (Pensacola)	Fort Myers Senior	3–2
	A	Palatka	Boca Raton	14–1
	B	Avon Park	Bonifay Holmes County	7–0

YEAR	CLASS	CHAMPION	RUNNER-UP	SCORE
1967	AA	Hillsborough (Tampa)	Colonial (Orlando)	7–2
	A	Bishop Moore (Orlando)	Cypress Lake (Ft. Myers)	4–3
	B	Hernando (Brooksville)	Central Catholic (Melbourne)	2–0
1968	AA	Ribault (Jacksonville)	Melbourne	2–0
	A	Tate (Gonzalez)	Seminole (Sanford)	4–0
	B	Tampa Catholic	Monsignor Pace (Opa-Locka)	13–3
1969	AA	Hialeah	Robinson (Tampa)	7–4
	A	Key West	Kathleen Senior (Lakeland)	3–0
	B	Florida (Tallahassee)	Zephyrhills	8–7
1970	AA	Miami Beach Senior	Leto (Tampa)	4–0
	A	Lakewood (St. Petersburg)	Rickards (Tallahassee)	4–0
	B	Jay	Central Catholic (Melbourne)	3–2
1971	AA	Robinson (Tampa)	Miami Beach Senior	5–2
	A	Tampa Catholic	Milton	5–0
	B	Ernest Ward (McDavid)	Dunnellon	12–2
	C	Clearwater Central Catholic	Mary Immaculate Star (Key West)	1–0
1972	AAAA	Escambia (Pensacola)	Robinson (Tampa)	5–2
	AAA	Bishop Barry (St. Petersburg)	Key West	5–0
	AA	Avon Park	Santa Fe (Alachua)	6–3
	A	Mary Immaculate Star (Key West)	Clearwater Central Catholic	12–4
1973	AAAA	Sarasota Senior	Pensacola Senior	1–0
	AAA	Tampa Catholic	Christopher Columbus (Miami)	5–3
	AA	Ocoee	Edward Pace (Opa-Locka)	3–2
	A	John Carroll (Ft. Pierce)	Pensacola Christian	2–0
1974	AAAA	Escambia (Pensacola)	Miami Beach	7–2
	AAA	Tampa Catholic	Leesburg	3–0
	AA	Century	St. Petersburg Catholic	3–1
	A	Loyola (Miami)	University Christian (Jacksonville)	9–5

YEAR	CLASS	CHAMPION	RUNNER-UP	SCORE
1975	AAAA	Miami Carol City (Opa-Locka)	Colonial (Orlando)	4–2
	AAA	Palatka South	Milton	6–4
	AA	Santa Fe (Alachua)	Port St. Joe	9–5
	A	Miami Christian	University Christian (Jacksonville)	6–4
1976	AAAA	Tate (Gonzalez)	South Dade (Homestead)	8–6
	AAA	Tampa Catholic	Atlantic (Delray Beach)	9–4
	AA	John Carroll (Ft. Pierce)	Union County (Lake Butler)	6–2
	A	Berkeley (Tampa)	North Florida Christian (Tallahassee)	7–0
1977	AAAA	Hialeah-Miami Lakes	Robinson (Tampa)	2–0
	AAA	Leesburg	Edward Pace (Opa-Locka)	4–2
	AA	St. Cloud	Palmetto	7–1
	A	Loyola (Miami)	University Christian (Jacksonville)	11–1
1978	AAAA	Miami Coral Park	Riverview-East Bay	3–1
	AAA	Edward Pace (Opa-Locka)	Bishop Kenny (Jacksonville)	9–2
	AA	John Carroll (Ft. Pierce)	S. Sumter (Bushnell)	6–4
	A	University Christian (Jacksonville)	Loyola (Miami)	2–1
1979	AAAA	Hialeah-Miami Lakes	Forest Hill (West Palm Beach)	5–4
	AAA	Tampa Catholic	Bolles (Jacksonville)	3–0
	AA	Clearwater Central Catholic	Newberry	6–3
	A	University Christian (Jacksonville)	Jupiter Christian	2–1
1980	AAAA	Hialeah-Miami Lakes	Lake Worth	5–2
	AAA	Edward Pace (Opa-Locka)	Bishop Kenny (Jacksonville)	4–1
	AA	Avon Park	Bolles (Jacksonville)	4–1
	A	Loyola (Miami)	Berkeley (Tampa)	2–1
1981	AAAA	Boone (Orlando)	Jackson (Miami)	8–1

YEAR	CLASS	CHAMPION	RUNNER-UP	SCORE
	AAA	Edward Pace (Opa-Locka)	Lake Wales	2–1
	AA	Westminster (Miami)	Avon Park	2–1
	A	Loyola (Miami)	Aucilla (Monticello)	10–0
1982	AAAA	Miami Carol City	Tate (Gonzalez)	8–7
	AAA	Tampa Catholic	Charlotte (Punta Gorda)	7–0
	AA	Florida (Tallahassee)	Avon Park	6–4
	A	Ernest Ward (McDavid)	Interamerican (Miami)	14–10
1983	AAAA	Riverview (Sarasota)	Sandalwood (Jacksonville)	13–11
	AAA	St. Brendan (Miami)	Auburndale	7–3
	AA	Bolles (Jacksonville)	Clermont	8–2
	A	Intramerican (Miami)	Shorecrest (St. Petersburg)	13–1
1984	AAAA	Tate (Gonzalez)	Miami Southridge	4–2
	AAA	Key West	Palm Bay (Melbourne)	7–5
	AA	Avon Park	St. Cloud	6–0
	A	Shorecrest (St. Petersburg)	Chattahoochee	9–8
1985	AAAA	Hialeah Miami Lakes	Mosley (Panama City)	4–2
	AAA	Edward Pace (Opa-Locka) Leesburg		2–1
	AA	Pace	Tampa Catholic	18-17
	A	Interamerican (Miami)	St. John Neumann Catholic (Naples)	12–5
1986	A	Tate (Gonzalez)	Lake Mary	9–3
	AAA	Satellite (Satellite Beach)	St. Thomas (Ft. Lauderdale)	4–3
	AA	Florida (Tallahassee)	Edward Pace (Opa-Locka)	4–3
	A	Interamerican (Miami)	Temple Christian (Jacksonville)	3–0
1987	AAAA	Sarasota	Miami Southridge	9–8
	AAA	Cardinal Gibbons (Ft. Lauderdale)	Auburndale	6–1
	AA	Avon Park	Edward Pace (Opa-Locka)	8–5

YEAR	CLASS	CHAMPION	RUNNER-UP	SCORE
	A	Loyola (Miami)	Grand Ridge	8–4
1988	AAAA	Sandalwood (Jacksonville)	Sarasota	4–2
	AAA	Plant (Tampa)	Ft. Pierce Westwood	12–2
	AA	Edward Pace (Miami)	Florida (Tallahassee)	3–1
	A	Westminster Christian (Miami)	Wewahitchka	11–8
1989	AAAA	Sarasota	Sandalwood (Jacksonville)	9–0
	AAA	Lely (Naples)	Plant (Tampa)	8–6
	AA	Bolles (Jacksonville)	Florida (Tallahassee)	6–4
	A	Shorecrest (St. Petersburg)	Westminster Christian (Miami)	9–3
1990	AAAA	Lake Brantley (Altamonte Springs)	Brandon	10–9
	AAA	Pace	Satellite	13–3
	AA	Westminster Chr. (Miami)	Bolles (Jacksonville)	3–2
	A	University Christian (Jacksonville)	Miami-Dade Christian	4–3
1991	AAAA	Terry Parker (Jacksonville)	Miami Southridge	7–4
	AAA	Escambia (Pensacola)	Barron Collier (Naples)	7–5
	AA	Bolles (Jacksonville)	Clearwater Central Catholic	13–2
	A	Maclay (Tallahassee)	Lafayette (Mayo)	5–2
1992	AAAA	Riverview (Sarasota)	Miramar	10–0
	AAA	Seminole (Sanford)	Jesuit (Tampa)	7–5
	AA	Westminster (Miami)	Florida Air (Melbourne)	5–1
	A	King's (West Palm Beach)	Maclay (Tallahassee)	4–1
1993	AAAA	Sarasota	Wellington (West Palm Beach)	4–1
	AAA	Lake Wales	Leon (Tallahassee)	2–1
	AA	Florida Air (Melbourne)	Cardinal Newman (West Palm Beach)	8–4
	A	Maclay (Tallahassee)	Brito Miami Private School (Miami)	9–1

YEAR	CLASS	CHAMPION	RUNNER-UP	SCORE
1994	AAAAA	Sarasota	Coconut Creek	9–2
	AAAA	Jesuit (Tampa)	Clearwater	10–2
	AAA	Palmetto	Key West	7–6
	AA	Bishop Verot (Ft. Myers)	Florida (Tallahassee)	5–3
	A	Westminster (Miami)	Santa Fe Catholic (Lakeland)	12–5
1995	AAAAAA	Lyman (Longwood)	Brandon	2–1
	AAAAA	St. Thomas Aquinas	Jesuit (Tampa)	4–3
	AAAA	Key West	Seminole Osceola	6–4
	AAA	North Florida Christian	Keystone Heights	2–0
	AA	Santa Fe Catholic (Lakeland)	Westminster Christian	3–1

Beginning in 1995, the Class-A schools with baseball programs played on the AA level.

APPENDIX B

1960 — Manatee Community College
1961 — Manatee Community College
1962 — Manatee Community College
1963 — Manatee Community College
1964 — Miami-Dade North Community College
1965 — Gulf Coast Community College
1966 — Miami-Dade North Community College
1967 — Miami-Dade North Community College
1968 — Manatee Community College
1969 — Manatee Community College
1970 — Miami-Dade South Community College
1971 — Miami-Dade North Community College
1972 — Manatee Community College
1973 — Gulf Coast Community College
1974 — Miami-Dade North Community College
1975 — Brevard Community College
1976 — Miami-Dade Wolfson Community College
1977 — Valencia Community College
1978 — Miami-Dade South Community College
1979 — Indian River Community College
1980 — Central Florida Community College
1981 — Miami-Dade South Community College
1982 — Manatee Community College
1983 — Chipola Junior College
1984 — Palm Beach Community College
1985 — Santa Fe Community College
1986 — Brevard Community College
1987 — Florida Community College at Jacksonville
1988 — Hillsborough Community College
1989 — Brevard Community College
1990 — Florida Community College at Jacksonville
1991 — Manatee Community College
1992 — Polk Community College
1993 — Indian River Community College
1994 — Manatee Community College
1995 — Indian River Community College

APPENDIX C

Florida Sites in the Minor Leagues

Site	League	Dates
Bartow	Florida State	1919–20
Baseball City	Florida State	1988–92
Bradenton	Florida State	1919–20, 23–24, 26
Charlotte (see Port Charlotte)		
Clearwater	Florida State	1985–
Cocoa	Florida East Coast	1941–42
	Florida State	1951–58, 65–72, 77
Crestview	Alabama-Florida	1954–56
Daytona Beach	Florida State	1920–24, 28, 1936–41, 1946–73, 1977–87, 1993
Deerfield Beach	Florida State	1966
DeLand	Florida State	1936–41, 1946–54, 70
	Florida East Coast	1942
Dunedin	Florida State	1978–79, 1987–
Ft. Lauderdale	Florida State	1928, 1962–
	Florida East Coast	1940–42
	Florida International	1947–53
Ft. Myers	Florida State	1926, 1978–87, 1992–
Ft. Pierce	Florida East Coast	1940–42
Ft. Walton Beach	Alabama-Florida	1953–62
Gainesville	*FLAG	1915
	Florida State	1936–41, 1946–52, 1955–58

Site	League	Dates
Graceville	Alabama-Florida	1952–58
Hollywood	Florida East Coast	1940
Jacksonville	SALLY	1904–17, 1936–42, 1946–61
	Florida State	1921–22
	Southeastern	1926–30, 1932
	International	1962–68
	Southern	1970–
Jacksonville Beach	Florida State	1952–54
Key West	Florida International	1952
	Florida State	1969,1971–75
Kissimmee (Osceola)	Florida State	1969, 1971–75
Lakeland	Florida State	1919–26, 1953–55, 1960, 1962–64, 1967–
	Florida International	1946–52
Leesburg	Florida State	1937–41, 1946–53, 1956–57, 1960–61, 1965–68
Miami	Florida State	1927–28, 1962–91
	Florida East Coast	1940–42
	Florida International	1946–54
	International	1956–1960
	Inter-American	1979
Miami Beach	Florida East Coast	1940–42
	Florida International	1946–52, 1954
Ocala	Florida State	1940–41

Site	League	Dates
Orlando	Florida State	1919–24, 1926–28, 1937–41, 1946–61, 1963–72
	Florida East Coast	1942
	Southern	1973–
Osceola (see Kissimmee)		
Palatka	Florida State	1936–39, 1946–53, 1956–62
Panama City	Georgia-Florida	1935
	Alabama-Florida	1936–39, 1951–61
Pensacola	Cotton States	1913
	Southeastern	1927–30, 1934–42, 1946–50
	Alabama-Florida	1957–62
Pompano Beach	Florida State	1969–73, 1976–78
Port Charlotte	Florida State	1987–
St. Augustine	Southeastern	1926–27
	Florida State	1936–41, 1946–50, 1952
St. Lucie	Florida State	1988–
St. Petersburg	Florida State	1920–28, 1955–
	Florida International	1947–54
Sanford	Florida State	1919–20, 1925–28, 1936–41, 1946–53, 1955, 1959–60

SITE	LEAGUE	DATES
Sarasota	Florida State	1926–27, 1961–65, 1989–
Tallahassee	Georgia-Florida	1935–42, 1946–50
	Alabama-Florida	1939,1951
	Florida International	1954
Tampa	Florida State	1919–27, 1957–88
	Southeastern	1928–30
	Florida International	1946–54
Vero Beach	Florida State	1980–
West Palm Beach	Florida State	1928, 1955–56, 1965–
	Florida East Coast	1940–42
	Florida International	1946–54
Winter Haven	Florida State	1966–67, 1969–92

* Florida-Alabama-Georgia, Class D, 1915; successor of the Georgia State League, 1914; started the season as the Georgia State League, but changed its name at the end of May when Americus transferred to Gainesville, Florida.

[Source: Lloyd Johnson and Miles Wolff, editors, *The Encyclopedia of Minor League Baseball*]

APPENDIX D

I. Listed by team

NATIONAL LEAGUE

Astros
1964–84 Cocoa Beach
1985– Kissimmee

Braves
1906 Jacksonville
1916–18 Miami
1922–37 St. Petersburg
1938–40, 1948–62 Bradenton
1942 Sanford
1946–47 Fort Lauderdale
1963– West Palm Beach

Cardinals
1914 St. Augustine
1923–24, 1930–36 Bradenton
1927–29 Avon Park
1937 Daytona Beach
1938–42, 1946– St. Petersburg

Cubs
1913–16 Tampa

Dodgers
1907–09, 1919–20, 1922
  Jacksonville
1915–16, 1946 Daytona Beach
1923–32, 1936–40 Clearwater
1933 Miami
1934–35 Orlando
1949– Vero Beach

Expos
1969–72, 1981– West Palm
  Beach
1973–80 Daytona Beach

Giants
1919 Gainesville
1924–27 Sarasota
1934–35 Miami Beach
1936 Pensacola
1940 Winter Haven
1941–42, 1946 Miami
1951 St. Petersburg

Marlins
1993 Cocoa
1994– Melbourne

Mets
1962–87 St. Petersburg
1988– Port St. Lucie

Phillies
1915–18 St. Petersburg
1921 Gainesville
1922–24 Leesburg
1925–27 Bradenton
1928–37 Winter Haven
1940–42, 1946 Miami Beach
1947– Clearwater

Pirates
1918 Jacksonville
1947 Miami Beach
1954 Fort Pierce
1955–68 Fort Myers
1969– Bradenton

Reds
1905 Jacksonville
1920 Miami
1923–30 Orlando
1931–42, 1946–87 Tampa
1988– Plant City

AMERICAN LEAGUE

Athletics
1903, 1914–18 Jacksonville
1925–36 Fort Myers
1946–62 West Palm Beach
1963–68 Bradenton

Blue Jays
1977– Dunedin

Indians
1913 Pensacola
1923–27 Lakeland
1940–41 Fort Myers
1942, 1946 Clearwater
1993– Winter Haven

Orioles (Browns)
1914 St. Petersburg
1925–27 Tarpon Springs
1928–36 West Palm Beach
1942 DeLand
1947, 1959–88 Miami
1955 Daytona Beach
1989–90 Miami/Sarasota
1991 Sarasota
1993– St. Petersburg/Sarasota

Rangers (Senators)
1961–86 Pompano Beach
1987– Port Charlotte

Red Sox
1919 Tampa
1928–29 Bradenton
1930–31 Pensacola
1933–42, 1946–58 Sarasota
1966–92 Winter Haven
1993– Fort Myers

Royals
1969–87 Fort Myers
1988– Baseball City

Tigers
1930 Tampa
1934–42, 1946– Lakeland

Twins (Senators)
1920–29 Tampa
1936–42, 1946–90 Orlando
1991– Fort Myers

White Sox
1924 Winter Haven
1954–59 Tampa
1960– Sarasota

Yankees
1919–20 Jacksonville
1925–42, 1946–50 St. Petersburg
1952–61 St. Petersburg
1962– Fort Lauderdale

II. Listed by site

Avon Park: Cardinals, 1927–29
Baseball City: Royals, 1988–
Bradenton: Braves, 1938–40,
   1948–62; Cardinals, 1923–24,
   1930–36; Phillies, 1925–27;
   Pirates, 1969–; Athletics,
   1963–68; Red Sox, 1928–29
Clearwater: Dodgers, 1923–32,
   1936–40; Phillies, 1947–;
   Indians, 1942, 1946
Cocoa: Marlins, 1993
Cocoa Beach: Astros, 1964–84
Daytona Beach: Cardinals, 1937;
   Dodgers, 1915–16, 1946; Expos,
   1973–80; Orioles, 1955
DeLand: Orioles (Browns), 1942
Dunedin: Blue Jays, 1977–
Fort Lauderdale: Braves,
   1946–47; Yankees, 1962–
Fort Myers: Pirates, 1955–68;
   Athletics, 1925–36; Indians,
   1940–41; Red Sox, 1993–;
   Royals, 1969–87; Twins,
   1991–
Fort Pierce: Pirates, 1954
Gainesville: Giants, 1919;
   Phillies, 1921
Jacksonville: Braves, 1906;
   Dodgers, 1907–09, 1919–20,
   1922; Pirates, 1918; Reds,
   1905; Athletics, 1903,
   1914–18; Yankees, 1919–20
Kissimmee: Astros, 1985–
Lakeland: Indians, 1923–27;
   Tigers, 1934–42, 1946–
Leesburg: Phillies, 1922–24
Melbourne: Marlins, 1994–

Miami: Braves, 1916–18;
   Dodgers, 1933; Giants,
   1941–42, 1946; Reds, 1920;
   Orioles (Browns), 1947,
   1959–90*
Miami Beach: Giants, 1934–35;
   Phillies, 1940–42, 1946; Pirates,
   1947
Orlando: Dodgers, 1934–35;
   Reds, 1923–30; Twins
   (Senators), 1936–42, 1946–90
Pensacola: Giants, 1936;
   Indians, 1913; Red Sox,
   1930–31
Plant City: Reds, 1988–
Pompano Beach: Rangers
   (Senators), 1961–86
Port Charlotte: Rangers, 1987–
Port St. Lucie: Mets, 1988–
St. Augustine: Cardinals, 1914
St. Petersburg: Braves, 1922–37;
   Cardinals, 1938–42, 1946–;
   Giants, 1951; Mets, 1962–87;
   Phillies, 1915–18; Orioles
   (Browns), 1914, 1993–*;
   Yankees, 1925–42, 1946–50,
   1952–61
Sanford: Braves, 1942
Sarasota: Giants, 1924–27;
   Orioles, 1989–93*; Red Sox,
   1933–42, 1946–58; White Sox,
   1960–
Tampa: Cubs, 1913–16; Reds,
   1931–42, 1946–87; Red Sox,
   1919; Tigers, 1930; Twins
   (Senators), 1920–29; White Sox,
   1954–59

Tarpon Springs: Orioles
  (Browns), 1925–27
Vero Beach: Dodgers, 1949–
West Palm Beach: Braves, 1963–;
  Expos, 1969–72, 1981–;
  Athletics, 1946–62; Orioles
  (Browns), 1928–36

Winter Haven: Giants, 1940;
  Phillies, 1928–37; Indians,
  1993–; Red Sox, 1966–92;
  White Sox, 1924

* The Orioles split the 1989–90
spring–training season between Miami
and Sarasota; they split the 1993 season
between St. Petersburg and Sarasota.

III. Teams with the most years in one Florida site*

Detroit Tigers in Lakeland (59 years)
St. Louis Cardinals in St. Petersburg (55 years)
Cincinnati Reds in Tampa (53 years)
Washington Senators/Minnesota Twins in Orlando (52 years)
Philadelphia Phillies in Clearwater (49 years)
Brooklyn/Los Angeles Dodgers in Vero Beach (47 years)
Chicago White Sox in Sarasota (36 years)
New York Yankees in Fort Lauderdale (34 years)
Milwaukee/Atlanta Braves in West Palm Beach (33 years)
Baltimore Orioles in Miami (33 years)
New York Yankees in St. Petersburg (33 years)
Pittsburgh Pirates in Bradenton (27 years)
Boston Red Sox in Winter Haven (27 years)
New York Mets in St. Petersburg (26 years)
Washington Senators/Texas Rangers in Pompano Beach (26 years)
Boston Red Sox in Sarasota (23 years)
Houston Astros in Cocoa Beach (21 years)

* Years accumulated, not necessarily continuous

Source: Myles E. Friedman, "Spring Training." (see Biliography.)

APPENDIX E

FLORIDA-BORN MAJOR LEAGUERS

Non Pitchers

NAME	BIRTHPLACE	BORN	POSITION	BATTING AVERAGE	SEASONS	TEAM	(LEAGUE)
Jack Albright	St. Petersburg	1921	S	.232	1	Phi	(N)
Horace Allen	DeLand	1899	O	.000	1	Bro	(N)
Frank Baker	Bartow	1944	O	.232	2	Cle	(A)
Billy Beane	Orlando	1962	O	.219	6	Min	(A)
Derek Bell	Tampa	1968	O,D	.275	4	SD	(N)
Jay Bell	Eglin A.F.B.	1965	S	.268	9	Pit	(N)
Butch Benton	Tampa	1957	C	.162	4	NY	(N)
Kurt Bevacqua	Miami Beach	1947	3,2,1	.236	15	SD	(N)
Dante Bichette	W. Palm Beach	1963	O	.277	7	Col	(N)
Elliot Bigelow	Tarpon Sps.	1897	O	.284	1	Bos	(A)
Jimmy Bloodworth	Tallahassee	1917	2	.248	11	Was	(A)
Greg Blosser	Bradenton	1971	O	.077	2	Bos	(A)
Rod Brewer	Eustis	1966	1,O	.270	3	StL	(N)
Randy Brown	Leesburg	1944	C,O	.138	2	Cal	(A)
Don Bryant	Jasper	1941	C	.220	3	Hou	(N)
Johnny Burnett	Bartow	1904	S,3,2	.284	9	Cle	(A)
Ray Busse	Daytona Beach	1948	S,3	.148	3	Hou	(N)
Ed Charles	Daytona Beach	1933	3	.263	8	KC	(A)
Steve Christmas	Orlando	1957	C,1	.162	3	Chi	(N)
Choo Choo Coleman	Orlando	1937	C	.197	4	NY	(N)
Vince Coleman	Jacksonville	1961	O	.264	10	StL	(N)
Warren Cromartie	Miami Beach	1953	O,1	.281	10	Mon	(N)
Jack Daugherty	Hialeah	1960	O	.258	5	Tex	(A)
Glenn Davis	Jacksonville	1961	1,D	.262	9	Hou	(N)
Andre Dawson	Miami	1954	O	.280	19	Mon	(N)
Paul Dicken	DeLand	1943	H	.000	2	Cle	(A)
Nick Esasky	Hialeah	1960	1,3	.250	8	Cin	(N)
Carl Everett	Tampa	1970	O	.186	2	Fl	(N)

NAME	BIRTHPLACE	BORN	POSITION	BATTING AVERAGE	SEASONS	TEAM	(LEAGUE)
Jorge Fabregas	Miami	1970	C	.283	1	Cal	(A)
Lenny Faedo	Tampa	1960	S	.251	5	Min	(A)
Scott Fletcher	Ft. Walton Beach	1958	S,2	.263	14	Chi	(A)
Mike Fuentes	Miami	1958	O	.250	2	Mon	(N)
Bob Gandy	Jacksonville	1893	O	.000	1	Phi	(N)
Adrian Garrett	Brooksville	1943	D,C,0,1	.185	8	Chi	(N)
Wayne Garrett	Brooksville	1947	3,2	.239	10	NY	(N)
Steve Garvey	Tampa	1948	1,3	.294	19	LA	(N)
Chuck Goggin	Pompano Beach	1945	2,O,S,C	.293	3	Pit	(N)
Alex Gonzalez	Miami	1973	S	.151	1	Tor	(A)
Luis Gonzalez	Tampa	1967	O	.269	5	Hou	(N)
Lee Graham	Summerfield	1959	O	.000	1	Bos	(A)
Ricky Gutierrez	Miami	1970	S	.247	2	SD	(N)
Bob Hale	Sarasota	1933	1	.273	7	Bal	(A)
Garry Hancock	Tampa	1954	O	.247	6	Bos	(A)
Lenny Harris	Miami	1964	3,2	.278	7	LA	(N)
Ed Hearn	Stuart	1960	C,D	.263	3	KC	(A)
Mike Heath	Tampa	1955	C,D	.252	14	Oak	(A)
Phil Hiatt	Pensacola	1969	3	.218	1	KC	(A)
Mark Higgins	Miami	1963	1	.100	1	Cle	(A)
Roge Holt	Daytona Beach	1956	2	.167	1	NY	(A)
David Howard	Sarasota	1967	S	.226	4	KC	(A)
Dick Howser	Miami	1936	S	.248	8	Cle	(A)
Reggie Jefferson	Tallahassee	1968	1,D	.269	4	Cle	(A)
Charles Johnson	Fort Pierce	1971	C	.455	1	Fl	(N)
Davey Johnson	Orlando	1943	2,1	.261	13	Bal	(A)
Howard Johnson	Clearwater	1960	3,S,O	.251	13	NY	(N)
Randy Johnson	Miami	1958	D,O,1	.244	2	Chi,Min	(A)
Chipper Jones	DeLand	1972	S	.667	1	Atl	(N)
Ross Jones	Miami	1960	S,2,3,D	.221	3	KC	(A)
John Kennedy	Jacksonville	1926	3,2	.000	1	Phi	(N)
Hal King	Oviedo	1944	C	.214	7	Cin	(N)
Bobby Kline	St. Petersburg	1929	S	.221	1	Was	(A)
Jeff Kunkel	W. Palm Beach	1962	S	.221	8	Tex	(A)
Tony La Russa	Tampa	1944	2,S,3	.199	6	Oak	(A)
Al Lopez	Tampa	1908	C	.261	19	Bro,Pit	(N)
Gordon MacKenzie	St. Petersburg	1937	C	.125	1	KC	(A)
Max Macon*	Pensacola	1915	P,1,O	.265	6	Bro	(N)
Scotti Madison	Pensacola	1959	3,D,C, 1,O	.163	5	Det,KC	(A)

Name	Birthplace	Born	Position	Batting Average	Seasons	Team	(League)
Dave Magadan	Tampa	1962	3,1	.288	9	NY	(N)
Tom Magrann	Hollywood	1963	C	.000	1	Cle	(A)
Tino Martinez	Tampa	1967	1	.254	5	Sea	(A)
Oddibe McDowell	Hollywood	1962	O	.253	7	Tex	(A)
Fred McGriff	Tampa	1963	1,D	.285	9	Tor	(A)
Terry McGriff	Fort Pierce	1963	C	.206	6	Cin	(N)
Ralph McLaurin	Kissimmee	1885	O	.227	1	StL	(N)
Brian McRae	Bradenton	1967	O	.262	5	KC	(A)
Hal McRae	Avon Park	1945	D,O	.290	19	KC	(A)
Jackie Moore	Jay	1939	C	.094	1	Det	(A)
Jim Morrison	Pensacola	1952	3,2	.260	12	Pit	(N)
Bitsy Mott	Arcadia	1918	S,2	.221	1	Phi	(N)
Reid Nichols	Ocala	1958	O	.266	8	Bos	(A)
Nate Oliver	St. Petersburg	1940	2	.226	7	La	(N)
Ralph Onis	Tampa	1908	C	1.000	1	Bro	(N)
Dean Palmer	Tallahassee	1968	3	.229	5	Tex	(A)
Larry Parrish	Winter Haven	1953	3,O,D	.263	15	Mon	(N)
John Patterson	Key West	1967	2	.220	3	SF	(N)
Herb Perry	Live Oak	1969	1,3	.111	1	Cle	(A)
Lou Piniella	Tampa	1943	O,D	.291	18	KC,NY	(A)
Whitey Platt	W. Palm Beach	1920	O	.255	5	Chi	(N)
Boog Powell	Lakeland	1941	1,O	.266	17	Bal	(A)
Jim Presley	Pensacola	1961	3	.247	8	Sea	(A)
Rich Puig	Tampa	1953	2,3	.000	1	NY	(N)
Tim Raines	Sanford	1959	O	.296	16	Mon	(N)
John Ramos	Tampa	1965	C,D	.308	1	NY	(A)
Jody Reed	Tampa	1962	2,S	.278	8	Bos	(A)
Lance Richbourg	DeFuniak Springs	1897	O	.308	8	Bos	(N)
Mickey Rivers	Miami	1948	O,D	.295	15	Cal	(A)
Deion Sanders	Fort Myers	1967	O	.263	6	Atl	(N)
Russ Scarritt	Pensacola	1903	O	.285	4	Bos	(A)
Donnie Scott	Dunedin	1961	C	.217	4	Tex	(A)
Danny Sheaffer	Jacksonville	1961	C,D,3,O	.228	4	Col	(N)
Gary Sheffield	Tampa	1968	3,S,O,D	.284	7	Mil	(A)
Dennis Sherrill	Miami	1956	S,2,D,3	.200	2	NY	(A)
Dwight Smith	Tallahassee	1963	O	.284	6	Chi	(N)
George Smith	St. Petersburg	1937	2	.205	4	Det	(A)
Keith Smith	Palmetto	1953	O	.207	3	StL	(N)
Mike Stanley	Fort Lauderdale	1963	C	.271	9	Tex	(A)

NAME	BIRTHPLACE	BORN	POSITION	BATTING AVERAGE	SEASONS	TEAM	(LEAGUE)
Stuffy Stewart	Jasper	1894	2,3,O	.238	8	Was	(A)
Ken Suarez	Tampa	1943	C	.227	7	Cle	(A)
John Tamargo	Tampa	1951	C	.242	5	StL	(N)
Carl Taylor	Sarasota	1944	C,O	.266	6	KC	(A)
Zack Taylor	Yulee	1898	C	.261	16	Bro	(N)
Herb Thomas	Sampson City	1902	O,2,S	.221	3	Bos	(N)
Robby Thompson	W. Palm Beach	1962	2	.263	9	SF	(N)
Bob Thorpe	Caryville	1926	O	.251	3	Bos	(N)
Rusty Tillman	Jacksonville	1960	O	.232	3	SF	(N)
Jack Voigt	Sarasota	1966	O,D	.270	3	Bal	(A)
Turner Ward	Orlando	1965	O,D	.235	5	Tor	(A)
Bill White	Lakewood	1934	1,O	.286	13	StL	(N)
Mark Whiten	Pensacola	1966	O	.259	5	Stl	(N)
Rick Wilkins	Jacksonville	1967	C	.263	4	Chi	(N)
Larry Wolfe	Melbourne	1953	3	.230	4	Bos	(A)
Woody Woodward	Miami	1942	S,2	.236	9	Cin	(N)
Hugh Yancy	Sarasota	1949	2,3,D	.105	3	Chi	(A)

Pitchers

NAME	BIRTHPLACE	BORN	RECORD	ERA	SEASONS	TEAM	(LEAGUE)
Vic Albury	Key West	1947	18-17	4.11	4	Min	(A)
Jose Alvarez	Tampa	1956	8-9	2.99	4	Atl	(N)
Ray Bare	Miami	1949	16-26	4.79	5	Det	(A)
Rich Barnes	Palm Beach	1959	1-3	5.65	2	Cle	(A)
Frank Barrett	Ft. Lauderdale	1913	15-17	3.51	5	Bos	(A)
Rick Behenna	Miami	1960	3-10	6.12	3	Cle	(A)
Don Bessent	Jacksonville	1931	14-7	3.33	4	Bro	(N)
Jack Billingham	Orlando	1943	145-113	3.83	13	Cin	(N)
William Brennan	Tampa	1963	2-2	5.18	2	Chi	(N)
Rod Brewer	Eustis	1966	0-0	45.00	1	StL	(N)
Pete Broberg	W. Palm Beach	1950	41-71	4.56	8	Tex	(A)
Curt Brown	Fort Lauderdale	1960	2-4	4.88	4	Mon	(N)
Charlie Butler	Green Cove Spgs.	1906	0-0	9.00	1	Phi	(N)
Marty Bystrom	Coral Gables	1958	29-26	4.26	6	Phi	(N)
Steve Carlton	Miami	1944	329-244	3.22	24	Phi	(N)
Cris Carpenter	St. Augustine	1965	27-22	3.83	7	StL	(N)
Jeff Carter	Tampa	1964	0-1	5.25	1	Chi	(A)

Name	Birthplace	Born	Record	ERA	Seasons	Team	(League)
Red Causey	Georgetown	1893	39-35	3.59	5	NY	(N)
Nardi Contreras	Tampa	1951	0-0	5.93	1	Chi	(A)
Doug Corbett	Sarasota	1952	24-30	3.32	8	Cal	(A)
Ray Corbin	Live Oak	1949	36-38	3.84	5	Min	(A)
Tim Crews	Tampa	1961	11-13	3.44	6	LA	(N)
Charlie Cuellar	Ybor City	1917	0-0	33.75	1	Chi	(A)
Steve Curry	Winter Park	1965	0-1	8.18	1	Bos	(A)
Joel Davis	Jacksonville	1965	8-14	4.91	4	Chi	(A)
Tim Davis	Marianna	1970	2-2	4.01	1	Sea	(A)
Tom Dixon	Orlando	1955	9-14	4.33	4	Hou	(N)
Dave Eiland	Dade City	1966	5-14	5.23	6	NY	(A)
Alex Fernandez	Miami Beach	1969	51-45	3.88	5	Chi	(A)
Gar Finnvold	Boynton Beach	1968	0-4	5.94	1	Bos	(A)
Jeff Fischer	W. Palm Beach	1963	0-1	9.53	2	LA	(N)
Dwight Gooden	Tampa	1964	157-85	3.10	11	NY	(N)
Tom Gordon	Sebring	1967	67-59	3.94	7	KC	(A)
Joe Grahe	W. Palm Beach	1967	17-23	4.34	5	Cal	(A)
Mudcat Grant	Lacoochee	1935	145-119	3.63	14	Cle	(A)
Johnny Gray	W. Palm Beach	1927	4-18	6.18	4	Phi	(N)
Mike Hampton	Brooksville	1972	3-4	5.40	2	Hou	(N)
Garry Hancock	Tampa	1954	0-0	0.00	1	Oak	(A)
Preston Hanna	Pensacola	1954	17-25	4.61	8	Atl	(N)
Andy Hansen	Lake Worth	1924	23-30	4.22	9	NY	(N)
Jack Hardy	St. Petersburg	1959	0-0	6.57	1	Chi	(A)
Gene Harris	Sebring	1964	10-16	4.75	6	Sea	(A)
Hilly Hathaway	Jacksonville	1969	4-3	5.29	2	Cal	(A)
Bill Henderson	Pensacola	1901	0-0	4.50	1	NY	(A)
Bobby Hogue	Miami	1921	18-16	3.97	5	Bos	(N)
John Hope	Fort Lauderdale	1970	0-2	4.50	2	Pit	(N)
David Howard	Sarasota	1967	0-0	4.50	1	KC	(A)
Jay Howell	Miami	1955	58-53	3.34	15	LA	(N)
John Hudek	Tampa	1966	0-2	2.97	1	Hou	(N)
James Hurst	Plantation	1967	0-0	10.13	1	Tex	(A)
Dane Johnson	Coral Gables	1963	2-1	6.57	1	Chi	(A)
Hank Johnson	Bradenton	1906	63-56	4.75	12	NY	(A)
Jerry Johnson	Miami	1943	48-51	4.31	10	SD	(N)
Ken Johnson	W. Palm Beach	1933	91-106	3.46	13	Atl	(N)
Rick Jones	Jacksonville	1955	6-9	4.02	3	Sea	(A)
Bobby Kline	St. Petersburg	1929	0-0	27.00	1	Was	(A)

NAME	BIRTHPLACE	BORN	RECORD	ERA	SEASONS	TEAM	(LEAGUE)
Jeff Kunkel	W. Palm Beach	1962	0-0	13.50	2	Tex	(A)
Dennis Lewallyn	Pensacola	1953	4-4	4.48	8	LA	(N)
Jim Lewis	Miami	1955	0-1	8.77	4	Sea	(A)
Derek Lilliquist	Winter Park	1966	23-33	4.00	6	Cle	(A)
Vance Lovelace	Tampa	1963	0-0	5.79	3	Cal	(A)
Max Macon*	Pensacola	1915	17-19	4.24	6	Bro	(N)
Lance McCullers	Tampa	1964	28-31	3.25	7	SD	(N)
Andy McGaffigan	W. Palm Beach	1956	38-33	3.38	11	Mon	(N)
Rusty Meacham	Stuart	1968	17-10	3.63	4	KC	(A)
Sam Militello	Tampa	1969	4-4	3.89	2	NY	(A)
Alan Mills	Lakeland	1966	20-17	3.49	5	Bal	(A)
Rich Monteleone	Tampa	1963	23-14	3.83	8	NY	(A)
Jim Morrison	Pensacola	1952	0-0	0.00	1	Atl	(N)
Rob Murphy	Miami	1960	31-36	3.49	10	Cin	(N)
Gene Nelson	Tampa	1960	53-64	4.13	13	Oak	(A)
Don Newhauser	Miami	1947	4-3	2.39	3	Bos	(A)
Dan O'Brien	St. Petersburg	1954	1-3	5.90	2	StL	(N)
Bob Patterson	Jacksonville	1959	29-28	4.27	9	Pit	(N)
Ned Porter	Apalachicola	1905	0-0	2.25	2	NY	(N)
Marshall Renfroe	Century	1936	0-0	27.00	1	SF	(N)
Carlos Reyes	Miami	1969	0-3	4.15	1	Oak	(A)
Rick Rhoden	Boynton Beach	1953	151-125	3.59	16	Pit	(N)
Scott Ruskin	Jacksonville	1963	11-9	3.95	4	Cin	(N)
Kevin Saucier	Pensacola	1956	15-11	3.31	5	Phi	(N)
Paul Schreiber	Jacksonville	1902	0-0	3.98	3	Bro	(N)
Jeff Schwarz	Fort Pierce	1964	2-2	4.17	2	Chi	(A)
Manny Seoane	Tampa	1955	1-0	5.65	2	Chi	(N)
Randy Sterling	Key West	1951	1-1	4.82	1	NY	(N)
Bill Swaggerty	Sanford	1956	4-3	4.76	4	Bal	(A)
Billy Taylor	Monticello	1961	1-3	3.50	1	Oak	(A)
Terry Taylor	Crestview	1964	0-1	6.26	1	Sea	(A)
Bobby Thigpen	Tallahassee	1963	31-36	3.43	9	Chi	(A)
Tim Wakefield	Melbourne	1966	14-12	4.17	2	Pit	(N)
Tom Walker	Tampa	1948	18-23	3.87	6	Mon	(N)
Gabe White	Sebring	1971	1-1	6.08	1	Mon	(N)
Kerry Woodson	Jacksonville	1969	0-1	3.29	1	Sea	(A)
Ken Wright	Pensacola	1946	11-15	4.54	5	KC	(A)
Floyd Youmans	Tampa	1964	30-34	3.74	5	Mon	(N)

Abbreviations

POSITION:	PRINCIPAL TEAM:	LEAGUE:

POSITION:

1 - first base
2 - second base
3 - third base
C - catcher
D - designated
   hitter
H - pinch-hitter
O - outfield
R - pinch-runner
S - shortstop
P - pitcher

PRINCIPAL TEAM:

Atl - Atlanta
Bal - Balitmore
Bos - Boston
Bro - Brooklyn
Cal - California
Chi - Chicago
Cin - Cincinnati
Cle - Cleveland
Col - Colorado
Det - Detroit
Fl - Florida
Hou - Houston
KC - Kansas City
LA - Los Angeles
Mil - Milwaukee
Mon - Montreal
NY - New York
Oak - Oakland
Phi - Philadelphia
Pit - Pittsburgh
SD - San Diego
Sea - Seattle
SF - San Francisco
StL - St. Louis
Tex - Texas
Tor - Toronto
Was - Washington, D.C.

LEAGUE:

A - American
N - National

OTHER:

ERA - earned run
average

* Player played in the field and as a pitcher

[This information is from the 1995 edition of *Total Baseball*, edited by John Thorn and Pete Palmer.]

QUOTATION SOURCES

Chapter 1

p. 3 "The national game . . ." *The Weekly Floridian* [Tallahassee], May 5, 1874, p. 3.

p. 7 "each separate base . . ." *The Weekly Floridian* [Tallahassee], May 5, 1874, p. 3.

p. 8 "If the sole object . . ." *The Weekly Floridian* [Tallahassee], September 15, 1874, p. 3.

p. 9 ". . . in all times . . ." *Florida Times-Union* [Jacksonville], May 19, 1883, p. 4.

p. 11 "Palatka hit the ball . . ." *The Florida Times-Union* [Jacksonville], July 29, 1897, p. 5.

p. 13 "I'd fill him full of shot . . ." *Morning News* [Jacksonville], June 4, 1886, as quoted in Bess Beatty, "Baseball," p. 67.

p. 14 "Wild applause . . ." *The Times-Herald* [Palatka], July 19, 1895, p. 5.

p. 15 "first baseman Bard . . ." *The Times-Herald* [Palatka], May 10, 1895, p, 5.

p. 16 "was wild about big league baseball . . ." James McGovern, *The Emergence of a City in the Modern South: Pensacola 1900–1945*, p. 100.

p. 19 "More real interest . . ." Stuart McIver, "Florida's grass roots," *Sun-Sentinel* [Fort Lauderdale], April 4, 1993, BB 24.

p. 20 "Sunday baseball . . ." *The Palm Beach Post*, October 22, 1920, p. 1.

p. 22 "When it comes to playing baseball . . ." *The Miami Herald*, April 1, 1922, p. 6.

Chapter 2

p. 25 "Playing youth baseball . . ." Alan Schwarz, "Sarasota Programs Flourish," *Baseball America*, March 21–April 3, 1994, p. 40.

p. 26 "There is evident material . . ." *The Weekly Floridian* [Tallahassee], August 11, 1874, p. 3.

p. 26 "took him . . ." Wes Singletary, "Opportunity Knocks Once: A Conversation with Manuel 'Curly' Onis," *The Sunland Tribune*, vol. 20 (November 1994), pp. 55–57.

p. 30 "We're really glad . . ." Mike Stephenson, "Baseball is special to disabled," *The Florida Times-Union*, June 9, 1991, C-1.

p. 36 "A lot of kids . . ." Alex Marvez, "Going to bat for Clemente Park kids," *The Miami Herald*, Northwest edition, "Neighbors" section, July 17, 1994, p. 1+.

p. 39 "Maybe it's in the water . . ." Alan Schwarz, "Sarasota Programs Flourish," *Baseball America*, March 21–April 3, 1994, p. 40.

Chapter 3

p. 45 "As the games begin . . ." Rick Lawes, "Solid State," *USA Today Baseball Weekly*, February 12–25, 1992, p. 28.

p. 46 "Jacksonville could be . . ." Greg Larson, "College baseball teams thriving in Jacksonville," *The Florida Times-Union* [Jacksonville], April 14, 1988, C-1.

p. 47 "I don't know . . ." Jo. Campbell, "Florida's Fireball on the Hill," *Baseball Magazine*, vol. 48, no. 4 (August 1956), p. 55.

p. 62 "the hardest-working recruiter . . ." *Baseball America*, December 12–15, 1994, p. 35.

Chapter 4

p. 65 "An axiom of the times . . ." Barbara Gregorich, *Women at Play: The Story of Women in Baseball* (San Diego: Harcourt Brace, 1993), p. 3.

p. 67 "The All-Americans were heroes . . ." Susan E. Johnson, *When Women Played Hardball* (Seattle, Wash.: Seal Press, 1994), p. xiii.

p. 73 "My ballplaying was . . ." Johnson, p. 226.

p. 76 "I started pitching . . ." Rick Lawes, "Haller was first of coed hurlers," *USA Today Baseball Weekly*, March 2–8, 1994), p. 32.

Chapter 5

p. 85 "A good Negro team . . ." James Weldon Johnson, *Along This Way: The Autobiography of James Weldon Johnson* (New York: Viking, 1933), p. 37.

p. 85 "The colored employees . . ." *St. Augustine Weekly News*, January 17, 1889.

p. 86 "I went over . . ." Stuart McIver, "Cooks to Catchers, Bellhops to Batters," *Sunshine News/Sun-Sentinel*, Fort Lauderdale, August 22, 1993, p.23+.

p. 89 "They called John Henry Lloyd . . ." John B. Holway, *Blackball Stars: Negro League Pioneers* (Westport, Conn.: Meckler, 1988), p. 36.

p. 89 "On bases . . ." Al Stump, *Cobb: A Biography* (Chapel Hill, N.C.: Algonguin Books of Chapel Hill, 1994), p. 200.

p. 89 "I do not consider . . ." Robert Peterson, *Only the Ball Was White: A History of Legendary Black Players and All-black Professional Teams* (New York: McGraw-Hill, 1984), p. 79.

p. 90 "I'd never heard a bat . . ." Charlie Huisking, "Heading For Home," *Sarasota Herald-Tribune*, March 5, 1995, p. 16A.

p. 92 "If I was going to be bitter . . ." John Holway, *Black Diamonds: Life in the Negro Leagues from the Men Who Lived It* (Westport, Conn.: Meckler, 1989), p. 104. See also Wulf's article, "The Guiding Light," and "First Negro Coach in Majors" in bibliography.

p. 97 "No race prejudice . . ." Henry Aaron with Lonnie Wheeler, *I Had a Hammer: The Hank Aaron Story* (New York: HarperCollins, 1991), p. 51.

p. 99 " . . . in all the years . . ." Aaron, p. 56.

p. 99 "When the pitchers . . ." Aaron, p. 58.

p. 99 "We stayed at a very nice home . . ." Jackie Robinson, *Baseball Has Done It*, edited by Charles Dexter (Philadelphia: J.B. Lippincott Company, 1964), p. 124.

p. 99 "We had played . . ." Aaron, p. 75.

p. 102 "running like a scared rabbit . . ." *Daytona Beach Evening News* (March 18, 1946), p. 10.

p. 103 "To me, Jackie represents . . ." Steve Moore, "Robinson: A hero honored," *The News-Journal* [Daytona Beach], September 16, 1990, p. 2C.

p. 104 "1919 dash 1972 . . ." Harvey Frommer, *Rickey & Robinson: The Men Who Broke Baseball's Color Barrier* (New York: Macmillan, 1982), p. 226.

pp. 104,101 "Mr. Rickey said . . ." "We complained . . ." "There were

beaches . . ." "It was watch my step . . ." These quotes are
from Robinson, *Baseball Has Done It,* pp. 85, 91, 115, 115.

p. 105 "huddled together . . ." Jules Tygiel, *Baseball's Great
Experiment: Jackie Robinson and His Legacy* (New York: Oxford
University Press, 1983), p. 316.

p. 105 "I got a taste . . ." Robinson, p. 75.

p. 107 "This thing keeps gnawing . . ." Jack E. Davis, "Baseball's
Reluctant Challenge: Desegregating Major League Spring
Training Sites, 1961–1964," *Journal of Sport History,* vol. 19,
no. 2 (Summer 1992), p. 144.

p. 107 "A major highway . . ." David Halberstam, *October 1964* (New
York: Villard Books, 1994), p. 59.

p. 108 "We drove from Omaha . . ." Bob Gibson with Phil Pepe,
From Ghetto to Glory: The Story of Bob Gibson (Englewood
Cliffs, N.J.: Prentice-Hall, 1968), p. 42.

p. 109 "without gloves, real baseballs . . ." John Geiger, "For
Johnson, kids always come first," *Florida Keys Keynoter*
[Marathon], February 11, 1995, p. 1.

Chapter 6

p. 113 "His players spoke . . ." Pat Jordan, *A False Spring* (New York:
Dodd, Mead, 1975), p. 197.

p. 116 "When you can't make it . . ." Paul Hemphill, "'I Gotta Let
the Kid Go,'" *Life,* September 1, 1972, p. 48.

p. 127 "There is no doubt . . ." William Leggett, "Where the majors
find new (and old) stars," *Sports Illustrated,* December 1,
1969, p. 88.

p. 128 "Palatka was a suffocating place . . ." Jordan, p. 264.

p. 130 "possibly the largest jazz café . . ." Mark Ribowsky, *Don't Look
Back: Satchel Paige in the Shadows of Baseball* (New York:
Simon & Schuster, 1994), p. 310.

p. 130 "had the greatest control . . ." Whitey Herzog and Kevin
Horrigan, *White Rat: A Life in Baseball* (New York: Harper &
Row, 1987), p. 54.

p. 131 "I wasn't running out . . ." LeRoy (Satchel) Paige, as told to
David Lipman, *Maybe I'll Pitch Forever* (Garden City, N.Y.:
Doubleday, 1962), p. 279.

Chapter 7

p. 138 "Of all the romantic datelines . . ." William Zinsser, *Spring Training* (New York: Harper & Row, 1989), pp. 1–2.

p. 139 "Spring training isn't for the players . . ." Ken Coleman with Dan Valenti, *Grapefruit League Road Trip: A Guide to Spring Training in Florida* (Lexington, Mass.: Stephen Greene Press, 1988), p. 5.

p. 140 "Spring training isn't what it used to be . . ." Roger Angell, "The Sporting Scene: State of the Art," *The New Yorker*, vol. 65 (May 8, 1989), p. 60.

p. 142 "As he basked . . ." Frederick G. Lieb. *Connie Mack: Grand Old Man of Baseball* (New York: Putnam's Sons, 1945), p. 29.

p. 143 "Al Lang, you must think . . ." Wythe Walker, "A History of the Grapefruit League," *Spring Training 1988*, p. 10.

p. 147 "minds of the players . . ." Walker, p. 12.

p. 147 "flirted with decadence . . ." Raymond Arsenault, *St. Petersburg and the Florida Dream, 1888–1950* (Norfolk, Va.: Donning Company, 1988), p. 204.

p. 147 "Al Lang certainly . . ." Melissa L. Keller, "Pitching for St. Petersburg: Spring Training and Publicity in the Sunshine City, 1914–1918," *Tampa Bay History*, vol. 15, no. 2 (Fall/Winter 1993), p. 36.

p. 148 "Jesus, I'm killed!" Robert W. Creamer, *Stengel: His Life and Times* (New York: Simon and Schuster, 1984), p. 87.

p. 148 "Underwood persuaded him . . ." Fred Lieb, *Baseball As I Have Known It* (New York: Coward, McCann & Geoghegan, 1977), p. 242.

p. 150 "was the longest home run . . ." James W. Covington, "Babe Ruth and His Record 'Home Run' at Tampa," *The Sunland Tribune*, vol. 17 (November 1991), p. 49.

p. 150 "If [Ruth] plays every day . . ." Charles C. Alexander, *John McGraw* (New York: Viking, 1988), p. 213.

p. 150 "How's that . . ." Babe Ruth, as told to Bob Considine. *The Babe Ruth Story* (New York: E.P. Dutton, 1948), p. 70.

p. 151 "Hey, Damon . . ." Ruth, p. 87.

p. 153 "My boy stood up . . ." Ruth, p. 172.

p. 153 "the Boston Brave . . ." Ruth, p. 208.

p. 159   "Wicker furniture . . ." Roger Kahn, *The Boys of Summer* (New York: Harper & Row, 1971), p. 166.

p. 160   "There is nothing . . ." Arthur Daley, "Automation on the Diamond," *The New York Times Magazine*, March 18, 1956, p. 19.

p. 165   "the facility's budget . . ." "Marlins Make Their Pitch," *Florida Trend*, March 1, 1992, p. 60.

Chapter 8

p. 178   "First, because the area . . ." Hank Hersch, "Tale of Four Cities," *Sports Illustrated*, vol. 77, no. 8 (August 24, 1992), p. 25.

p. 180   "Now, champagne for everyone . . ." Ed Giuliotti, "Big catch: Florida Marlins," *Sun-Sentinel* [Fort Lauderdale], July 6, 1991, p. 1A.

p. 180   "When we picked out that name . . ." Giuliotti, p. 8A.

p. 181   "where America began . . ." John Krich, *El Béisbol* (New York: The Atlantic Monthly Press, 1989), p. 3.

p. 183   "I think this is the greatest day . . ." Marc Topkin, "HOOO-RAYS!" *St. Petersburg Times*, March 10, 1995, p. 1A.

p. 183   "I actually feel kind of sad . . ." Joe Henderson and Bill Chastain, "HOO-RAYS!" *The Tampa Tribune*, March 10, 1995, Nation/World, p. 5.

p. 187   "swept the late precincts . . ." John Helyar, *Lords of the Realm: The Real History of Baseball* (New York: Villard Books, 1994), p. 25.

Chapter 9

p. 189   "Tallahassee honored Red . . ." Bob Edwards, *Fridays with Red: A Radio Friendship* (New York: Simon & Schuster, 1993), p. 225.

p. 192   "The money was nice . . ." Peter Golenbock, *The Forever Boys* (New York: Carol Publishing Group, 1991), p. 383.

p. 194   "actually became a tourist attraction . . ." Claire Smith, "Baseball's Angry Man," *The New York Times Magazine*, October 13, 1991, p. 56.

p. 200 "I cannot think of a better place . . ." Fred Lieb, *Baseball As I Have Known It* (New York: Coward, McCann & Geoghegan, 1977), p. 232.

p. 206 "I didn't have my heart in it . . ." Ted Williams with John Underwood, *My Turn At Bat: The Story of My Life* (New York: Simon & Schuster, Inc., 1988), p. 97.

BIBLIOGRAPHY

Aaron, Henry, with Lonnie Wheeler. *I Had a Hammer: The Hank Aaron Story.* New York: HarperCollins, 1991.

Adams, Frank. "The twilight boys" [about the Senior Professional Baseball Association]. In *Maclean's* (November 13, 1989): pp. 58–59.

Alexander, Charles C. *John McGraw.* New York: Viking, 1988.

Andelman, Bob. *Stadium For Rent: Tampa Bay's Quest for Major League Baseball.* Jefferson, N.C.: McFarland & Co., 1993.

Angell, Roger. "The Sporting Scene: State of the Art" [about spring training]. In *The New Yorker* 65 (May 8, 1989): pp. 54–76.

Arsenault, Raymond. *St. Petersburg and the Florida Dream, 1888–1950.* Norfolk, Va.: Donning Company, 1988.

Ashe, Arthur R. Jr. *A Hard Road to Glory: A History of the African-American Athlete Since 1946.* New York: Warner Books, Inc., 1988.

Bakewell, George A. *The History of the Kids and Kubs, 3/4 Century Softball Club, Inc., 1931–1973.* St. Petersburg: n.p., n.d.

Beatty, Bess. "Baseball: Jacksonville's Gilded Age Craze." In *Apalachee* [Tallahassee Historical Society] (1971–1979): pp. 50–68.

Berlage, Gai. *Women in Baseball.* Westport, Conn.: Praeger, 1994.

———. "Women Umpires as Mirrors of Gender Roles," In *The National Pastime: A Review of Baseball History*, no. 14 (1994): pp. 34–38.

Black Diamonds: Life in the Negro Leagues from the Men Who Lived It. Westport, Conn.: Meckler, 1989.

Blake, Mike. *The Minor Leagues.* New York: Wynwood Press, 1991.

Blaylock, Debbie. "The lady was an ump" [about Bernice Gera]. In *The (Fort Lauderdale) Sun-Sentinel*, 19 August 1985, p. 1C+ [for more about Gera, see Davis, Pratt, and Vernon].

Bloodgood, Clifford. "Snuffy — and His School" [about George Stirnweiss's baseball school in Bartow]. In *Baseball Magazine* 81, no. 1 (June 1948): pp. 239–40+.

Brandmeyer, Gerard A. "Baseball and the American Dream: A Conversation with Al Lopez," In *Tampa Bay History* 3, no. 1 (spring/summer, 1981): pp. 48–73.

Brooks, Ken. *The Last Rebel Yell: The Zany but True Misadventures of Baseball's Forgotten Alabama-Florida League.* Lynn Haven, Fla.: Seneca Park Publishing, 1986.

Callahan, Tom. "Baseball Picks a Pioneer" [about Bill White]. In *Time* 133, no. 7, (13 February 1989): p. 76.

Campbell, Jo. "Florida's Fireball on the Hill" [about Florida Senator Spessard Holland]. In *Baseball Magazine* 48, no. 4 (August 1956): pp. 55, 59.

Carter, John. "Rachel Robinson: 'I love the statue'" [about the Jackie Robinson statue in Daytona Beach]. In *The (Daytona Beach) News-Journal* (15 September 1990): p. D1.

Clark, Dick, and Larry Lester, editors. *The Negro Leagues Book*. Cleveland, Ohio: Society for American Baseball Research, 1994.

Coleman, Ken, with Dan Valenti. *Grapefruit League Road Trip: A Guide to Spring Training in Florida*. Lexington, Mass.: Stephen Greene Press, 1988.

Corliss, Richard. "Never Having to Grow Up" [about the Senior Professional Baseball Association]. In *Time* (18 December 1989): p. 76.

Covington, James W. "Babe Ruth and His Record 'Home Run' at Tampa," In *The Sunland Tribune* [Journal of the Tampa Historical Society] 17 (November 1991): pp. 47–49.

———. "The Chicago Cubs Come to Tampa" [in 1913]. In *Tampa Bay History* 8, no. 1 (spring/summer 1986): pp. 38–46.

Creamer, Robert W. *Stengel: His Life and Times*. New York: Simon & Schuster, 1984.

Crepeau, Richard. "Reflections on a Diamond: Spring Training's Impact on Florida." In *Florida Connections Magazine*, no. 7 (March/April 1990): pp. 20–23.

———. *Baseball: America's Diamond Mind, 1919–1941*. Orlando: University Presses of Florida, 1980.

Culp, Stanley. "Memories of Baseball in DeLand." In *Reflections: West Volusia County, 100 Years of Progress*. DeLand: West Volusia Historical Society, 1976, pp. 281–85.

Daley, Arthur. "Automation on the Diamond" [about Dodgertown in Vero Beach]. In *The New York Times Magazine* (18 March 1956): p. 19+.

Davis, Craig. "Called Out" [about Bernice Gera]. In *The (Fort Lauderdale) News/Sun-Sentinel* (15 September 1989): p. 1C+.

Davis, Jack E. "Baseball's Reluctant Challenge: Desegregating Major League Spring Training Sites, 1961–1964." In *Journal of Sport History* 19, no. 2 (summer 1992): pp. 144–62.

DeFreitas, Howard. "St. Petersburg has wealth of baseball history." In *St. Petersburg Times* (8 November 1990): City Times section, p. 2.

Dews, Robert P. *Ga.-Fla. League 1935–1958*. New York: Gifford/Shestack, 1979.

Drebinger, John. "Spring Training Becomes Streamlined." In *Baseball Magazine* 80, no. 4 (March 1948): p. 329+.

Durso, Joseph. *The Days of Mr. McGraw*. Englewood Cliffs, N.J.: Prentice-Hall, 1969.

The Economic Impact of Major League Baseball Spring Training on the Florida Economy. York, Maine: Davidson-Peterson Associates, Inc., 1987.

Edwards, Bob. *Fridays with Red: A Radio Friendship*. New York: Simon & Schuster, 1993.

Esch, Harold. "Waddell and Schreck in College" [about Rube Waddell and Ossee Schreckengost at Rollins in 1903]. In *Baseball Research Journal* (1980): pp. 144–45.

Everson, David. *Suicide Squeeze*. New York: Ivy Books, 1991.

"First Negro Coach in Majors" [about Buck O'Neil]. In *Ebony* 17 (August 1962): pp. 29–30.

Foley, Bill. "Half-century baseball career had moment in Jacksonville Beach sun" [about Spud Chandler]. In *The Florida Times-Union* (4 February 1990): p. C-3.

Forman, Ross. "B.U.D.ding Umps" [about the training of umpires]. In *Referee* (January 1994): p. 36+.

Fowler, Connie May. *Sugar Cage*. New York: Putnam's Sons, 1992.

Frayne, Trent. "Children of the springtime" [about records in spring training]. *Maclean's* 104, no. 14 (8 April 1991): p. 46.

Friedman, Myles E. "Spring Training." In *Total Baseball*, edited by John Thorn and Pete Palmer, with Michael Gershman. 4th ed. New York: Viking, 1995, pp. 573–76.

Frommer, Harvey. *Growing up at Bat: 50 Years of Little League Baseball*. New York: Pharos Books, 1989.

————. *Rickey & Robinson: The Men Who Broke Baseball's Color Barrier*. New York: Macmillan, 1982.

Gagnon, Cappy. "College Baseball." In *Total Baseball*, edited by John Thorn and Pete Palmer, with Michael Gershman. 4th ed. New York: Viking, 1995, pp. 577–81.

Geiger, John. "For Johnson, kids always come first" [about Lawrence Johnson of Key Largo]. In *(Marathon) Florida Keys Keynoter* (11 February 1995): p. 1+.

Giamatti, A. Bartlett. *Take Time for Paradise: Americans and Their Games*. New York: Summit Books, 1989.

Gibson, Bob, with Phil Pepe. *From Ghetto to Glory: The Story of Bob Gibson*. Englewood Cliffs, N.J.: Prentice-Hall, 1968.

Giuliotti, Ed. "Big catch: Florida Marlins" [about Huizenga's landing of the Marlins' franchise]. In *The (Fort Lauderdale) Sun-Sentinel* (6 July 1991): p. 1A.

Gleason, William F. (Red). "Fred Merkle . . . He Was No Bonehead." In *Baseball Magazine* (October 1953): pp. 26+.

Golenbock, Peter. *The Forever Boys* [about the Senior Professional Baseball Association]. New York: Carol Publishing Group, 1991.

Gordon, Jabbo. "It's Grapefruit League Time Again." In *Florida Trend* 18, no. 11 (March 1976): pp. 22–27.

Graham, Frank. *McGraw of the Giants, An Informal Biography*. New York: G.P. Putnam's Sons, 1944.

Gregorich, Barbara. *Women at Play: The Story of Women in Baseball*. San Diego: Harcourt Brace, 1993.

Halberstam, David. *October 1964*. New York: Villard Books, 1994.

Hall, Donald, and others. *Playing Around: The Million-Dollar Infield Goes to Florida*. Boston: Little, Brown, 1974.

"Hall of Fame Grave Sites." In *The Whole Baseball Catalogue*, edited by John Thorn and Bob Carroll with David Reuther. New York: Simon & Schuster, 1990, p. 142.

Hawkins, Richard Lee Jr. *N-O-L-E-S: The History of Florida State Baseball*. Thesis, Florida State University. Tallahassee, Fla.: 1989.

Helyar, John. *Lords of the Realm: The Real History of Baseball*. New York: Villard Books, 1994.

Hemphill, Paul. *The Good Old Boys*. New York: Simon & Schuster, 1974.

———. "'I Gotta Let the Kid Go.'" In *Life* (1 September 1972): pp. 41–48.

———. *Long Gone*. New York: Viking, 1979.

Henderson, Joe, and Bill Chastain, "HOO-RAYS!" [about the Devil Rays of Tampa Bay]. In *The Tampa Tribune* (10 March 1995): Nation/World, p. 5+.

Hersch, Hank. "Tale of Four Cities" [about efforts by cities, including Miami and St. Petersburg, to lure a major league team]. *Sports Illustrated* 77, no. 8 (24 August 1992): pp. 24–31.

Hersch, Valerie. "Field of Dreams?" [about the cost of luring the Red Sox to Fort Myers] In *Florida Trend* (1 March 1992): pp. 59–62.

Herzog, Whitey, and Kevin Horrigan. *White Rat: A Life in Baseball*. New York: Harper & Row, 1987.

Holway, John B. *Black Diamonds: Life in the Negro Leagues from the Men Who Lived It*. Westport, Conn.: Meckler, 1989.

———. *Blackball Stars: Negro League Pioneers*. Westport, Conn.: Meckler, 1988.

Huisking, Charlie. "Heading For Home" [about "Buck" O'Neil]. In *Sarasota Herald-Tribune* (5 March 1995): p. 1A+.

Hurley, June. *The Don Ce-Sar Story*. Edited by Ken Hurley. St. Petersburg Beach, Fla.: Partnership Press, 1974.

Johnson, Arthur T. *Minor League Baseball and Local Economic Development*. Urbana: University of Chicago Press, 1993.

Johnson, James Weldon. *Along This Way: The Autobiography of James Weldon Johnson*. New York: Viking, 1933.

Johnson, Lloyd, and Miles Wolff, editors. *The Encyclopedia of Minor League Baseball*. Durham, N.C.: Baseball America, Inc., 1993.

Johnson, Susan E. *When Women Played Hardball*. Seattle, Wash.: Seal Press, 1994.

Johnston, Joey. "Tony Saladino Award." In *The Tampa Tribune* (18 June 1995): Sports section, pp. 8–9.

Jordan, Pat. *A False Spring*. New York: Dodd, Mead, 1975.

Kahn, Roger. *The Boys of Summer*. New York: Harper & Row, 1971.

Keetz, Frank. "The Board" [about the replica of a baseball diamond outside newspaper offices]. In *The National Pastime: A Review of Baseball History*, no. 13 (1993): pp. 3–4.

Keller, Melissa L. "Pitching for St. Petersburg: Spring Training and Publicity in the Sunshine City, 1914–1918." In *Tampa Bay History* 15, no. 2 (fall/winter 1993): pp. 35–53.

Kiefer, Michael. "Hardball" [about the American Women's Baseball Association]. *Women's Sports & Fitness* 14 (April 1992): pp. 56–60+.

Kirk, Cooper. "Fort Lauderdale High School Athletics and the 'Flying L' Symbol," In "Baseball Comes to Southeast Florida." *Broward Legacy* 12, nos. 3–4 (summer/fall 1989): pp. 3–4.

Kleinberg, Howard. "Play Ball! — Florida's Romance with Baseball." In *South Florida History Magazine* 21, no. 1 (winter 1993): pp. 16–23.

Koenig, Bill. "Facing the Odds" [about how few players ever reach the majors]. In *Baseball Weekly* (31 August-6 September 1994): p. 16.

Krich, John. *El Béisbol*. New York: The Atlantic Monthly Press, 1989.

Lamb, David. "The Minors." In *Baseball: An Illustrated History* by Geoffrey C. Ward. New York: Alfred A. Knopf, 1994, pp. 146–49.

Larson, Greg. "College baseball teams thriving in Jacksonville." In *The (Jacksonville) Florida Times-Union* (14 April 1988): p. C-1+.

———. "1.5 million attendance." In *Baseball America* (15 May 1984): p. 2.

Lawes, Rick. "Haller was first of coed hurlers" [about Jodi Haller]. In *USA Today Baseball Weekly* (2–8 March 1994): p. 32.

———. "Solid State" [about the high quality of Florida baseball]. In *USA Today Baseball Weekly* (12–25 February 1992): pp. 28–29.

Lawson, Steven F. "Ybor City and Baseball: An Interview with Al Lopez." In *Tampa Bay History* 7, no. 2 (fall/winter 1985): pp. 59–76.

Leggett, William. "Where the majors find new (and old) stars" [about the instructional leagues]. In *Sports Illustrated* (1 December 1969): pp. 86–91.

Lidz, Franz. "Ol' Man Rivers" [about Mickey Rivers of the Senior Professional Baseball Association]. *Sports Illustrated* 72, no. 4 (29 January 1990): pp. 36–38.

Lieb, Fred. *Baseball As I Have Known It*. New York: Coward, McCann & Geoghegan, 1977.

———. *Connie Mack: Grand Old Man of Baseball*. New York: Putnam's Sons, 1945.

Livingston, Joe. "How Sam Wolfson Saved The Jacksonville Braves" [how a local financier bought the Jacksonville team and revived it]. In *Baseball Magazine* (November/December 1954): p. 14+.

Logan, Rayford W., and Michael R. Winston, editors. *Dictionary of American Negro Biography*. New York: Norton, 1982, p. 397+.

Lowry, Philip J. *Green Cathedrals*. Cooperstown, N.Y.: Society for American Baseball Research, 1986.

Macht, Norman L. "Ruth mightiest when he stooped to help kids." In *USA Today Baseball Weekly* (26 February–3 March 1992): p. 6.

Malloy, Jerry. "The Birth of the Cuban Giants: The Origins of Black Professional Baseball." In *Nine* 2, no. 2 (spring 1994): pp. 233–47.

"Marlins Make Their Pitch" [about the Marlins' seeking a spring training site]. In *Florida Trend* (1 March 1992): p. 60.

Marti, Chris. "A day in the life of the Minor League." In *The Tampa Tribune* (3 July 1994): BayLife, pp. 1–2.

Martin, Harold. "Real Baseball Provided by the East Coast League." In *Broward Legacy* 5, nos. 1–2 (winter/spring 1982): pp. 2–4.

Martz, Jim. *Hurricane Strikes! University of Miami Baseball*. Huntsville, Ala.: Strode Publishers, 1983.

Marvez, Alex. "Going to bat for Clemente Park kids." In *The Miami Herald*. Northwest ed. (17 July 1994): "Neighbors" section, p. 1+.

McGovern, James. *The Emergence of a City in the Modern South: Pensacola 1900–1945*. DeLeon Springs, Fla.: Painter, 1976.

McIver, Stuart. "Big Hit at the Hitler Games" [about Les McNeece at the 1936 Olympics]. In *Sunshine, (Fort Lauderdale) News/Sun-Sentinel* (1 May 1994): pp. 16, 18.

———. "Cooks to Catchers, Bellhops to Batters" [about African-American baseball at Henry Flagler's hotels]. In *Sunshine, (Fort Lauderdale) News/Sun-Sentinel* (22 August 1993): p.23+.

———. "Florida's grass roots" [about baseball in south Florida]. In *(Fort Lauderdale) News/Sun-Sentinel* (4 April 1993): p.24. BB

McKay, D. B. "A Sportive Chapter of Florida History — How the Grapefruit League Came to St. Petersburg." In *Tampa Sunday Tribune* (26 December 1954): p. 12-C.

Millburg, Steve. "Field of Dreamers" [about baseball fantasy camps]. In *Southern Living* 28, no. 3 (March 1993): pp. 22–23.

Moore, Steve. "Robinson: A hero honored" [about Jackie Robinson], In *The (Daytona Beach) News-Journal* (16 September 1990): p. C-1+.

Morgenson, Gretchen. "Where the fans still come first" [about the minor leagues]. In *Forbes* 149, no. 9 (27 April 1992): pp. 40–42.

Nack, William. "Dodgertown" [about the Dodgers' camp in Vero Beach]. In *Sports Illustrated* (14 March 1983): pp. 44–55.

"The National League's New Boss" [about Bill White]. In *Ebony* 44, no. 7 (May 1989): pp. 44, 46.

Obojski, Robert. *Bush League: A History of Minor League Baseball.* New York: Macmillan, 1975.

Oliver, Peter. "Spring Training: The Second Hundred Years." *Travel-Holiday* 171, no. 2 (February 1989): pp. 63–67.

Olson, Gordon L., and Frank N. Schubert, "The Detroit Tigers Move to Lakeland, Florida, in 1934." In *Polk County Historical Quarterly* 21, no. 1 (June 1994): pp. 1–3.

O'Neal, Bill. *The International League.* Austin, Texas: Eakin Press, 1992.

———. *The Southern League: Baseball in Dixie, 1885–1994.* Austin, Texas: Eakin Press, 1994.

O'Neil, Buck with Steve Wulf. *I Was Right on Time.* New York: Simon & Schuster, 1995.

Paige, LeRoy (Satchel), as told to David Lipman. *Maybe I'll Pitch Forever.* Garden City, N.Y.: Doubleday, 1962.

Pepe, Phil. "Farewell, Fort Lauderdale" [about the Yankees' changing spring training sites]. In *Yankees* [official publication of the New York Yankees] 15, issue 12 (31 March 1995): pp. 6–16.

Peterson, Robert. *Only the Ball Was White: A History of Legendary Black Players and All-black Professional Teams.* New York: McGraw-Hill, 1984.

Plimpton, George. "The Curious Case of Sidd Finch," In *Sports Illustrated* (1 April 1985): pp. 58–76.

———. *The Curious Case of Sidd Finch.* New York: Macmillan, 1987.

Porter, David L., editor. *Biographical Dictionary of American Sports: Baseball.* Westport, Conn.: Greenwood Press, 1987, p. 333+.

Postema, Pam, and Gene Wojciechowski. *You've Got to Have Balls to Make It in This League.* New York: Simon & Schuster, 1992.

Pratt, Benjamin. "Ernest's Gera: the first woman pro baseball umpire" [about Bernice Gera]. In *The Indiana Gazette* (23 May 1988): p. 16.

Punnett, Dick & Yvonne. *Thrills, Chills & Spills*. New Smyrna Beach, Fla.: Luthers, 1990.

Puro, George, and Kyle Veltrop, editors. *The Sporting News Official Baseball Register: 1995 Edition*. St. Louis, Mo.: The Sporting News Publishing Co., 1995.

Reflections: West Volusia County, 100 Years of Progress. DeLand, Fla.: West Volusia Historical Society, 1976.

Ribowsky, Mark. *Don't Look Back: Satchel Paige in the Shadows of Baseball*. New York: Simon & Schuster, 1994.

Richards, J. Noble. *Florida's Hibiscus City: Vero Beach*. Melbourne, Fla.: Brevard Graphics, Inc., 1968.

Riley, James A. *The Biographical Encyclopedia of the Negro Baseball Leagues*. New York: Carroll & Graf Publishers, Inc., 1994.

Ritter, Lawrence S. *The Glory of Their Times: The Story of the Early Days of Baseball Told by the Men Who Played It*. New York: William Morrow, 1984.

Robinson, Jackie. *Baseball Has Done It*. Edited by Charles Dexter. Philadelphia: J.B. Lippincott Company, 1964.

———. *Jackie Robinson: My Own Story*. New York: Greenberg Publisher, 1948.

———. "Jackie Robinson's First Spring Training." In *The American Sporting Experience*, edited by Steven A. Riess. West Point, N.Y.: Leisure Press, 1984, pp. 365–70.

——— as told to Alfred Duckett. *I Never Had It Made*. New York: Putnam, 1972.

Rooney, John F. Jr., "Geography of Sports." In *Encyclopedia of Southern Culture*. Chapel Hill, N.C.: University of North Carolina Press, 1989, pp. 564–65.

———. "The Pigskin Cult and Other Sunbelt Sports." *American Demographics* 8, no. 9 (September 1986): pp. 38–43.

——— and Richard Pillsbury. In *Atlas of American Sport*. New York: Macmillan, 1992.

Roush, Chris. "Back in Swing" [about the big business of baseball]. In *The Tampa Tribune* (8 April 1991): pp. 12, 14.

———. "Communities, teams playing hardball over training sites." In *The Tampa Tribune* (8 April 1991): pp. 13, 15.

Rowan, Carl, with Jackie Robinson. *Wait Till Next Year*. New York: Random House, 1960.

Ruth, Babe, as told to Bob Considine. *The Babe Ruth Story*. New York: E.P. Dutton, 1948.

Scher, Jon. "Reaching out for new ideas" [about the Kansas City Royals Baseball Academy]. In *Baseball America* (25 April 1990): pp. 20–21.

Schoor, Gene. *Jackie Robinson, Baseball Hero*. New York: Putnam's Sons, 1958.

Schwarz, Alan. "The Holdout From Hell" [about Jason Varitek's holding out for a big bonus]. In *Baseball America* (9–22 January 1995): pp. 4–5.

———. "Sarasota Programs Flourish." In *Baseball America* (21 March-3 April 1994): p. 40.

Shaara, Michael. *For Love of the Game*. New York: Carroll & Graf, 1991.

Shatzkin, Mike, and Jim Charlton. *The Baseball Fan's Guide to Spring Training*. Reading, Mass.: Addison-Wesley Publishing Company, 1988.

Simons, Art. "Baseball in Early Miami." In *Update* [Historical Association of Southern Florida] 4, no. 1 (October 1976): p. 3.

Singletary, Wes. "The Inter-Social League: 1943 Season" [about baseball in Tampa]. In *The Sunland Tribune* [Journal of the Tampa Historical Society] 18 (November 1992): pp. 82–83.

————. "Opportunity Knocks Once: A Conversation with Manuel 'Curly' Onis" [about Tampa Baseball]. *The Sunland Tribune* [Journal of the Tampa Historical Society] 20 (November 1994): pp. 55–57.

————. "Señor: The Managerial Career of Al Lopez." In *The Sunland Tribune* [Journal of the Tampa Historical Society] 19 (November 1993): pp. 57–66.

Smith, Claire. "Baseball's Angry Man" [about Bill White]. In *The New York Times Magazine* (13 October 1991): pp. 28–31+.

Smits, Garry. "Rossi Weeks plays way into Cooperstown" [about Rossi Weeks of the All-American Girls Professional Baseball League]. In *The (Jacksonville) Florida Times-Union* (24 December 1988): p. 5.

Stavro, Barry. "Gambling on a Game Plan for Baseball" [about the efforts by Tampa and St. Petersburg to lure a major league team]. In *Florida Trend* 26, no. 3 (July 1983): pp. 38–43.

Stephenson, Mike. "Baseball is special to disabled" [about the Little League's efforts for the physically and mentally handicapped]. In *The (Jacksonville) Florida Times-Union* (9 June 1991): p. C-1.

Stern, William. "Buy me some arepa and media noche" [about the Florida Marlins' efforts to attract Hispanics]. In *Forbes* 151, no. 11 (24 May 1993): p. 184.

Stockton, J. Roy. "Spring Training in Florida." In *The Florida Historical Quarterly* 39, no. 3 (January 1961): pp. 221–30.

Stout, Wesley W. "Geo. Andrews, Big Leaguer." In *Fort Lauderdale Daily News* (23 February 1954): p. 6.

Strouse, Charles. "A league *apart*" [about the Negro Leagues]. In *The Miami Herald* (27 September 1994): p. 1E+.

Stump, Al. *Cobb: A Biography*. Chapel Hill, N.C.: Algonquin Books of Chapel Hill, 1994.

Sullivan, Neil J. *The Minors*. New York: St. Martin's Press, 1990.

Thorn, John, and Pete Palmer, editors, with Michael Gershman. *Total Baseball*. 4th ed. New York: Viking, 1995.

Thrift, Syd. *The Game According to Syd*. New York: Simon & Schuster, 1990.

Topkin, Marc. "HOOO-RAYS!" [about the Devil Rays of Tampa Bay]. In *St. Petersburg Times* (10 March 1995): p. 1A+.

Tygiel, Jules. *Baseball's Great Experiment: Jackie Robinson and His Legacy*. New York: Oxford University Press, 1983.

✓———. "Black Ball." In *Total Baseball*, edited by John Thorn and Pete Palmer, with Michael Gershman. 4th ed. New York: Viking, 1995, pp. 516–31.

Vernon, Amy. "Bernice Gera, 61, first female ump in pro ball." In *The Miami Herald* (24 September 1992): Broward Edition, p. 9

Vincent, Ted. *Mudville's Revenge.* New York: Seaview Books, 1981.

Walker, Wythe. "A History of the Grapefruit League." In *Spring Training 1988*, vol. 1, pp. 8–17.

Ward, Geoffrey C. *Baseball: An Illustrated History.* New York: Alfred A. Knopf, 1994.

Weidling, Philip J., and August Burghard. *Checkered Sunshine: The Story of Fort Lauderdale, 1793–1955.* Gainesville, Fla.: University of Florida Press, 1966.

Whitford, David. *Playing Hardball: The High-Stakes Battle for Baseball's New Franchises.* New York: Doubleday, 1993.

✓Wiggins, David K. "Wendell Smith, the *Pittsburgh Courier-Journal* and the Campaign to Include Blacks in Organized Baseball, 1933–1945." In *Journal of Sport History* 10, no. 2 (summer 1983): pp. 5–29.

Wilber, Cynthia J., editor. *For the Love of the Game.* New York: William Morrow & Co., 1992.

Will, George F. *Men at Work: The Craft of Baseball.* New York: Macmillan, 1990.

Williams, Ted, with John Underwood. *My Turn At Bat: The Story of My Life.* New York: Simon & Schuster, 1988.

Wills, Chuck, and Pat Wills. *Beyond Home Plate: On the Trail of Yesterday's Baseball Heroes.* Ocala, Fla.: Special Publications, Inc., 1993.

Winston, Lisa. "Female trainer is trying to mend gender barrier." In *USA Today Baseball Weekly* (27–28 March 1995): p. 31.

Wulf, Steve. "The Boys of Winter" [about the Senior Professional Baseball Association]. In *Sports Illustrated* 71, no. 21 (20 November 1989): pp. 28–33.

———. "The Guiding Light" [about Buck O'Neil]. In *Sports Illustrated* 81, no. 12 (19 September 1994): pp. 148–58.

———. "You Aren't My Sunshine" [that Florida does not deserve a major league team]. In *Sports Illustrated* 74, no. 1 (14 January 1991): p. 100.

Zinsser, William. *Spring Training.* New York: Harper & Row, 1989.

INDEX